OVER
THE
CLIFF

OVER THE CLIFF

HOW OBAMA'S ELECTION DROVE THE AMERICAN RIGHT INSANE

John Amato and David Neiwert

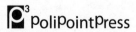 PoliPointPress

Over the Cliff:
How Obama's Election Drove the American Right Insane

Copyright © 2010 by John Amato and David Neiwert

14   13   12   11   10   1   2   3   4   5

Production management: BookMatters
Book design: BookMatters
Cover design: Nicole Hayward

Library of Congress Cataloging-in-Publication Data
   Amato, John.
      Over the cliff : how Obama's election drove the American right
   insane / John Amato and David Neiwert.
         p. cm.
      Includes index.
      ISBN 978-0-9824171-7-1 (alk. paper)
         1. Presidents—United States—Election—2008.   2. Obama,
   Barack.   3. Conservatism—United States.   4. Right and left
   (Political science)   5. United States—Politics and government.
   I. Neiwert, David A., 1956–   II. Title.
   JK5262008.A39   2010
   324.973'0931—dc22   2010011359

Published by:
PoliPointPress, LLC
80 Liberty Ship Way, Suite 22
Sausalito, CA 94965
(415) 339-4100
www.p3books.com

Distributed by Ingram Publisher Services
Printed in the USA

Contents

Foreword
Careening Far to the Right

When the liberal blogosphere formed in the early years of the Bush administration, it was a small community of dedicated political observers, reaching out to one another and the odd reader or two, trying desperately to make sense of what was going on around them. Of particular interest were the right-wing media, or what we called at the time "The Mighty Wurlitzer," and their amazing capacity to shape the political discourse. Author and journalist David Neiwert's blog Orcinus quickly rose to the top of our blogrolls; his series "Rush, Newspeak and Fascism" was a seminal insight into how right-wing extremist ideas made their way into the mainstream and helped us understand how the conservative movement had come to so dominate our political culture. A couple of years later, John Amato changed the way blogs themselves were constructed by offering commentary and videos online (well before YouTube) on his blog Crooks and Liars to expose the media's absorption of the right-wing agenda. It was only natural that they would team up to write together, as they do at Crooks and Liars every day, and now in this book. There are few people in the country who follow this subject more closely.

The last few years have been dramatic ones for the conservative movement. Just eight short years ago, drunk on vengeful bloodlust and convinced they had just ushered in a thousand-year reign, the right wing in America was united with their government as never before. Its members culturally enforced their peculiar form of chauvinistic patriotism and insisted that Americans unquestionably submit themselves to the power of the state. They said to trust the president, a man they deified as a warrior god, and condemned anyone who questioned his decisions as a traitor.

Today, they are hunkered down in a paranoid crouch, convinced that their country has been stolen from them by a usurper—a man so illegitimate that they believe he isn't even an American citizen, much less a qualified leader. But they aren't depressed—far from it. They are energized and excited, organizing around the extremist ideologies that have been bubbling for decades under the surface of conservative-movement thought. The election of a youthful black man from Chicago by way of Hawaii, a Harvard-educated lawyer, community organizer, and putative liberal, has unleashed the right-wing beast. And the groundwork they laid in the media over the past few decades, along with the organizing ability of the Internet, has given mainstream voice and support to what was once considered fringe ideology.

In one short year, beginning with the original Ron Paul Tea Party events during his ill-fated run for the Republican nomination, the Tea Party movement has become a political force to be reckoned with. Though its adherents once believed that every American should follow the government's lead unquestioningly, the election of Barack Obama has turned these right-wingers back into anti-government zealots. Inspired by Rush Limbaugh's ideological thuggishness, Glenn Beck's lugubrious, incoherent demagoguery, and the faux populism of financial elites like Rick Santelli, they see themselves as glamorous revolutionaries fighting to take their country back from people who have stolen it from them. Their "militia" is made up of former members of the "Patriot" movement, white supremacists, John Birchers, "Birthers," "Oathers," and various other permutations of the radical fringe, including "lone wolves" who are increasingly turning to violence. And it's financed by a secretive, sophisticated, corporate-sponsored astroturf operation that seeks to use them to destabilize the Obama administration and help pave the way for a Republican resurgence. The problem is that the tail may very well be wagging the dog, and the conservative political establishment may have unleashed a force that's beyond its control. When polls show that Glenn Beck is Americans' fourth-most-admired man in the world, it may be time to start taking them seriously.

Nobody knows where this is going. The Tea Partiers and their allies are tapping into the fear and anger that are washing over a country with over 10 percent unemployment and ongoing economic insecurity. And they are using the tried-and-true bogeymen and shibboleths of the paranoid strain in American politics to explain to their audiences who are and what is the cause of their angst: liberals, minorities, and big government (not incidentally led by the first African American president). In the absence of a strong counter-narrative, this deception may gain strength. However, if liberals remain alert to how the Tea Partiers' fringe ideas are mainstreamed, stay focused on solving problems, and tell people the real reasons for their economic anxiety, these radical wingnuts may finally be exposed and discredited. If not, this movement of crazies, cranks, and hucksters could end up taking over one of the two American political parties—and that outcome is not comforting.

There is no question that the American Right is running at full speed and hurtling itself over the cliff. It remains to be seen if they will take the rest of America with them.

—*Digby, Santa Monica, January 2010*

ONE

It's the End of the World as They Know It

On the day Barack Obama was elected president of the United States, much of the nation—particularly those who supported and voted for him—celebrated the election of the first African American to the country's highest office. For those who voted for his opponent, John McCain, there was naturally the usual bitterness and disappointment.

Among a certain subset of those Americans, however—especially those who opposed Obama precisely because he sought to become the nation's first black president—it went well beyond the usual despair. For them, November 5, 2008, was the end of the world. Or at least, the end of America as they knew it.

So maybe it wasn't really a surprise that they responded that day with the special venom and violence peculiar to the American Right.

Like the noose strung in protest from a tree limb in Texas. Students at Baylor University in Waco discovered the noose hanging from a campus tree the evening of election day, near a site where angry Republican students had gathered Obama yard signs and burned them in a big bonfire. That same evening, a riot nearly broke out when Obama supporters, chanting the new president's name, were confronted outside a residence hall by white students who told them: "Any nigger who walks by Penland [Hall], we're going to kick their ass, we're going to jump him." The Obama supporters stopped and responded, "Excuse me?"—and somehow managed to keep the confrontation confined to a mere shouting match until police arrived and broke things up.

There were also the students on the North Carolina State University campus, in Raleigh, who spent election night spraypainting such fun-loving messages as "Let's shoot that Nigger in the head" and "Hang Obama by a noose." The university's administration was so upset by this behavior that it protected the students' identities and refused to take any legal action against them or discipline them at all.

Those were just warm-ups from the student cheering section. The real thugs, exemplars of the dark side of the American psyche, were shortly to make their mark.

That night, four young white men from Staten Island "decided to go after black people" in retaliation for Obama's election. The men first drove to the mostly black Park Hill neighborhood and assaulted a Liberian immigrant, beating him with a metal pipe and a police baton, as well as their fists and feet. They drove next to Port Richmond, where they assaulted another black man and verbally threatened a Latino man and a group of black people. The hooligans finished up the night by attempting to drive next to a man walking home from his job as a Rite Aid manager and club him with the police baton. Instead, they simply hit him with their car, throwing him off the windshield and into a coma for over a month. The pedestrian was actually white, but this crew of geniuses managed to misidentify him as a black man. All four of the thugs wound up convicted of hate crimes and will spend the duration of Obama's first term in prison. Look for them to turn up on Fox News in a few years claiming to be victims of the oppressive Obama administration.

The day after the election in Midland, Michigan, a discarded Ron Paul activist named Randy Gray (he had been peremptorily dismissed from the Paul campaign when his white-supremacist activism was revealed), dressed in full Ku Klux Klan regalia, stalked the sidewalk in the middle of a heavily trafficked intersection and waved an American flag. He also toted a handgun. Police talked to Gray but let him continue his display after he told them his behavior had nothing to do with Obama winning the presidency.

A bus full of schoolkids in Rexburg, Idaho, started chanting "Assassinate Obama" just to tease the tiny minority of their fellow schoolkids who were Obama supporters. In Rexburg—where the population is more than 90 percent Mormon—that's about three kids in the entire school. District officials didn't discipline the children who had led the chants, but they did send a letter to the kids' parents reminding them that students are to be told such behavior is unacceptable.

Then there were the arsons.

On election night, a black family in South Ogden, Utah, came home from volunteering at their local polling station to discover that their American flag had been torched.

In Hardwick Township, New Jersey, a black man taking his eight-year-old daughter to school emerged from his front door the morning after the election to discover that someone had burned a six-foot-tall cross on his lawn, right next to the man's banner declaring Obama president. It had been torched too.

Another cross was burned on the lawn of the only black man in tiny Apolacon Township, Pennsylvania, the night after the election. A black church in Springfield, Massachusetts, was burned to the ground the night of the election; three white men were arrested and charged with setting the fire as a hate crime.

And if the election itself wasn't enough to bring the haters out of the woodwork, there was Obama's inauguration on January 21, 2009.

Two days before the big event, arsonists in Forsyth County, Georgia, burned down the home of a woman who was a public supporter of Obama; she was in DC for the inauguration at the time. Someone also painted a racial slur on her fence, along with the warning "Your black boy will die."

On inauguration day, someone taped newspaper articles featuring Obama onto the apartment door of a woman in Jersey City, New Jersey, and set fire to the door. Fortunately, the woman had stayed home to watch the inauguration on TV and smelled the burning, and she was able to extinguish the fire before it spread. If only she could have done the same for the hate that sparked the act.

The day after the inauguration, a large, 22-year-old skinhead from Brockton, Massachusetts, named Keith Luke decided it was time to fight the "extinction" of the white race, so he bashed down the door of an African American woman and her sister and shot them both; one died. Police cornered and arrested Luke before he could pull off the next phase of his shooting rampage. According to the district attorney, Luke intended to "kill as many Jews, blacks, and Hispanics as humanly possible . . . before killing himself." When he appeared in court a month later, Luke had carved a swastika into his forehead with a razor blade.

The pain and violence inflicted by these haters were just beginning.

In all, the Southern Poverty Law Center (SPLC), in Montgomery, Alabama, counted more than 200 "hate-related" incidents in the first weeks after the election of Barack Obama, a number that more than doubled after the inauguration. We called up the SPLC's Mark Potok for his thoughts on what was happening. Here's what he said:

> I think there's something remarkable happening out there. I think we really are beginning to see a white backlash that may grow fairly large. The situation's worrying.
>
> Not only do we have continuing nonwhite immigration, not only is the economy in the tank and very likely to get worse, but we have a black man in the White House. That is driving a kind of rage in a certain sector of the white population that is very, very worrying to me.
>
> We are seeing literally hundreds of incidents around the country—from cross-burnings to death threats to effigies hanging to confrontations in schoolyards, and it's quite remarkable.
>
> I think that there are political leaders out there who are saying incredibly irresponsible things that could have the effect of undamming a real flood of hate. That includes media figures. On immigration, they have been some of the worst.
>
> There's a lot going on, and it's very likely to lead to scapegoating. And in the end, scapegoating leaves corpses in the street.

Among the indicators of this spike in violent white racism was a sharp increase in business for white-supremacist Web sites like the neo-Nazi forum Stormfront. It collected more than 2,000 new members the day after the election. One poster to the Stormfront site, a North Las Vegas resident going by the moniker Dalderian Germanicus, reflected the consensus sentiment in the comments: "I want the SOB laid out in a box to see how 'messiahs' come to rest. God has abandoned us, this country is doomed."

That theme popped up a lot among the denizens of the extremist Right in the weeks after the election. One middle-aged Georgian, quoted by an Associated Press reporter, voiced the typical view: "I believe our nation is ruined and has been for several decades, and the election of Obama is merely the culmination of the change."

For the American Right, 2008 was indeed the end of the world.

The old racist Right made clear its hatred of Barack Obama early on. Obama formally announced his candidacy in February 2007. In June 2007, the Grand Dragon of the National Knights of the Ku Klux Klan—a fellow who went by the name of Ray Larsen (though his real name is Railston Loy)—declared:

> Well, I'm not going to have to worry about him, because somebody else down South is going to take him out. . . . If that man is elected president, he'll be shot sure as hell.

Well, white supremacists are nothing if not a deluded bunch. As Obama's candidacy marched forward, they began facing the prospect of the election of a black man to the presidency and, in short order, began changing their tune. Indeed, they began claiming that his imminent election was a good thing for them. August Kreis, national director of the notorious Aryan Nations, told a *Palm Beach Post* reporter: "Obama's done my group a lot of good. He's polarizing Americans, black and white. . . . Especially in Florida, affiliates have increased recently."

"I've gotten more calls in the last two months about interest in our organizations than I got in all the years in the past," said Tom Prater, Florida spokesperson for the white-power group Euro.

Don Black, founder and leader of the neo-Nazi group Stormfront, was optimistic when interviewed by the *Palm Beach Post* about the opportunities offered by Obama's candidacy: "I get nonstop e-mails and private messages from new people who are mad as hell about the possibility of Obama being elected," Black said.

"White people, for a long time, have thought of our government as being for us, and Obama is the best possible evidence that we've lost that. This is scaring a lot of people who maybe never considered themselves racists, and it's bringing them over to our side."

Mainstream conservatives chose to race-bait more subtly by using what are popularly known as "dog whistles"—code words that race-baiting politicians and pundits trot out to refer to red-meat issues for the rabid Right and that are audible only to those who have the right ears to hear. Conservative pundits in short order began using Obama's full name, including his middle name, Hussein, in an attempt to emphasize his "foreignness," as well as to link him mentally to the Iraqi tyrant American forces had toppled not so long ago. Rush Limbaugh ran ditties calling him "Barack the Magic Negro," claiming that his entire candidacy was built on a foundation of "white guilt." In the *Washington Times,* eugenics enthusiast Steve Sailer opined: "While some whites envisage Mr. Obama as the Cure for White Guilt, blacks are in no hurry to grant the white race absolution for slavery and Jim Crow, since they benefit from compensatory programs like affirmative action." In the eyes of conservative pundits, Obama's candidacy was all about race—and for the duration, that's all it ever would be.

Things became ugly quickly on mainstream Web sites. CBS had to shut down comments on any Obama story on its site because the comments inevitably attracted vicious race-baiters and death threats. In real life, matters were even worse: Obama's campaign attracted so many threats that he was assigned a Secret Service detail earlier than any candidate in history.

For most of the early stages of the campaign, John McCain and his organization openly decried the use of such rhetoric. McCain didn't need to use such rhetoric himself as long as Republicans had their longtime gutter-politics operatives doing it for him. Case in point: Floyd Brown.

Brown is perhaps best remembered as the man behind the notorious race-baiting Willie Horton ad. Horton, an African American in prison for murder, had escaped in 1986 during a weekend furlough and later committed further crimes. Conservative operatives used the ad in the 1988 presidential campaign to attack Democratic candidate Michael Dukakis by depicting him as "weak on crime" (see chapter 6). Since then, Brown has been a major player in nearly every right-wing smear of leading Democratic figures, including the Clinton impeachment fiasco and the Swift Boating of John Kerry. He also helped promote black-helicopter New World Order conspiracy theories about Clinton in the 1990s.

Brown got involved in the 2008 campaign with an organization called ExposeObama, which began running TV ads during the North Carolina primary that accused Obama of being "weak in the war on gangs." The ads' visuals depicted Obama as a sleazy gangster himself and implied that his "softness" was a product of his racial identity. McCain denounced the ads, which ensured that they would appear continually on cable-TV reports.

That's the Floyd Brown formula: Create an incendiary ad that is typically reverberant with far-right (often racist) themes repackaged for more mainstream consumption. Next, spend a little bit of money in a few precincts to let the Republicans involved officially denounce the ads. The Republicans look good with the soccer-mom contingent that is turned off by racially incendiary campaigns while reaching the closet-racist bloc with the ad, which gets national play in the mainstream media as the pundits discuss the outrage that ensues. The national exposure expands the audience exponentially—and for no added expense. It's diabolical, really, but clever as hell. Brown not only indulges in dog-whistle race-baiting but also consorts with all kinds of racists and extremists. That was the ExposeObama operation in a nutshell. The group's executive director, Bruce E. Hawkins, was disbarred in 2006 for peddling tax-fraud schemes that originated with the extremist "Patriot" Right. The schemes were based on the absurd notion that by filing certain "sovereignty" documents, citizens can exempt themselves from paying taxes. In 2007, the Justice Department filed suit against Hawkins to prevent him from peddling the schemes even after his disbarment; eventually, the federal courts enjoined Hawkins from promoting these schemes in any fashion, legal license or no. Hawkins's extremism wasn't confined to tax issues—on the front page of the ExposeObama site, a prominent link pointed visitors to a piece by Hawkins that compared Reverend Jeremiah Wright and black liberation theology to the Ebola virus.

Later in the campaign, Brown and Co. sent out a press release and e-mail announcing that one of Obama's half brothers had acknowledged that Obama was raised as a Muslim, an assertion Obama himself had denied. The problem was that the half brother never said any such thing. The quote on which the e-mail relied for the claim was a reporter's not-very-accurate paraphrase. The actual quotes made clear that Obama's half brother had converted to Islam well into adulthood; they never even hinted that he and Barack Obama had a Muslim upbringing. (They hadn't.) Nonetheless, Fox News's Brit Hume picked up the story and ran it credulously.

When it came to spreading anonymous and phony smears on the Internet, though, Brown's efforts were a mere drop in a vast ocean of garbage about Obama. Millions of Americans received e-mails that purported to contain "true" information revealing

Barack Obama to be an America-hating Muslim radical. Permutations on this theme included fake claims that Obama had the American flag removed from his jet and that he refused to wear flag lapel pins, as well as theories that he was secretly raised a Muslim at a madrasah in Indonesia and that in reality he was born not in Hawaii but in Kenya. Another favorite was a Photoshopped portrait that transformed Obama into a bearded bin Laden-type figure.

The viral anonymous e-mails became such a fixture of the campaign that Obama's organization was forced to create a Web site devoted to debunking the false information. A piece in the *Nation* written by Christopher Hayes described the campaign as "The New Right-Wing Smear Machine" and detailed how movement conservatives—using fringe far-right Web sites like NewsMax and WorldNetDaily as a kind of base of operations—spread hearsay rumors and wholly fabricated nonsense about Obama to millions of eager e-mail readers.

A typical e-mail forward that made the rounds during the 2008 campaign featured various "real quotes" from Barack Obama that painted him as a radical and anti-white racist. All of the quotes in question—as the debunking site Snopes.com laid out—were grotesquely twisted out of context and proportion or were jammed-up misquotes. In some cases, they were outright fabrications. One "quote" stood out: "I found a solace in nursing a pervasive sense of grievance and animosity against my mother's race." As Snopes noted, "No such sentence (nor anything close to it) appears anywhere in either *Dreams from My Father* or *The Audacity of Hope*." Nor could anything like it be found in any speech or article by Obama. He never said it, so who did?

The "quote" was actually taken (and slightly edited) from a line in a March 2007 *American Conservative* magazine article:

In reality, Obama provides a disturbing test of the best-case scenario of whether America can indeed move beyond race. He inherited his father's penetrating intelligence; was raised mostly by his loving liberal white grandparents in multiracial, laid-back Hawaii, where America's normal race rules never applied; and received a superb private school education. And yet, at least through age 33 when he wrote *Dreams from My Father,* he found solace in nursing a pervasive sense of grievance and animosity against his mother's race.

The author of the article, Steve Sailer, was intent on turning Obama's presidential candidacy into nothing but a referendum on race, and he insisted that Obama reflected a malignant "foreign" influence. (At one point, he even called Obama a "wigger.") It was *Sailer's* depiction of Obama being bandied about the Internet as Obama's own words. More sad and disturbing, many mainstream conservatives were eager to lap up and pass on the disinformation.

The intensity of the racial and ethnic animus directed at Obama picked up as Obama secured the Democratic Party nomination. Perhaps the clearest sign of this came in the days before the Democratic National Convention in Denver in late August, when three men with white-supremacist backgrounds were arrested in a nearby suburb for allegedly plotting to assassinate Obama, though they were never charged with the plot.

Obama's nomination also became a turning point in the tenor of the official campaigns—or more precisely, it coincided with John McCain's selection of Alaska governor Sarah Palin, a populist bomb thrower popular with the Religious Right, as his running mate. Upon hitting the hustings the week after the Republican National Convention unveiled her as America's newest right-wing heroine, Palin began lobbing rhetorical grenades in Obama's direction, accusing him of "palling around with terrorists" for his associations with onetime Weather Underground leader William Ayers. She also emphasized that the difference between Barack Obama and John McCain—and herself, of course—was that, being good Republicans, they preferred to campaign in "pro-American places." The tenor of Palin's campaign speeches was of the distinctly right-wing rabble-rousing kind, full of red meat meant to emphasize Obama's foreignness and his supposed radicalism.

The response was predictable: The crowds responded by shouting "terrorist" in reference to Obama, and at one rally the cry of "Kill him!" was heard in reference to Ayers. An Al Jazeera camera crew caught the honest sentiments of McCain/Palin supporters as they were leaving an Ohio rally:

> I'm afraid if he wins, the blacks will take over. He's not a Christian! This is a Christian nation! What is our country gonna end up like?

> When you got a Negra running for president, you need a first stringer. He's definitely a second stringer.

> He seems like a sheep—or a wolf in sheep's clothing to be honest with you. And I believe Palin—she's filled with the Holy Spirit, and I believe she's gonna bring honesty and integrity to the White House.

> He's related to a known terrorist, for one.

> He is friends with a terrorist of this country!

> He must support terrorists! You know, uh, if it walks like a duck and quacks like a duck, it must be a duck. And that to me is Obama.

> Just the whole, Muslim thing, and everything, and everybody's

still kinda—a lot of people have forgotten about 9/11, but . . . I dunno, it's just kinda . . . a little unnerving.

Obama and his wife, I'm concerned that they could be anti-white. That he might hide that.

I don't like the fact that he thinks us white people are trash . . . because we're not!

In Las Vegas, videographer Matt Toplikar captured footage of McCain/Palin supporters as they emerged from a rally featuring an appearance by Sarah Palin. One camouflage-capped fellow captured the spirit of the event:

Obama wins, I'm gonna move to Alaska. Haven't you ever heard that the United States is gonna be taken down from within? What better way to get taken down from within than having the President of the United States be the one that's going to do it?

The rally-goers became especially aggravated when they encountered anti-McCain protesters outside. The same Alaska-bound supporter started leading a chant in front of them: "Vote McCain, not Hussein!"

The video caught another McCain supporter declaring: "This country needs to wake up! Obama is dangerous! This man is a tyrant to this country. I mean, he has connections to Arabs! His education was paid for by Arabs! He's an abomination."

Another man warned, "Don't be afraid of me! Be afraid of Obama! Obama bin Laden, that's what you should be afraid of!" When accused of being a racist, he answered:

Yes, I am a racist. If you consider me a racist, well [unintelligible]. Those Arabs are dirtbags. They're dirty people, they hate

Americans, they hate my kids, they hate my grandkids. And people like him [points to another supporter], more power to them.

A *New York Observer* report from Florida told a similar story from outside another McCain/Palin event, quoting a 44-year-old calling herself "America Blanca" (White America) who said she didn't believe the polls showing Obama ahead. "I don't give a shit," she said. "I will never vote for a black man."

The week after the election, *Newsweek* carried a report describing how this was playing out on the ground:

> The Obama campaign was provided with reports from the Secret Service showing a sharp and disturbing increase in threats to Obama in September and early October, at the same time that many crowds at Palin rallies became more frenzied. Michelle Obama was shaken by the vituperative crowds and the hot rhetoric from the GOP candidates. "Why would they try to make people hate us?" Michelle asked a top campaign aide.

The answer: Because hate is what they do.

Representative Michelle Bachmann, a Republican from Minnesota's 6th District, made something of a name for herself in the 2008 campaign as a wingnut's wingnut. She'd always been eager to peddle conservative misinformation on the cable shows, but one October night on MSNBC's *Hardball with Chris Matthews,* she reached a special plateau of crazy.

Matthews tried to get Bachmann to tell his audience, per Sarah Palin's homage to "pro-American places," what parts of America are anti-American. Bachmann danced around the question and kept repeating the talking points programmed into her playback. So then Matthews tried another tack:

Matthews: How many Congresspeople, members of Congress are in that anti-American crowd you describe?

Bachmann: [Deer in the headlights]

Matthews: How many Congresspeople you serve with—I mean, there's 435 members of Congress—

Bachmann: Well, right now—

Matthews: —how many are anti-American in that Congress right now that you serve with?

Bachmann: You'd have to ask them, Chris, I'm focusing on Barack Obama and the people he's been associated with—

Matthews: But do you suspect that a lot of the people you serve with—

Bachmann: —and I'm very worried about their anti-American nature.

Matthews: Well, he's the United States Senator from Illinois, he's one of the people you suspect as being anti-American. How many people in the Congress of the United States do you think are anti-American? You've already suspected Barack Obama. Is he alone, or are there others?

Bachmann: [Deer in the headlights]

Matthews: How many of your colleagues do you suspect of being anti-American?

Bachmann: I would say, what I would say is that the news media should do a penetrating exposé and take a look—I wish they would. I wish the American media would take a great look at the views of the people in Congress and find out, are they pro-America or anti-America? I think the people would love to see an exposé like that.

Right after the break, Katrina vanden Heuvel, editor of the *Nation,* said precisely what needed saying:

> Chris, I fear for my country. I think what we just heard is a congresswoman channeling Joe McCarthy, channeling a politics of fear and loathing and demonization and division and distraction. Not a single issue mentioned. This is a politics at a moment of extreme economic pain in this country that is incendiary, that is so debased, that I'm almost having a hard time breathing, because I think it's very scary. Because this is a country I love, and this woman had no sense of the history of this nation, which is one of struggle, of trying to fulfill the great ideals of this nation, of movements that have brought about the civilizing advances of this country, and she doesn't even know who Saul Alinsky is—a community organizer who channeled the views of the people from below.
>
> I think Barack Obama is going to win, and he's going to have a lot of work because there is an extremism unleashed in this nation which you just heard on this program, which could lead to violence, and hatred, and toxicity. And against the backdrop of the Great Depression we're living through, it could lead—and I don't use this word lightly—to a kind of American fascism, which is against the great values of this nation, and which people like that are fomenting.

Even Patrick Buchanan was shaking his head, grimly acknowledging that he doubted any member of Congress could be called anti-American.

Bachmann was far from alone in indulging in this kind of McCarthyite rhetoric. At about the same time, Glenn Beck, while he was still at CNN's Headline News channel, offered his recipe for victory to John McCain—take off the kid gloves and start calling out Obama and "all of these guys" as Marxists:

He's bringing up these topics in the wrong way. Not as a political strategist or a politician or anything else, just as a guy who says, OK: The problem with all of these guys is they're all Marxists—they're all Marxists. They're all spread the wealth. . . . Now, you say to Joe the Plumber, I'm going to take some of your wealth and give it to somebody else, that's Marxism.

Similarly, CNN's Lou Dobbs, in his warm-up for that night's final presidential debate on October 15, hosted a discussion with right-wing pundit Diana West, who fretted about the prospects of an Obama electoral victory:

I find it amazing. I think that a lot of our traditional beliefs about the way people think and act are being shattered in this election. One of whom would be in a time of economic crisis, I am amazed that Americans seem to be turning to one, the one, Senator Obama of course, who is someone who embraces what I would increasingly describe as socialist policies. He spoke about it this week in terms of spreading wealth around.

At the time, this kind of talk was dismissed as silly and overheated hyperbole. In a few months, it became a standard part of the national discourse.

You couldn't help sensing that a lot of people pulled the levers or punched the chads for Barack Obama in the 2008 election precisely because of the ugliness that he stirred up among the denizens of the American Right. American voters were finally repelled by it and made their final decision based on the sense that it had gone too far.

Yet afterward, the Right's reliable pundit corps—particularly those who plied their trade at Fox News—were claiming that the country was still fundamentally a "center-right" nation and that Republicans lost because they weren't conservative enough. For many more—notably Rush Limbaugh and Glenn Beck—they weren't wingnutty enough. However, plenty of politicians and pundits were willing to oblige.

For instance, there was the Georgia Republican congressman who foresaw young Brownshirts emerging from Obama's proposal for a national civilian-service corps. "It may sound a bit crazy and off base, but the thing is, he's the one who proposed this national security force," Representative Paul Broun told an Associated Press reporter. "I'm just trying to bring attention to the fact that we may—may not, I hope not—but we may have a problem with that type of philosophy of radical socialism or Marxism." The story also included this information:

> Broun cited a July speech by Obama that has circulated on the Internet in which the then-Democratic presidential candidate called for a civilian force to take some of the national security burden off the military.
>
> "That's exactly what Hitler did in Nazi Germany and it's exactly what the Soviet Union did," Broun said. "When he's proposing to have a national security force that's answering to him, that is as strong as the U.S. military, he's showing me signs of being Marxist."

Then there was the member of the state education board of Texas who feared that Obama was secretly plotting with Muslim terrorists to destroy America. Cynthia Dunbar, writing for the Christian Worldview Network (CWN) Web site, fretted that a terrorist attack on America during the first six months of an Obama administration "will be a planned effort by those with whom Obama truly sympathizes to take down the America that is a threat to tyranny." Obama, she believed, would eventually declare martial law to impose a dictatorship. When called out by a citizens watchdog group that questioned the propriety of the piece, Dunbar was defiant—though the article was shortly removed from the CWN site.

Republican presidential candidate Ron Paul—who has a long history of promoting far-right conspiracy theories, particularly those involving a massive global-government plot—chimed in, casting Barack Obama as the new embodiment of the nefarious New World Order plot. Paul gave an interview to Alex Jones's conspiracy-mongering radio program in which he warned against "a cataclysmic shift toward a new world order":

> I think it's going to be an announcement of a new monetary order, and they'll probably make it sound very limited, they're not going to say this is world government, even though it is if you control the world's money and you control the military, which they do indirectly.
>
> A world central bank, worldwide regulation and world control of the whole system, of all the commodities and all the natural resources, what else can you call it other than world government?
>
> Obama wouldn't be there if he didn't toe the line, and when the meeting starts on November 15th for the new monetary system, this could be the beginning of the end of what's left of our national sovereignty.

Paul enjoyed substantial support from the extremist Right during the primary season—the neo-Nazi Web site Stormfront featured numerous pro-Paul campaign threads, and he notoriously refused to return a $100 campaign donation from Stormfront founder Don Black (with whom he was photographed at a campaign stop).

The real call to action for the extremist Right, however, came from Alan Keyes, the Republican candidate who opposed Obama for his Senate seat in 2004. In a February 2009 interview with a reporter from KHAS-TV, filmed outside a fund-raiser for the AAA Crisis Pregnancy Center in Hastings, Nebraska, Keyes said this:

> Obama is a radical communist, and I think it is becoming clear. That is what I told people in Illinois and now everybody realizes it's true. He is going to destroy this country, and we are either going to stop him or the United States of America is going to cease to exist.

To a significant segment of the American Right, 2008 indeed marked the end of the world as they knew it. Small wonder, then, that the most extreme among them erupted in violence.

TWO

Into the Abyss

The conservative movement—and especially its political wing, the Republican Party—was at a real crossroads in the weeks after Obama's election. Would the movement's members take the hard route—assess honestly and accurately the political wasteland before them (they had just lost both the presidency and any hope of having much influence in Congress) and remake themselves accordingly—or would they increase the racially and culturally divisive tactics that had led them to previous electoral glory in days gone by?

Perhaps it wasn't a surprise that they took the easy route. And no one on board seemed much concerned that it led directly over the cliff and into the abyss.

Immediately after the election, right-wing pundits began proclaiming, like a Greek chorus, their conviction that "America was still a center-right nation." On Fox News, on CNN, on MSNBC, the mantra was repeated endlessly. David Sirota began tracking this theme in the media and by mid-November reported:

> The media has exponentially increased the amount of times it claims that this country is a "center-right nation"—at the very same time public opinion data shows the country is a decidedly center-left nation. In short, we have the two hard data

points proving that as the country has become more progressive and validated its progressivism on election day, the media has increased its claims that the nation is conservative.

Leading the way were Rush Limbaugh and his chorus of imitators. Limbaugh began insisting that the problem for Republicans was that they weren't conservative enough. In an interview with Fox News's Sean Hannity, he explained:

> The reason they [the GOP] lost huge is because in a contest of group politics, the experts are gonna always get group votes before the pretenders will. And we were pretenders trying to get the groups. We gotta get the Hispanics, we gotta be moderate, we gotta prove we can walk across the aisle, the era of Reagan is over.

Limbaugh was soon joined by other conservatives, who were eager to proclaim their reembrace of the conservative values that had been lost during the Bush administration—even though nearly every one of the policy decisions that led to the electoral disaster, from economic to national-security and wartime decisions as well as domestic disaster-relief policy, was a product of ongoing conservative political philosophy. Still, that didn't keep people like former GOP presidential candidate Mike Huckabee from telling Alan Colmes on Fox News: "When Republicans stick to our stuff we win. It's when we run to the mushy middle, that's when we lose."

Some Republican voices of warning started to crop up: Former secretary of state Colin Powell told a group of business executives that the GOP is "getting smaller and smaller" and "that's not good for the nation." Powell also said, "I think what Rush does as an entertainer diminishes the party and intrudes or inserts into our public life a kind of nastiness that we would be better to do without." He added that Sarah Palin is "a very accomplished person" who became "a very polarizing figure."

The response from the hard-right sector of the GOP was swift and strong: Sean Hannity told Powell he should "go join the Democrats." Even former vice president Dick Cheney chimed in, saying he thought Powell was in fact a Democrat now. Powell promptly denied this.

Republican congresspeople began fanning out to try to "reconnect with their roots." On the first weekend of May 2009, a number of them held town-hall meetings designed to reach constituents—demonstrating in the process that they remained as clueless as ever. That same weekend, an interesting Rasmussen poll showed that those constituents basically despise them: At the time, a mere 21 percent of GOP voters believed Republicans in Congress had "done a good job representing their own party's values." Some 69 percent said congressional Republicans had lost touch with GOP voters throughout the nation. These findings were virtually unchanged from a survey just after election day. The report added:

> Seventy-two percent (72%) of Republicans say it is more important for the GOP to stand for what it believes in than for the party to work with President Obama. Twenty-two percent (22%) want their party to work with the President more.

In other words, the Republican base, by a large margin, was unhappy with its party's political leadership for *not being right wing enough*. And that happened to comport with what their real leadership—the right-wing punditocracy—had been saying.

Unfortunately for Republicans, the electorate at large has a distinctly different outlook. Polls at the same time showed that they strongly wanted Republicans to cooperate with President Obama and strongly believed they were not making a good-faith effort to do so. Republicans wanted to fight, but this was not a fight Republicans were winning.

However, they had experience in facing these kinds of daunting electoral opportunities and began turning back the pages of the playbook to 1993, the last time they were up against a popular new Democratic president and a solid Democratic Congress—which meant that it was time to fire up the ranks of the extremist Right.

No one's exactly certain where it originated, but somewhere in those e-mail forwards promoted by the likes of Floyd Brown—the ones with a long list of reasons why Barack Obama was secretly a Muslim radical—there first appeared the suggestion that Obama was not really an American citizen because of the circumstances of his birth. Some of these e-mails claimed that Obama actually was born in Kenya, whereas others suggested he was born in Indonesia.

So the Obama campaign—at a Web site called Fight the Smears set up specifically to combat the wild rumors that circulated through the e-mail forwards—obtained a copy of Obama's birth certificate showing that he was born in Hawaii in 1961 and published it for all to see. Problem solved, right?

Perhaps for rational people. For the conspiracy-mongers of the fringe Right, though, that was just the beginning.

Some of them noticed that what Obama had actually obtained was what the state of Hawaii calls a "Certification of Live Birth"—which is basically the state's short-form version of a person's original birth certificate. It includes time of birth, city, and so on, but lacks medical details, including the name of the hospital. To get those details, you have to get the original certificate itself. Obtaining a copy of the original requires making a special request to state officials.

Naturally, a fresh round of conspiracy theorizing erupted—the birth certificate on display, the Obama haters asserted, had been digitally altered with Adobe Photoshop. It also lacked a stamped seal of the state, a certain sign of forgery. Jerome Corsi—coauthor of the "Swift Boat" hoax that played a critical role in sinking John Kerry's presidential campaign in 2004, and more recently the author of a book he oh-so-cleverly titled *The Obama Nation: Leftist Politics and the Cult of Personality* (get it? Obama Nation/ Abomination?)—went on *Fox & Friends* and told Steve Doocy:

> The campaign has a false, fake birth certificate posted on their website. . . . it's been shown to have watermarks from Photoshop. It's a fake document that's on the website right now, and the original birth certificate the campaign refuses to produce.

The Obama campaign invited FactCheck.org to come see the certificate for themselves, and it subsequently reported:

> FactCheck.org staffers have now seen, touched, examined and photographed the original birth certificate. We conclude that it meets all of the requirements from the State Department for proving U.S. citizenship. Claims that the document lacks a raised seal or a signature are false. We have posted high-resolution photographs of the document as "supporting documents" to this article. Our conclusion: Obama was born in the U.S.A. just as he has always said.

Hawaii state officials subsequently confirmed that the state held Obama's original birth certificate on record, noting that "there have been numerous requests" for copies but explaining that the state's records department was prohibited by state law from releasing it to "persons who do not have a tangible interest in the vital record."

Of course, there are always the births listed in local newspapers—and sure enough, both the *Honolulu Advertiser* and the *Honolulu Star-Bulletin* (on August 13 and August 14, 1961, respectively) published a birth notice for Barack Obama, listing the home address as 6085 Kalanianaole Highway in Honolulu. Addressing the whole kerfuffle—which lasted through the summer of 2009—*Star-Bulletin* editors, in an unsigned editorial, scathingly wondered: "Were the state Department of Health and Obama's parents really in cahoots to give false information to the newspapers, perhaps intending to clear the way for the baby to someday be elected president of the United States?"

The birth-certificate controversy seemed largely laid to rest by the election results. Yet in spite of all the incontrovertible evidence proving that their various theories and hypotheses were bogus, the outer fringes of wingnuttia clung, even after the election, to the conspiracy theory as their last hope of stopping Barack Obama from becoming president. Some of them—primarily a pair of fringe right-wing lawyers named Leo Donofrio and Orly Taitz—even tried to take legal action to prevent Obama from being sworn in. The U.S. Supreme Court briefly considered Donofrio's lawsuit challenging Obama's U.S. citizenship—a continuation of a New Jersey case embraced by the birth-certificate conspiracy theorists (or "Birthers," as they came to be known)—but peremptorily dismissed it.

Also chiming in at this point were the conspiracists who had organized for the previous seven years around theories that the 9/11 terrorist attacks were actually the product of a nefarious plot by the Bush/Cheney cabal. While the "9/11 Truthers," as they came to be known (or, more derisively, "Troofers"), were often left-wing opponents of the Bush administration, by 2003 much of the movement had absorbed—and was being led by—right-wing extremists from the old Patriot/militia movement of the 1990s. The most prominent of these was Texas radio talk-show host Alex

Jones, whose broadcasts for most of the 1990s had been dedicated to theories about Bill Clinton's "New World Order"—including supposed plans to round up gun owners and place them in concentration camps—and who continued the conspiracist mind-set well into the Bush years with his *Prison Planet* TV show and Infowars Web site. Now, Jones and the rest of the "Truthers" began touting various theories about Barack Obama—including the birth-certificate claims. "Truther" Philip Berg filed the first attempt at a legal injunction against Obama running for the presidency, in August 2008, alleging that the "extensive forensic testing" of anonymous experts had proved the certificate a forgery. (Berg also claimed that Obama operatives had simply printed his name over that of his half sister, Maya—who was born in Indonesia.)

The convergence of old far-right conspiracists and the new anti-Obama fanatics gave birth, in the weeks after the election, to a campaign to prevent Obama from taking the oath of office in January. They formed online campaigns like RallyCongress.com, where more than 125,000 signatures were gathered demanding Obama's birth certificate, and WeMustBeHeard.com, which organized sit-ins outside the Supreme Court Building in Washington. The right-wing Web news site WorldNetDaily—which has a long history of promoting right-wing conspiracy theories dating back to the 1990s—organized a similar petition drive. A longtime far-right tax protester named Bob Schultz purchased full-page ads in the *Chicago Tribune* asserting that Obama's birth certificate was "forged," that his "grandmother is record[ed] on tape saying she attended your birth in Kenya," and that Obama had lost his citizenship by virtue of his mother's second marriage to an Indonesian man.

By the time of Obama's inauguration on January 20, 2009, however, all these efforts had come to naught. That didn't mean they had subsided. Rather the opposite—thanks in no small part to the mainstream media.

A California lawyer and dentist named Orly Taitz, who had filed a 2008 California suit over Obama's birth certificate that went nowhere, filed a lawsuit in July 2009 on behalf of an Army Reserve soldier named Stefan Cook, who claimed he could refuse deployment orders to Afghanistan because the president wasn't an American citizen. When the army responded by simply rescinding Cook's orders, Sean Hannity reported it on his Fox News program thus:

> Now we told you yesterday about an Army Reserve soldier who challenged his deployment orders on the grounds that President Obama has not proven that he is a U.S. citizen. Now that soldier, Maj. Stefan Frederick Cook, who was supposed to deploy to Afghanistan in the coming days, has now had his orders revoked. According to his lawyer, quote, "They just said order revoked. No explanation, no reasons, just revoked."
>
> Now, Major Cook and his lawyers expressed joy at this outcome, and they took it as an admission on the part of the military that the president is not, in fact, a legitimate citizen by birth.

That was the entirety of the report; Hannity simply gave the segment over to promoting Orly Taitz's claims. But all you had to do was read the actual news accounts to realize that Taitz was lying: The army in fact gave a clear reason for Cook's orders being revoked—namely, that Cook always had the option of requesting not to go on this duty.

Hannity shied away from any "Birther" reports from then on. Similarly, Rush Limbaugh briefly referenced it on his radio show: "God does not have a birth certificate, and neither does Obama— not that we've seen." But afterward, he made little mention of it.

However, the "Birthers" eventually found an ardent supporter in the mainstream media: CNN's Lou Dobbs.

Dobbs kicked off his coverage of the birth-certificate controversy in mid-July on his syndicated radio show by hosting Orly Taitz and asserting repeatedly that Obama "needed to produce" his birth certificate:

> Should he produce his birth certificate—the long form, the real deal? Should he be a little more forthcoming? . . . What is the deal here? I'm starting to think we have a—we have a document issue. Do you suppose he's un—no, I won't even use the word undocumented. It wouldn't be right.

Filling in for Dobbs on Dobbs's CNN program a few days later, CNN's Kitty Pilgrim ran a report debunking the theories. Nonetheless, on his CNN broadcast the next night, Dobbs asserted that Obama's birth-certificate questions "won't go away." He featured a video clip of a town-hall attendee berating Republican representative Mike Castle of Delaware about Obama's birth certificate: "He is not an American citizen! He is a citizen of Kenya!"

Dobbs commented: "A lot of anger in the audience, and a lot of questions remaining—seemingly, the questions won't go away because they haven't been dealt with, it seems possible, too straightforwardly and quickly."

The comments created an uproar; media critics from around the press—including Dobbs's colleague at CNN, Howard Kurtz—questioned Dobbs's journalistic sense in reporting the story as though it had any credibility. Dobbs also became an object of derision. On *The Daily Show,* Jon Stewart shouted at Dobbs in absentia: "Do you even *watch* CNN?!" Rather than back down, Dobbs doubled down: He went on CNN and charged that Obama could "make the whole . . . controversy disappear . . . by simply releasing his original birth certificate." On his radio show, Dobbs similarly persisted: "Where is that birth certificate? Why hasn't it been forthcoming?" When the resulting public firestorm produced calls from organizations like the Southern Poverty Law Center to remove Dobbs from his anchor's chair, CNN president Jon Klein defended Dobbs's coverage as "legitimate"—though Klein did e-mail Dobbs's staff to inform them that the birth-certificate story was "dead." That night, Dobbs persisted in arguing that Obama could "make the story go away." As the controversy raged on other channels—Fox's Bill O'Reilly knocked Dobbs for his credulousness but defended him against his attackers anyway—Dobbs tried claiming that he really didn't believe the theories: "How I could be wrong about that I don't know because all I said is the president is a citizen, but it would be simple to make all this noise go away with just simply producing the long form birth certificate?"

Eric Boehlert, writing for MediaMatters.org, captured the essence of what the "Birther" controversy was really all about:

> Viewed in a vacuum, the movement seems like the nutty fringe.
> But viewed in a larger historical context, birthers share obvious
> ties to traditional right-wing assaults on previous Democrats,
> and birthers have all the marks of a GOP Noise Machine cre-
> ation. The movement is about a larger, more sinister attempt
> to paint Obama as illegitimate, foreign, and suspect (i.e. not
> like you and me). To portray him as "a gratuitous interloper," as
> radio host G. Gordon Liddy put it. As someone who isn't who
> he says he is. As—let's face it—the Manchurian Candidate,
> with all the evil connotations that come with it. . . .
>
> And it's about the disturbing role media figures like Dobbs
> play when they act as the bridge—as the transmitter—between
> the radical and the mainstream. When they legitimize the crazi-
> ness, if only in the eyes of the crazies themselves. As MSNBC's
> Rachel Maddow noted this week, "The home run for conspira-

cists of any stripe is when their ideas can leave the lunatic fringe and enter the mainstream."

In that respect, the explosion of right-wing conspiracism and McCarthyite smears that followed Obama's election was remarkably similar to the events that followed Bill Clinton's election in 1993—the onslaught was predicated on a series of viral memes whose purpose was to delegitimize Obama's presidency. In the case of Clinton, the conspiracy theories created a narrative depicting the president as an amoral, womanizing conniver who was plotting to hand the national sovereignty over to a cabal of New World Order conspirators. For Obama, the meme evolved into a depiction of the president as a radical communist (or socialist or even fascist) who "hates America," a man with Muslim sympathies similarly plotting to resign our national sovereignty.

The groundwork for this meme, as we've seen, was laid during the 2008 campaign. But it took on a life of its own after the election.

Even before the inauguration, Sean Hannity went on his nationally syndicated radio show and announced he was organizing a would-be force to attempt to stop Obama from enacting "radical" policies, calling his show the outpost of "the conservative underground." Fellow radio host Mike Gallagher similarly promoted an effort by a far-right online group called Grassfire to present a petition announcing that signers were joining "the resistance" to Obama's presidency.

In mid-January 2009, Rush Limbaugh announced on his radio show his hope that Obama would fail:

> We're talking about my country, the United States of America, my nieces, my nephews, your kids, your grandkids. Why in the world do we want to saddle them with more liberalism and

socialism? Why would I want to do that? So I can answer it, four words, "I hope he fails." And that would be the most outrageous thing anybody in this climate could say. Shows you just how far gone we are. Well, I know, I know. I am the last man standing.

Limbaugh's wish for Obama's failure stirred outrage from liberals and centrists alike, but he was defiant. At the Conservative Political Action Conference in February, he justified it by explaining that Democrats did it too:

> Ladies and gentlemen, the Democrat Party has actively not just sought the failure of Republican presidents and policies and now wars, for the first time. The Democrat Party doesn't stop at failure. Talk to Judge Robert Bork, talk to Justice Clarence Thomas, about how they try to destroy lives, reputations, and character. And I'm supposed to say, I don't want the president to fail?

Then there was Glenn Beck. By 2009, Limbaugh was the elder statesman of the incendiary-pundit set. And as vicious and divisive as his rhetoric got, even he was overtaken that year in both those qualities by the hot new face on the right-wing scene: Beck. Not only did Beck build on and amplify the central themes established during the 2008 campaign—that Obama was a foreigner, a leftist, an America-hating radical who wanted to destroy the American way of life—but he opened up a whole new frontier in the transmission of right-wing extremist ideas into mainstream American discourse in the process.

Beck already had a reputation as a bomb thrower from his tenure at CNN's Headline News channel, where he was noted for such antics as asking newly elected representative Keith Ellison— the nation's first Muslim congressman—why he shouldn't consider him to be working for the enemy. He also was open in his sympathy for right-wing extremists and their ideas. While credulously interviewing a John Birch Society official about a supposed conspiracy to create a "North American Union," Beck said: "Sam, I have to tell you, when I was growing up, the John Birch Society, I thought they were a bunch of nuts, however, you guys are starting to make more and more sense to me."

Beck announced he was making the leap to Fox News in October 2008, though his show did not begin running regularly until January 2009. Still, he gave the public a preview of where he was going with his new show in a mid-November appearance with Bill O'Reilly on *The O'Reilly Factor*, ranting at length about the public's evident tolerance—judging by election results—of a presidential candidate who had "palled around" with terrorists like William Ayers. Beck explained away the election as the result of "[c]akes and circuses and too many dumb people. I mean, we should thin out the herd, you know what I mean?" He also set the table for what was to come:

> This is a total outrage, Bill. There is a disconnect in America. We are at the place where the Constitution hangs in the balance, and I think we're at a crossroads here. We're still about here [points to spot on hand], where the roads are just starting to split, but pretty soon, this side and this side are not gonna understand each other at all, because we're living in different universes.

It became clear early on, though, that Beck was not interested in bridging this gap but in exploiting it. No sooner did his show get started on Fox than he began focusing on the ideological aspects of Obama's supposed "radicalism." The show also featured an unusually maudlin tone; in his Fox debut on January 19, Beck became teary-eyed talking about Sarah Palin's candidacy and how it made him feel like he "was not alone." A couple of weeks later, he featured a segment in which he had the camera crop in tightly around his eyes as he delivered his monologue; when he was parodied for it a few days later by Stephen Colbert, Beck came on and explained that he did it because "we don't look each other in the eyes" enough these days. A few weeks after this, in an hour-long program set up like a town-hall meeting, Beck again got choked up: "I just love my country—and I fear for it!" he blurted out.

Beck devoted most of his energy to the theme that President Obama was a far-left radical who intended to remake America into a totalitarian state. He had a problem, though, in figuring out just what *kind* of totalitarianism Obama was bringing: socialist, communist, or fascist. Over the course of the next several months, Beck began using all three terms—which, by anyone's lights but Beck's, actually represent profoundly different and distinct ideologies—to describe Obama's agenda, often interchangeably.

On his February 4 Fox News show, Beck launched into a scathing attack on Obama after he signed into law the State Children's Health Insurance Program (SCHIP), which provides matching funds to states to cover health-insurance costs to families with children. Beck saw this as proof of the new administration's incipient socialism:

> Hey, has anybody noticed this crazy thing that we're on the road to socialism? I'm just sayin'—wow, we got that SCHIPs thing goin' for us—that's great, there's the change that we were all hoping for, seriously. Hey, I got an idea, if we're gonna go down the road to socialism, I mean, why not really go for it, hah?

The screen then displayed an animated graphic showing the road from "Capitalism" (in big block letters) to "Socialism" to "Communism." When we returned to Beck, he was accompanied by a large graphic declaring this a "Comrade Update" (with the R reversed and a chryon with a Cyrillic script running beneath, in case you didn't get that this was supposed to be a faux Soviet-propaganda broadcast):

> Comrades! Good news from the Western Front! Our glorious revolution is starting to take hold. Oh, the revolution of Change. Our fearless leader has just signed in SCHIPs, and earlier today, he spoke out against capitalism. Listen up!

Then he played a clip of Obama announcing a cap on executive salaries for banks receiving bailout funds. In other words, for Beck, limiting the amount that corporate-bailout recipients can take from taxpayers for their personal enrichment is tantamount to "speaking out against capitalism."

Two nights later, appearing on *The O'Reilly Factor* with fill-in Laura Ingraham, Beck took it to the next illogical step:

> Beck: We are really, truly, stepping beyond socialism and we're starting to look at fascism. We are putting business and government together!

> Ingraham: Glenn, you're throwing a lot of terms around, and I'm going to play devil's advocate, because this is fair and balanced. Now, moving from socialism to communism, that's, that's a pretty big leap—socialism, obviously, the economic system, communism the political system. How are we right now moving toward state ownership of all, for instance, heavy industry?

> Beck: Let me first of all just explain first what happened in Nazi Germany. It was National—Socialism. We're talking now about nationalizing the banks, and socialized programs. National. Socialism. At first in Nazi Germany, everybody was so panicked, they were so freaked. Remember—don't take

anytime to think about it, we've just got to do, do, do. At first all the big companies and the big capitalists in Germany said, "Oh thank goodness there's a savior! OK, great! We'll do that, yes!" It didn't take too long before—like here in America, now Goldman Sachs. They've started to see the writing on the wall and went, "Whoa, whoa whoa! You guys are getting out of control here. What are you guys doing?" And they couldn't get out of it fast enough. Unfortunately, for those in Germany, you could never go back. I don't know if this is the system that we're headed towards or not, where they're not going to let you out, but let me tell you something, I don't want to play this game. This is becoming extraordinarily dangerous.

About this time, Beck began featuring Jonah Goldberg, the author of *Liberal Fascism,* on his programs as a guest to discuss the "fascist" tendencies of populist liberals angered by bonuses handed out to executives of bailed-out insurance companies and similar issues. Finally, on his March 4 broadcast, Beck announced that he had been wrong: America was on the road to fascism, not socialism.

He opened the segment ranting about how Obama, in his campaign, decried "the politics of fear," while running on a screen behind Beck was grainy black-and-white footage of German Nazis in World War II, marching en masse.

It doesn't matter which administration we have in office. It all adds up . . . to me, now having to admit that I was wrong. Our government is not marching down the road towards communism or socialism. I was convinced, for a long time, we were headed towards socialism, that they were marching us toward a brand of socialism we hadn't seen for awhile, maybe except in France. But now I have to tell you that they're not marching us in that direction. They're marching us to a brand of non-violent fascism—or to put it another way, they're marching us toward *1984.*

Big Brother. He's watching! They're controlling. They're telling you how to run your business, who to hire, who to fire, how much to pay 'em. They're controlling your life. And suggesting now, in the G-20 and the U.N., even how to parent your own children. . . .

Like it or not, fascism is on the rise. And that doesn't mean the Adolf Hitler kind of fascism. It's fascism with a happy face. I'll explain the exact definition of fascism in a second, and it will boggle your mind.

Beck, parroting Goldberg, gave a mangled libertarian definition of fascism as an economic system. But fascism is an economic phenomenon only secondarily at best. Primarily, fascism is a political and cultural pathology; its leading ideologues explicitly rejected economics as a driver in human affairs. Fascism is all about blood and iron and will, a love of violence, and a contempt for the weak. Only in its mature stages—when it has actually obtained power—does economics come into play for fascism. Thus only in the fevered imaginations of right-wing ideologues could the manifestly moderate politics of the Obama administration be construed as "fascist."

Beck never really could settle on an ideological direction for his warnings about Obama. By that fall, he would be attacking Obama administration officials again as "Marxist radicals" and "Maoists."

It was more than fitting that, from the beginning, Beck's show also featured an overarching apocalyptic sensibility. After all, if Obama's election meant the end of the world for conservatives, then nowhere was that more evident than on Beck's show on Fox.

At various times, different dooms confronted the nation, according to Beck. He frequently fretted about the epidemic of violent crime by Mexican drug cartels south of the border and hosted a hysterical discussion with prominent right-wing blogger Michelle Malkin about the existential threat this posed to the United States. At other times, he saw a global nuclear apocalypse looming in the form of a potential confrontation with Iran. But consistently the greatest threat to America, by Beck's hallucinatory lights, was President Obama and his administration. Whether it was the road to socialism or communism or fascism, Beck knew one thing: Obama was taking America to hell in a handbasket.

Soon the paranoia began reaching a fever pitch—including a flirtation with conspiracy theories that Obama was using the Federal Emergency Management Administration (FEMA) to secretly prepare concentration camps into which conservatives were about to be rounded up. On March 3, Beck went on the morning show *Fox & Friends* and talked about his fears with the co-hosts:

> We don't even understand freedom anymore. We are a country that is headed toward socialism, totalitarianism, beyond your wildest imagination.
>
> I have to tell you, I am doing a story tonight, that I wanted to debunk these FEMA camps. I'm tired of hearing about them—you know about them? I'm tired of hearing about them. I wanted to debunk them.
>
> Well we've now for several days been doing research on them—I can't debunk them! And we're going to carry the story tonight....
>
> It is our government—if you trust our government, it's fine. If you have any kind of fear that we might be headed toward a totalitarian state, there is something going on in our country that it's—it ain't good.

He also reported it credulously, twice, on his own Fox News program. As he promised on *Fox & Friends,* he announced on the air that night that he couldn't disprove the FEMA concentration-camps story. He also discussed them in an interview with Ron Paul, who told him his office could find no evidence the camps existed but Beck's "underlying concerns" with government power were well founded anyway.

Funny thing about "not debunking" the FEMA camps: As Beck no doubt discovered upon trying to look into them, it's not easy to "debunk" the existence of something for which there is simply no evidence of its existence in the first place. In reality, these claims originated back in the 1990s with the far-right Patriot/militia movement. We first heard about them in 1994, while attending a militia meeting in Maltby, Washington, featuring Militia of Montana spokesman Bob Fletcher. The map Fletcher displayed on the stage during his talk featured what he claimed was a "United Nations reserve" being created just to the east of Seattle, in the northern Cascade Range, in which the feds were busy creating concentration camps, run by FEMA, which he assured us were being built to hold gun owners after the government rounded them all up.

Of course, no such camps existed. When asked to help pinpoint the camps' exact location, neither Fletcher nor Militia of Montana leader John Trochmann ever got back to us. Trochmann had largely originated these conspiracy theories, though they quickly spread to other Patriot outlets. He described how Clinton's "New World Order" would enact its totalitarian regime: Guns would be confiscated. Urban gangs like the Bloods and the Crips would be deployed to conduct house-to-house searches and round up resisters. Thousands of citizens would be shipped off to concentration camps and liquidated, all in the name of reducing the population.

These theories came to be believed on a broad basis among militia followers. Another national militia leader, Linda Thompson, began selling the theories by videotaping scenes from inside facilities that she said were future concentration camps being organized under the rubric of FEMA.

A month after repeatedly telling his audience he "couldn't debunk" the existence of the FEMA camps, Beck finally featured on his April 6 show a ten-minute segment with Jim Meigs, a journalist from *Popular Science,* who looked into the veracity of the claims. It was something akin to running a single correction on page A23 for a series of sensationally bannered stories on A1, but at least it offered some closure: Meigs reported unequivocally that a "detention center" depicted in one of the key "FEMA camp" videos making the rounds was actually an abandoned rail station, and that the people making the videos and the claims had been doing so since the 1990s. One of the key figures, Meigs said, was a longtime militia figure named Linda Thompson, who had created the video in question.

Beck was hardly chastened by the episode and continued promoting militia-style beliefs in other arenas. On March 24, he had hosted former United Nations ambassador John Bolton for a discussion of the globalist propensities of the Obama White House.

> You know, let's not throw Barack Obama under the bus solely. I
> think George Bush was not as bad, but he was on the same road.
> I mean, you know, we've been playing the game with the United
> Nations—thank God George Bush put you into the United
> Nations! I know you, you were extremely unpopular there—I
> cheered for that!
>
> I mean, I think these guys—these guys, they'll take away
> guns, they'll take away our sovereignty, they'll take away our,
> our, our currency, our money! They're already starting to put all

the global framework in with this bullcrap called global warm-ing! This is an effort to globalize and tie together everybody on the planet, is it not?

Taking away guns—that was one of the militias' chief sources of paranoia in the 1990s, and now Beck was raising it against Obama, too. He regularly warned his audience that "our rights are under attack," including "the right to keep and bear arms" under the Second Amendment.

The notion that Obama and his administration intended to go on a gun-grabbing spree—while not having any factual basis in reality, beyond a handful of quotes suggesting a sympathy for gun-control measures—became a recurring theme on Beck's show. Twice he featured the president of the National Rifle Association (NRA), Wayne LaPierre, in segments with a large chryon titled "Constitution Under Attack." On March 18, he and LaPierre dis-cussed administration plans to crack down on gun traffic along the Mexican border as a potential opening for Attorney General Eric Holder to "reinstate" the expired federal ban (enacted by Clinton) on assault-style weapons—even though no administration officials ever indicated they would. A month later, on April 16, LaPierre suggested that administration support for international efforts to adopt strict gun-licensing standards amounted to a United Nations plot: "They're trying to pass, basically, a global gun ban on all individual possession of firearms ownership."

Mind you, the paranoia whipped up by the NRA had no known basis in reality. In the list of 13 priorities for action in Obama's first year and beyond (leaked to the *New York Times*), jobs and the economy completely predominated. Gun control not only was not on the list, it wasn't anywhere near it. Nor was there even a whisper of it from any Obama administration official in 2009. Which, for the paranoid at heart, only proved once and for all that something nefarious was afoot.

Whether grounded in reality or not, Beck was tapping into something very real by promoting gun paranoia. Indeed, one of the remarkable ways the fringe hysteria manifested itself in the real world after the election was in the astonishing surge in gun sales.

The initial spike occurred before the election, when firearms groups began noticing a surge in federal background checks for new gun purchases. There was an even sharper spike in background checks in the last three months of 2008. In November alone, the number—some 378,000 checks—was 42 percent greater than in the same month a year before. One gun-friendly news service that covers the outdoors named the new president its "Gun Salesman of the Year."

The only time gun rights really made their way into the news was during the confirmation hearings for then attorney general nominee Eric Holder, where one of the voices testifying against his confirmation was a "gun rights expert" named Stephen Halbrook, who also happened to have authored a recent book about the Second Amendment. What upset the gun crowd about Holder was his position supporting the gun ban in DC, as well as an op-ed piece he wrote in October 2001 for the *Washington Post* titled "Keeping Guns Away from Terrorists" in which he lobbied for closing gun-sales loopholes because many terrorists use them to obtain weapons.

When the gun-sales data emerged, the Obama camp had this to say, as reported by CNN:

> "What people do is their own business, and if they decide to go out and buy guns they'll go out and buy guns, assuming that

they are eligible to buy guns," John Podesta, the co-chairman of Obama's transition team, told reporters Sunday. "But I think that President-elect Obama has been clear in his campaign that what he wants to focus on is the economy, trying to get jobs growing again, dealing with the health care crisis, and dealing with our dependence on foreign oil."

Nonetheless, the fears that Obama was a closet gun grabber became widespread, particularly in the rural areas where gun rights have been a favorite bugaboo since the days of gas-station attendants and Beaver Cleaver. The fear that "Liberal President [insert name here] is gonna take our guns away" has been commonplace in rural America at least since the days of Lyndon Johnson, and probably before then too. But Obama's election produced a lightning bolt of fear among gun-friendly citizens, and they responded by snapping up every gun in sight—as well as every piece of ammunition. Soon, gun dealers were reporting a shortage of certain models of guns as well as a serious shortage of ammunition and even manual-loading supplies like gunpowder.

"Barack Obama would be the most anti-gun president in history—bar none," NRA chief lobbyist Chris Cox wrote in a *Washington Times* op-ed. Warnings like that—as well as Glenn Beck's paranoid musings with Wayne LaPierre—produced predictable results among gun owners. "They're like, 'Hey, maybe I should buy one of these before they become illegal,'" one gun-shop owner told a reporter. "If you look in any NRA magazine or you're into guns, you see a lot of bills that are in the works."

The NRA's annual convention in Arizona in May 2009 became an extended exercise in wallowing in groundless paranoia. All the raging talk at the convention was about the gun-sales spike. The footage coming out of Arizona from the NRA's big convention was striking for the amount of paranoia purveyed versus the actual cause for such fearfulness. Michael Steele, chairman of the Republican National Committee, warned conventiongoers: "Whenever they can, wherever they can, the Democrats want to take away the rights of law-abiding citizens to own and purchase a gun, a right that is guaranteed under the United States Constitution."

"Right now is a pivotal time in our history with a president and a total administration that is anti-gun," a 56-year-old trucker and Republican Party organizer from Tucson named Leonard Junker told a Reuters reporter. "I truly believe that they want to disarm us," he added.

It was more than just fear of Obama, however, driving people to buy guns; it was also fear of the social chaos they believed would result from his administration. Video footage from the NRA convention featured a number of white, conservative women who were drawn to the NRA via fearmongering. In one video, a woman explained that she was determined to get as much ammo as she could at the show. Another talked about why women are buying guns—because they fear Obama will take them away, but also because of a fear that society is about to fall apart. Glenn Beck's apocalyptic scenarios of a dog-eat-dog society had obviously struck a chord.

If gun paranoia was flying high among the more mainstream NRA set, it was at exospheric levels within the Patriot/militia ranks, where concocting the most far-flung conspiracy theories imaginable is not just a way of life but a competition. On the fringes of right-wing thought, the fearfulness became virulent and the rhetoric became threatening and violent.

By late February 2009, there were signs that the militia movement was ratcheting up after being largely dormant for most of the Bush years. The newer militias had a broader menu of fears to choose from—to their groundless fears about guns they added President Obama's supposedly "socialist" plans for stimulating the economy and reforming health-care insurance. The new militias that started forming also were constituted of a different base—younger, more militant, more paranoid, and more likely to have an actual military background.

A lot of this organizing occurred quietly, and the Internet played a key role. Among the more common places you could find militiamen online was at Web social-networking platforms like MySpace. Much of the networking occurred on private pages that required permission to access, but others were public. For instance, one site, run evidently by a former U.S. Marine from Colorado, featured discussions such as "Training a Survival of Militia Group, Part 1."

A common organizational theme among the new militiamen is "Μολών λαβέ"—or "Molon labe," Greek for "Come and take them," which is reportedly what the Spartan king Leonidas replied when the Persian king Xerxes demanded the surrender of their weapons before the battle of Thermopylae in 480 BC. It's roughly equivalent in sentiment to "Over my dead body." The film *300,* about this famous battle, enjoys a great deal of popularity among the Patriots because many see themselves as potential martyrs. A couple of the would-be militiamen organized broadcasts of "Come and Take It Radio," hosted online at a MySpace page, where they published the following rant:

> Join hosts Matt Conner and Erin Cassity as they proudly
> lead the way into the dark bleak abyss that will be the Obama
> Presidency as the drum-beating leftys that have joined with us
> for the past eight years run off into the shadows to backpedal

and support Obama's wars for the Elite. We will speak the truth that the true "Conservative" will be so desperately seeking in this new age of world governance. Everything from preserving our gun rights to how to prepare for the fun of the looming depression, these Texas Nationalists will cover in this Sunday evening show.

There was a disturbing component to this trend: Among the would-be militia organizers were a substantial number of military veterans voicing Patriot-movement beliefs, including threats of violent resistance to the Obama administration.

One of these veterans made the news in late February. Kody Brittingham, a 20-year-old Marine lance corporal based at Camp Lejeune, was arrested on charges that he threatened the life of the president. Brittingham was first arrested by civilian authorities on breaking-and-entering charges in December 2008. When navy investigators searched his barracks after his arrest, they discovered a journal he wrote containing plans on how to kill the president. There was white-supremacist material in the journal as well.

The talk about violent resistance to Obama's presidency kept building and metastasizing. It was only a matter of time before talk became action.

When an Alabama man named Michael McLendon went on a lethal shooting rampage on March 11 in the small town of Samson, near the Florida border, and killed 10 people before dying in a blazing gun battle with police, investigators afterward were unable to discern any apparent motive, beyond personal and professional vendettas. But the death toll and violence left people shocked and looking for answers.

Glenn Beck, of course, had an idea. In conversation with Bill

O'Reilly the next day on *The O'Reilly Factor,* Beck speculated that the cause of the rampage might have been the shooter's frustration with "political correctness":

> Beck: But as I'm listening to him, I'm thinking about the American people that feel disenfranchised right now. That feel like nobody's hearing their voice. The government isn't hearing their voice. Even if you call, they don't listen to you on both sides. If you're a conservative, you're called a racist. You want to starve children.
>
> O'Reilly: Sure.
>
> Beck: Yada yada yada. And every time they do speak out, they're shut down by political correctness. How do you not have those people turn into that guy?
>
> O'Reilly: Well, look, nobody, even if they're frustrated, is going to hurt another human being unless they're mentally ill. I think.
>
> Beck: I think pushed to the wall, you don't think people get pushed to the wall?

If Beck was warning that disenfranchised and angry right-wingers were about to start taking their frustrations out in a wave of violence, well, he was being downright prophetic. Three weeks later in Pittsburgh, it all started coming true.

THREE

Reaping the Whirlwind

U ntil his dog peed on his mother's carpet, Richard Poplawski was just another ordinary Pittsburgh schlub living in his parents' home—albeit one who liked to spend his time hanging out on white-supremacist Web sites, fretting about the looming New World Order crackdown under Obama, posting Glenn Beck videos, and collecting guns. Lots of guns.

But then his dog relieved itself on the carpet of the home he shared with his mom. And the next thing everyone knew, three cops were dead, two more were wounded, and Poplawski's home in a quiet neighborhood was being barraged, from within and without, by about a hundred rounds of ammunition.

April 4, 2009, was supposed to be a typically quiet Saturday morning in the neighborhood. But when Margaret Poplawski awoke sometime around 7 a.m., she discovered that one of the two pit-bull puppies belonging to her 23-year-old son, Richard, had left a puddle on the floor. She woke him up and yelled at him to clean up the mess. A violently verbal shouting match erupted, and Margaret decided she'd had enough from her layabout son, who'd washed out of the Marines the previous year after only a few weeks. So she called the cops to have him thrown out of the house.

She evidently forgot that her son had been stockpiling guns and ammunition "because he believed that as a result of economic collapse, the police were no longer able to protect society," she later told authorities.

So when two Pittsburgh police officers—Paul Sciullo III and Stephen Mayhle, both beat cops who had been on the force for two years—arrived at her front door, she invited them in and asked them to remove her son.

What she didn't realize was that Richard Poplawski was standing directly behind her holding an AK-47 and wearing a bulletproof vest. When the cops came in, he opened fire on them at point-blank range, killing Sciullo with a round to the skull and Mayhle with rounds to the body and head.

Margaret Poplawski ran from the room, shouting: "What the hell have you done?" She hid in the basement and remained there for the duration of the armed standoff that followed.

Another Pittsburgh cop, Eric Kelly, had cruised up to the Poplawski home on his own to act as backup for his two friends. When he heard the shots, he got out of the car and headed straight for the front door. He only made it about halfway; Richard Poplawski mowed him down from the front window of the house with his AK-47. Kelly fell to the lawn, still alive, and was able to radio for help: "Shots fired! Officer down! Need assistance!"

When dozens more police arrived on the scene and surrounded the house, Kelly was still alive, but Poplawski opened fire on any officer trying to rescue him. One officer was wounded in the hand in the attempt. Kelly wound up bleeding to death on the lawn before he could be retrieved. Another officer broke his leg trying to get in the house from the rear.

Poplawski freely fired at the cops, and they returned the fire, riddling the house with bullets. Eventually, hunkered down and wounded himself, Poplawski surrendered and was taken alive into custody by the tactical-unit cops who had negotiated with him. He was taken to a hospital and placed under police guard.

Outside the home, neighbors and other lookers-on mingled with news crews, everyone trying to figure out what had happened. A young man named Eddie Perkovic piped up that he was Poplawski's best friend and explained that Poplawski feared "the Obama gun ban that's on the way" and "didn't like our rights being infringed upon." Perkovic told reporters he got a call at work from Poplawski earlier that morning and was told: "Eddie, I am going to die today.... Tell your family I love them and I love you." Said Perkovic: "I heard gunshots and he hung up.... He sounded like he was in pain, like he got shot."

Perkovic himself was an interesting "best friend": His MySpace page was rife with anti-Semitic hate talk and extolled white-supremacist propaganda like William Pierce's neo-Nazi race-war blueprint, *The Turner Diaries,* as well as the old Jewish-conspiracy hoax *The Protocols of the Elders of Zion.*

Poplawski, it turned out, was largely of the same mold. He left an easily followed trail of postings on the Internet that gave the public a good deal of insight into his motives for gunning down three police officers. Many of these, as it happened, were on white-nationalist Web sites like Don Black's Stormfront.org, where Poplawski had an account to which he regularly posted, especially in discussion forums. What many of his posts indicated was an increasing paranoia about a coming economic and political collapse under President Obama. And yes, he not only was a fan of conspiracy-theory salesman Alex Jones, he also liked to watch Glenn Beck's Fox News show.

Mark Pitcavage of the Anti-Defamation League (ADL) surveyed Poplawski's postings and concluded:

- Poplawski believed that the federal government, the media, and the banking system are all largely or completely controlled by Jews. He thought African Americans were "vile" and non-white races inferior to whites.

- He also believed that a conspiracy led by "evil Zionists" and "greedy traitorous goyim" was "ramping up" a police state in the United States for malign purposes.

- Web sites like the neo-Nazi Stormfront forums and the anti-government conspiracy Infowars site fueled his racist, anti-Semitic, and conspiratorial mindset. . . .

Poplawski bought into the SHTF/TEOTWAWKI [S--t Hits The Fan/The End Of The World As We Know It] conspiracy theories hook, line and sinker, even posting a link to Stormfront of a YouTube video featuring talk show host Glenn Beck talking about FEMA camps with Congressman Ron Paul. When the city of Pittsburgh got a Homeland Security grant to add surveillance cameras to protect downtown bridges, Poplawski told Stormfronters that it was "ramping up the police state." He said, too, that he gave warnings to grocery store customers he encountered (but only if they were white) to stock up on canned goods and other long-lasting foods.

However, an astonishing thing happened to the Poplawski case when it was picked up and reported on by the mainstream media: Most of the information relating to his white-supremacist background and motivations vanished or simply did not appear. Instead, the leads of the news stories around the country focused on Poplawski's dog peeing on his mother's carpet as the incident that sparked the killings. The *New York Times* at first completely ignored the white-supremacy aspect of the story, running an Associated Press story that only briefly alluded to Poplawski's paranoiac fears, and instead focused on the role of his peeing dog; only later, when its own reporter filed a story, did any discussion of the killer's background appear. Read the headline at MSNBC. com: "Fight over urinating dog got police to ambush." At CNN, it read: "Urinating dog triggered argument resulting in 3 officers' deaths."

The dog-pee angle, in fact, became a fat red herring tossed into the discourse by the people most implicated by the case. Alex Jones, whose videos were a Poplawski favorite, angrily dismissed on his radio show any talk of conspiracy theories causing Poplawski's rage by pointing to the puddle on the floor. Far-right blogger Robert Stacy McCain argued: "The key witness in the case blames . . . the family dog. . . . Now, you can blame the dog. Or you can blame Mrs. Poplawski. Or you can blame Glenn Beck. Or you can blame a 'gun culture.' Me? I blame Richard Poplawski."

Then there was Glenn Beck himself, who dismissed it as the random happenstance of a nutjob. Moreover, he attacked anyone who suggested otherwise—including us.

Crooks and Liars reported the Poplawski case closely and posted some of the earliest information about Poplawski's background. Like a number of liberal blogs—including DailyKos—we made the fairly commonsensical connection between Poplawski's unhinged beliefs and the unhinging rhetoric that was being marketed to an audience of millions by Glenn Beck. So on the Monday after the shooting, Beck went on Fox News and denounced us in his keynote "The One Thing" segment:

> Blaming anyone except the nutjob for what happened in
> Pittsburgh is crazy. Police officers over the weekend were
> killed by a crazy man with a gun, and blaming anybody else
> besides him is like blaming a flight attendant after a terrorist
> takes down a plane. Giving passengers a nice little safety talk

to prepare them for a worst-case scenario doesn't mean you're responsible should a terrorist actually make that worst-case scenario happen. One person is providing important information and the other . . . *is a nutjob!* Who would have acted that way no matter what!

Before any facts came out on the Pittsburgh shooting, the Left—I mean, like this! [Snaps]—the blogs started burning up. The DailyKos, Media Matters, and The Atlantic decided this maniac was worried that President Obama was gonna take away his guns. Therefore—conservative talk shows were to blame! [Laughs] I mean, what else could it be? You know? Bloggers rushed to paint this killer as a conservative, presumably one who is clinging to his God and his guns.

Well, the truth is, this guy in Pittsburgh was about as much of a conservative as, um, as Stalin was cuddly. He's a *neo-Nazi,* for the love of Pete! A white supremacist! And more importantly, he's a premeditated killer. Allegedly, of course. That's why I'm not even going to waste any time addressing the people who lump in everybody who questions Obama's policies into the same hate group. Let me talk to some rational people like, I don't know, *you* instead.

Civil unrest for a number of reasons is coming. Lone nutjobs and people who are just angry and frustrated and have had enough. You've got to seek those people out. You've got to start asking people in your own neighborhood, "How are you?" And actually care about the answer. . . .

People who think that radio, or people who espouse their opinions—that are taken out of context—those are the people who are trying to start a revolution, are just as crazy!

Beck invited on a right-wing blogger named Noel Sheppard from a self-proclaimed "liberal media bias" watchdog site called Newsbusters to assist with the denunciation. Sheppard told Beck:

The incident actually ended probably somewhere around 11 o'clock, 11:30 Eastern time, and by oh, I guess about 2 o'clock Eastern time, a gentleman had clipped a Fox News report—Fox had reported that a friend of the assailant apparently was worried about his gun rights because of Obama—so a liberal blogger took a piece of this video, posted it at a very, very popular liberal website called CrooksandLiars, and now the game was on and every liberal blogger was linking to this post.

Beck concluded the segment with a long rant about how "freedoms" always entail "responsibilities"—and we heartily agree. But he forgot to mention freedom of speech and the responsibilities that come with it. Those responsibilities include the ethical obligation not to use words that scapegoat and demonize and incite needless fear in people, especially when there is no evidence to support those fears—that is, shouting "Fire!" in a crowded theater. Those responsibilities are magnified a thousandfold when you hold a major media megaphone like Glenn Beck does.

Pretending that the hysterical hyperbole that became a fixture of right-wing rhetoric on mainstream conservative programs like Beck's had no discernible effect on its audience—that it had no role in inflaming the irrational beliefs of extremists and unstable characters likely to explode into violence—became a standard mainstream response to the flood of right-wing violence that ensued. Inherent in the dismissal by Beck and others of the role of their own hyperbole in inflaming white-supremacist ideologues—that these were just nutcases, mentally ill people, anomalies—was the underlying contention that right-wing extremism didn't really exist as a serious threat to the well-being of Americans.

The dismissal reflected the growing propensity among mainstream conservatives to obscure and deny the existence of white supremacists, militiamen, Patriots, and various other far-right extremists, as well as their role in instigating violence across the American landscape—even as those same extremists were being enabled, condoned, and inflamed by movement conservatives.

The propensity to minimize the threat posed by far-right extremists had manifested itself in the previous year, during the campaign, in a disturbing way—as the de facto law-enforcement policy of the Bush administration. Especially disturbing was the specific threat that was minimized: a conspiracy to assassinate Barack Obama.

Denver was just starting to swarm with jubilant conventioneers on Monday, August 25, 2008, when the news reports started coming in of three men arrested for supposedly plotting to assassinate Barack Obama. The account from local TV station CBS4, reported by Brian Maass, was gripping:

> Maass reported earlier Monday that one of the suspects told authorities they were "going to shoot Obama from a high vantage point using a . . . rifle . . . sighted at 750 yards."
>
> Law enforcement sources told Maass that one of the suspects "was directly asked if they had come to Denver to kill Obama. He responded in the affirmative."
>
> The story began emerging Sunday morning when Aurora police arrested Tharin Gartrell, 28. He was driving a rented pickup truck in an erratic manner, according to sources.
>
> Sources told CBS4 police found two high-powered, scoped rifles in the car along with camouflage clothing, walkie-talkies, wigs, a bulletproof vest, a spotting scope, licenses in the names of other people and 44 grams of methamphetamine. One of the rifles is listed as stolen from Kansas.
>
> Aurora police alerted federal officials because of heightened

security surrounding the Democratic convention, Aurora police Det. Marcus Dudley said. . . .

Subsequently authorities went to the Cherry Creek Hotel in Glendale to contact an associate of Gartrell's. But that man, identified as Shawn Robert Adolf, 33, who was wanted on numerous warrants, jumped out of a sixth-floor hotel window. Law enforcement sources say Adolf broke an ankle in the fall and was captured moments later. Sources say he had a handcuff ring and was wearing a swastika, and is thought to have ties to white supremacist organizations.

Nathan Johnson, 32, an associate of Gartrell and Adolf, was also arrested Sunday morning. He told authorities that the two men had "planned to kill Barack Obama at his acceptance speech."

"He don't belong in political office. Blacks don't belong in political office. He ought to be shot," Johnson told Maass.

What motivated them? At least two of the men, as details emerged, were reported to be white supremacists described as members of the Sons of Silence, a radical hate group. One of the women who knew them described all three men as racists.

Federal court records released a week later gave the details of the plot: Essentially, they planned to sneak into one of Obama's events at the convention and shoot him with a gun hidden inside a camera. Nathan Johnson's girlfriend told a Denver TV station that it would have had to be a suicide mission.

According to the federal affidavit filed in the case, Johnson, Adolf, and Gartrell had a room on the third floor of the Hyatt hotel, where they discussed the plot with two women while doing methamphetamine. Adolf, who already had seven pending warrants for his arrest on a variety of drug and theft charges, told the women "it would not matter if he killed Senator Obama because police would simply add a murder charge to his pending charges."

Adolf also talked about using "a high-powered rifle 22-250 from a high vantage point" to shoot Obama during his acceptance speech.

Even more significant, beyond the details of the plot, was the fact that, as the *Colorado Independent* noted, the FBI asked for more serious charges to be filed and were turned down:

> When police searched the hotel rooms and cars the men were using, they confiscated meth, needles, laptops, cell phones, a black mask, books indicating check fraud and forgery, bags of new clothes, tactical pants and bar coupons.
>
> Based on the evidence, FBI special agent Robert Sawyer believed there was probable cause to charge the men with conspiracy to kill Senator Obama.

Those charges were never filed. Instead, the men were arraigned on a more mundane series of drugs, weapons, and probation-violation charges.

Why? You'd have to ask Colorado's U.S. attorney, Troy Eid.

The day after news of the arrests hit, Eid announced there would not be any charges brought on the supposed conspiracy—because even if they were plotting such an event, they weren't really capable of it and therefore there was "no credible threat." When questioned further about the decision, Eid defended it by saying the men's plot was "more aspirational, perhaps, than operational."

This was an interesting choice of language, considering that similar words were used by the FBI to describe a group of black Muslim radicals in Florida who became known as the "Liberty Seven." They were arrested in June 2006 on charges of plotting to blow up the Sears Tower in Chicago. Even though they were described by the FBI as "aspirational rather than operational," there was no hesitation by the Justice Department in bringing charges.

That was not the case in Denver. Police had uncovered a clique of white men with rifles, ammunition, disguises, maps, walkie-talkies, and all the accoutrements of a conspiracy—as well as open admissions to just such a conspiracy and witness accounts that they had talked about it—but the U.S. attorney in Colorado decided there wasn't enough evidence to pursue charges.

Another funny thing: When a black man in prison sent a letter purportedly containing white powder to John McCain, Troy Eid brought down the full force of the law, complete with press conferences and public declarations against such threats. And he did it the Friday before Johnson, Adolf, and Gartrell were arrested.

Marc Ramsey was, at the time of his indictment on charges of threatening McCain, in the custody of the Arapahoe County Jail for allegedly threatening a police officer. He sent a letter to McCain protesting his supposed nonchalance for the victims of Agent Orange among his fellow Vietnam veterans. It began with the line, "If you are reading this then you are already dead." McCain staffers claimed that the envelope contained a white powder (Ramsey denied this), which created a brief scare at campaign offices as hazmat teams were called in.

In fact, there wasn't any powder. Andy Lyon of the Parker South Metro Fire Rescue Authority told a local news station that what they found was described to him as "maybe . . . a couple of granules of something. It tested positive for protein, what was described to me as a weak positive. Well, protein could be a protein shake."

Troy Eid charged Ramsey on August 22 with knowingly threatening to harm or kill through the U.S. mail. "We won't stand for threats of this kind in Colorado," Eid said. "A death threat is not a legitimate form of political expression."

A number of legal experts questioned Eid's handling of both cases, and in particular the way he turned a blind eye to the would-be Obama plot. Eid's refusal to proceed in this case ultimately sent a chilling message: If you're a white supremacist who wants to target Obama for assassination, Bush's Justice Department would give you a slap on the wrist and look the other way should you get caught. This almost certainly was not intentional, but in the insular and paranoid world of neo-Nazi skinheads, silence and inaction were usually interpreted as a green light.

It's unknown whether Daniel Cowart and Paul Schlesselman had the Denver plotters—and Troy Eid's slap on the wrist for them—in mind when they concocted their own plan to assassinate President Obama. Nonetheless, only a few weeks after the Denver plot was foiled, the two skinheads were ready to put into action a plan of their own: Go on a cross-country killing spree targeting over a hundred African Americans and culminate the rampage with an armed assault on Obama's motorcade while wearing white tuxedos and top hats. You couldn't say they didn't have active imaginations.

Fortunately, they decided to try robbing a gun shop in Tennessee first to obtain the needed weaponry and ran into federal Alcohol, Tobacco, Firearms and Explosives agents, who broke up the attempt and arrested both men outside Jackson on October 26, a little over a week before the election. Upon making the bust, the agents ascertained that the two men had met online and concocted the plan for mass murder and assassination and were in the opening stages of actually carrying it out—Schlesselman, an 18-year-old who lived in Arkansas, had traveled to Tennessee (where 20-year-old Cowart lived) to begin their operations. This time, there was no hesitation on the part of the U.S. attorney to file conspiracy charges.

Of course, the plot more resembled a dumb fantasy out of a bad action flick than anything likely ever to become a reality. But that's what anyone who might've stumbled onto Timothy McVeigh and Terry Nichols before April 19, 1995, likely would have concluded too. Moreover, both of these young men were serious, they were heavily armed, and they took concrete steps to begin making their fantasy into a reality.

In his story for the online news site the Daily Beast, Max Blumenthal detailed Cowart's and Schlesselman's ties to the institutionalized skinhead underground, noting that "one of the would-be assassins, Daniel Cowart, was a 'probate member' of an incipient youth group of the neo-Nazi movement, Supreme White Alliance [SWA]. Cowart also maintained a friendship with the SWA's founder, Steven Edwards. Steven Edwards is the son of Ron Edwards, the founder of the Imperial Klans of America, a neo-Nazi outfit best known for the 'Nordic Fest' white power concerts it holds at its 15-acre compound in Kentucky."

The ADL reported more details about the SWA, including the group's advocacy of "lone wolf" attacks to inspire a race war:

> One member, Jarod Anderson, declared his determination to "re-light the Fire in the Movement." He added that SWA was his "Crew and Life," and that he would die for it "as much as I would for my Family." Ohio SWA member Richard Kidd claimed, in May 2008 in an Internet posting titled "Its time for war," that "We will all die one day so lets die for some thing not nothing."

While the election of a liberal Democrat as president had already energized and aggravated the worst tendencies of the extremist Right—notably the militiamen who formed the ranks of the Patriot movement—the fact that Barack Obama is also an African American sent the racist Right into a near-psychotic frenzy, embodied by plots such as Cowart and Schlesselman's. At the same time, these same racist hate groups were working hard to bolster their recruitment by trying to appeal to the public as mainstream conservatives.

The *Philadelphia Daily News* carried a story examining how one such group—the Keystone State Skins (KSS)—was recruiting by presenting its roster as being ordinary, taxpaying, job-holding members of society with kids and families. One of the skinheads—a man named Steve Smith, who was director of the Scranton/Wilkes-Barre chapter of the KSS—told the reporter that the Cowart/Schlesselman plot was the type of scheme that

> makes us look like we're a bunch of loonies. . . . They're a couple of loony bins that give our movement a bad name. . . . I don't know anybody who would even think that killing Barack Obama would solve anything. . . . Anyone who tries to kill Barack Obama does a lot more harm to the white movement than anything.

When mainstreaming themselves is the game, white supremacists are nothing if not disingenuous. After all, their ideology specifically is devoted to inspiring race war—a point they take pains to disguise when recruiting from the mainstream. Yet when the masks are off and they speak freely among themselves—as they often do on Internet forums and in private gatherings—the cold reality is that for hard-core white supremacists, assassinating Obama became widely viewed as the ticket for inspiring a race war. Any "race warrior" who happened to succeed in that mission would earn himself permanent Aryan glory.

Michael Ward, the FBI's deputy assistant director for counter-terrorism, told *Newsweek* that law-enforcement officers were seeing a significant uptick in angry and threatening rhetoric from white supremacists, both in Internet postings and in the threats reported to law-enforcement agencies. Ward said the greatest concern was "lone wolf"-type terrorists "who might be seething with anger and armed to the teeth but who do not show up on any government radar screens."

And it was quite a tide, according to *Newsweek:*

> Since last February, a presidential-campaign-threat task force created by the FBI and Secret Service has conducted more than 650 "threat assessments" to evaluate reports that could involve threats to presidential or vice-presidential contenders or any others connected to the election. About 100 of those threats have been assessed to be "racially motivated" and are thought to be directed at Obama. Another 100 of the reports received since last winter are deemed to be "political" and come from across the ideological spectrum. They include pro-gun groups and anti-abortion extremists. Other categories used by the task force to track threats don't break down along ideological or political lines.

In February 2009, the Southern Poverty Law Center—which carefully tracks the activities of hate groups across the country—released its annual "State of Hate" report, finding that the country was in the middle of a sudden surge of racist organizing:

> From white power skinheads decrying "President Obongo" at a racist gathering in rural Missouri, to neo-Nazis and Ku Klux Klansmen hurling epithets at Latino immigrants from courthouse steps in Oklahoma, to anti-Semitic black separatists calling for death to Jews on bustling street corners in several East Coast cities, hate group activity in the U.S. was disturbing and widespread throughout 2008, as the number of hate groups operating in America continued to rise. Last year, 926 hate groups were active in the U.S., up more than 4% from 888 in 2007. That's more than a 50% increase since 2000, when there were 602 groups.

As in recent years, hate groups were animated by the national immigration debate. But two new forces also drove them in 2008: the worsening recession, and Barack Obama's successful campaign to become the nation's first black president. Officials reported that Obama had received more threats than any other presidential candidate in memory, and several white supremacists were arrested for saying they would assassinate him or allegedly plotting to do so.

The visceral and violent reaction among right-wing extremists to Obama's election soon began manifesting itself, as the FBI feared, in a series of violent incidents involving lone-wolf extremists around the country.

The case of James Cummings—a 29-year-old trust-fund millionaire, the scion of a California real-estate magnate, who lived in a quiet neighborhood in Belfast, Maine—was part of this trend. Because he was independently wealthy, Cummings stayed at home and evidently began occupying himself with conspiracy theories, Nazi and fascist belief systems, and his mounting collection of guns—as well as various chemicals. Cummings had a history of violence—he was associated with a number of assault cases in his hometown of Fort Bragg, California, though he had no criminal record after moving to Maine in 2007. But once there, he had a reputation among those who came in contact with the family for verbally abusing his 31-year-old wife, Amber, and being "extremely controlling" when it came to his wife and their nine-year-old daughter.

After years of enduring mental and physical abuse, Amber shot him to death in their home in the presence of their daughter, reportedly to defend herself from another of Cummings's beatings. When police arrived and began combing through the house, they were shocked at what they found, sealed the place off, and called the hazmat teams.

Police found Nazi memorabilia (including a prominently displayed swastika flag), a large collection of white-supremacist literature (Cummings had even printed out an application to join the neo-Nazi National Socialist Movement), instructions for building a "dirty bomb," and information on radioactive materials. In the basement were "four 1-gallon containers of 35 percent hydrogen peroxide, uranium, thorium, lithium metal, thermite, aluminum powder, beryllium, boron, black iron oxide and magnesium ribbon"—all components for making a "radiological dispersal device," or dirty bomb, which will contaminate a large area and kill anyone within the immediate blast zone.

Amber told police her husband was "very upset" by the election of Barack Obama and began obsessing about dirty bombs, sometimes mixing chemicals in their kitchen sink.

Obama's election appeared to feed extremist right-wing paranoia and inspire violent fantasies of a "revolution." On February 27 in Florida, for example, a mentally ill man named Dannie Baker walked up to the window outside the recreation room of a Miramar Beach apartment complex and opened fire on the gathering of Chilean exchange students therein, killing two people—Nicolas Corp, 23, and Racine Balbontin, 22—and wounding three others. After police arrested the 60-year-old Baker at his apartment, neighbors told reporters that Baker had asked them if they were ready for a "revolution"—and warned them that if they were harboring illegal immigrants, to get them out.

Baker had worked as a local volunteer for the Republican Party during George W. Bush's 2000 and 2004 campaigns. However, when Baker turned out to volunteer in 2008, his mental state had apparently deteriorated; a county GOP official said he "just made people feel uncomfortable," so they asked him to stay away. Baker fired off a number of angry e-mails to GOP officials, which so disturbed and alarmed them that they turned them over to the Walton County sheriff, who did nothing. In one e-mail, Baker wrote: "The Washington D.C. Dictators have already confessed to rigging elections in our States for their recruiting dictators to overthrow us with foreign illegals here, and have allowed them to kill and run for office in the States to extend their influence into our States." In another missive, Baker claimed there is a plot to "give our homeland to foriegn states and their representatives here in America. Lets exacute them and reinstate a legal government that will do something for us."

Especially remarkable about the Baker case was how little attention it attracted in the United States. In Chile and much of Latin America, the Miramar Beach shootings were front-page national news. Francisco Vidal, the Chilean government minister, denounced the crime as "macabre" and "brutal." The deputy consul general personally oversaw the return of the two students' bodies to their homeland. One of the ironies of the murders was that the students were not "illegal immigrants"—they were studying abroad as part of an exchange program, and all of them planned to return to Chile. In the end, Baker was found incompetent to stand trial and remanded to the custody of the Florida State Hospital in Chattahoochee for treatment; if he regains competency within five years, he will then stand trial. The story again received no attention outside of Walton County.

Similarly, the case of James Cummings received little national attention. After a day or so of headlines, the case of the Tennessee skinheads and their assassination plot disappeared from the news. And no one, outside of a handful of reporters, followed up on the Denver would-be assassins and Troy Eid's nonfeasance.

That's because the mainstream media have their preferred narratives and stick to them like glue. The preferred narrative when it came to these violent acts committed by right-wing extremists was that these were all "isolated incidents" with no connection, no set of radical belief systems that wove them together, and, most of all, nothing to connect them to the hyperbole from mainstream conservatives. As Glenn Beck said, these were just nutcases who had nothing to do with anything he or his fellow right-wing pundits told people.

Perish the thought. If you dared harbor or express it—as Beck also made abundantly clear—then you were just trying to silence and oppress poor helpless right-wing pundits. That was the conservative way, and it was about to become one of their favorite and most repeated themes.

We'd wager that Glenn Beck, like a lot of people, has heard the famous Thomas Jefferson quote: "The tree of liberty must be refreshed from time to time with the blood of patriots and tyrants."

Maybe he's even seen one of the T-shirts bearing that inscription. One of these shirts is especially notable: the one Timothy McVeigh was wearing when he was arrested for blowing up 168 people at the Murrah Federal Building in Oklahoma City on April 19, 1995.

Does this mean that anyone wearing one of these shirts, or expressing the sentiment, is a crazed militiaman eager and willing to blow up government workers and their children? No—but the broader meaning of that T-shirt is critical to understanding what happened in Oklahoma City as well as the mind-set of violent right-wing extremists like McVeigh.

For people who simply admire the Founding Fathers' love of liberty, Jefferson's quote is a clear warning to those who would undermine American democracy. For people on the far right who believe that the federal government is actively conspiring not merely to undermine but to tyrannically overthrow the republic, and thereby enslave millions, Jefferson's sentiments become an admonition to resort to violence to stop it.

To encounter someone wearing a shirt or carrying a sign bearing the Jefferson quote can be a kind of red flag: Given the current political environment—in which T-shirt admiration of the Founding Fathers is rare and in which their written words increasingly are conflated with right-wing radical sentiments—there's a high likelihood the person shares McVeigh's attitudes about the supposed tyranny of the federal government.

It's a critical red flag for people working in law enforcement. As the ADL explained:

> Any time law enforcement officers encounter people with extreme ideologies, safety issues potentially arise. However, for a variety of reasons, certain circumstances pose a heightened threat of violent confrontation. Some situations, for instance, are particularly stressful for extremists, increasing the chances that they may lash out or overreact.

In 2009, the Missouri State Highway Patrol's information arm compiled a report about militias, largely as a way of helping to inform their officers in the field—the people most at risk when it comes to random encounters with armed right-wing extremists. The February 20 report was titled "The Modern Militia Movement," and it specifically mentioned such warning signs as political bumper stickers for third-party candidates, including Republican representative Ron Paul of Texas (who attracted a significant bloc of support from white nationalists) and Chuck Baldwin, the official presidential candidate of the Patriot-friendly Constitution Party. It also pointed to talk of conspiracy theories (such as the supposed plan for a "North American Union" and a "NAFTA superhighway") and possession of white-supremacist and subversive literature.

> Due to the current economical and political situation, a lush environment for militia activity has been created. Unemployment rates are high, as well as cost-of-living expenses. Additionally, President . . . Barack Obama is seen as tight on gun control and many extremists fear that he will enact firearms confiscations. White supremacists from within the militia movement have further become angered due to the election of the first African American President. Many constitutionalists have claimed that President . . . Obama does not meet the residency requirements to hold the office of president, and therefore his election is unconstitutional.

The report created a small firestorm among conservatives and libertarians, who suddenly found they had more of a resemblance to right-wing extremists than they thought. "It seems like they want to stifle political thought," Roger Webb, president of the University of Missouri campus Libertarians, told the *Kansas City Star.* "There are a lot of third parties out there, and none of them express any violence. In fact, if you join the Libertarian Party, one of the things you sign in your membership application is that you don't support violence as a means to any ends."

The *Star* also quoted a GOP delegate and military veteran named Tim Neal—whose bumper bore a Ron Paul sticker— musing that the next time he is pulled over by a police officer, he wouldn't know whether it was for speeding or for his political views.

> I was going down the list and thinking, "Check, that's me." I'm a Ron Paul supporter, check. I talk about the North American union, check. I've got the "America: Freedom to Fascism" video

loaned out to somebody right now. So that means I'm a domestic terrorist? Because I've got a video about the Federal Reserve?

The report was created not to highlight reasons for engaging subjects—it didn't suggest that any of the signs were cause to pull someone over—but rather to give police officers some potential warning signs of trouble when they did engage people for ordinary law-enforcement situations, such as traffic stops. State law-enforcement officials defended the report, pointing out that it was being misinterpreted. The report, they said, was compiled by the Missouri Information Analysis Center in Jefferson City, a "fusion center" that combines resources from the state law-enforcement agency, the federal Department of Homeland Security, and other entities. The center was set up in 2005 to collect local intelligence to better combat terrorism and other criminal activity. The report simply comprised publicly available trend data on militias and other far-right extremists.

"All this is an educational thing," Lieutenant John Hotz of the Missouri State Highway Patrol told the *Star*. "Troopers have been shot by members of groups, so it's our job to let law enforcement officers know what the trends are in the modern militia movement."

The conspiracist right—led by radio talk-show host Alex Jones—saw the report as an indication of a looming government crackdown on right-wing extremists. Then Glenn Beck chimed in, and the controversy went national.

On his March 19 Fox News show, Beck featured a segment in which he and Penn Jillette (of the duo Penn & Teller) discussed how crazy it was for law enforcement to be profiling people as potential domestic terrorists for behaviors that ordinary citizens like themselves indulge in happily, as they should. They noticed, at one point, that there's actually very little about Patriot-movement beliefs to which they subscribe. It's just that their libertarianism might trip some of the outward indicators suggested in the report.

The catch—unmentioned by Beck—was that there was nothing even remotely inaccurate in the report. While there were some legitimate concerns about its methodology, every fact in it could be readily substantiated. More to the point, there was nothing in it suggesting that any of these traits were cause for arrest or evidence of criminal intent or radical behavior; rather, the report was compiled to provide officers with advance warning of potential dangers in their law-enforcement work.

The report reflected a reality that law enforcement trying to deal with domestic terrorism in America must confront: Their subjects are thoroughly American, and many of the people drawn into these movements are, if anything, "hyper-normal." Their version of "patriotism," for instance, is so extreme that they actually hate not just their government but their fellow citizens—in essence, their country, because it has been "perverted" from its original purposes.

The hyper-normality is intentional camouflage. The Patriot movement, and militias in particular, used a very specific and intentional strategy adopted in the 1990s by the white supremacists and radical tax protesters of the American far right. The purpose of the strategy was to mainstream their belief systems and their agendas by adopting the appearance of normal, "red-blooded" Americanism as a way of presenting their radical beliefs as "normal" too.

In the process, they often adopted time-worn "patriotic" sayings and symbols—such as the "Don't Tread on Me" flag Beck once wore on his show as a T-shirt—though with a much more menacing meaning. After Timothy McVeigh was arrested wearing a shirt bearing the Jefferson quote, its deeper ramifications have never been quite the same, either.

Nothing in the Missouri report even suggested that anyone of the Patriot persuasion should be arrested or treated as a terrorist—because it's perfectly legal in this country to hold beliefs as radical as one likes. What's not legal is to act criminally on behalf of those beliefs. The report simply tries to give a factual overview of some of the motivations of right-wing extremists and what kinds of things are likely to set them off. The police officers whose job it is to stop such criminality need to be able to assess what they're dealing with on the ground—whether someone they've pulled over for not having license plates on their car is likely to pull something stupid.

Nonetheless, on his March 24 show, Beck continued to disparage the report, comparing the concerns of Missouri law enforcement to events the day before in Oakland, California, where a black parolee had killed a police officer:

> Next, look at the government's priorities. This is an actual cop killer [in Oakland], who clearly wasn't rehabilitated. But the Missouri State Troopers now—and wait until you hear the rest of the story, the update on this one coming up in a few minutes—they're worried about militias. . . .
>
> Let's put this into perspective here: Our researchers couldn't find a single report of a single death specifically linked to a militia group, or an individual member of a militia, in over a decade. Yet an average of more than 150 officers die every year nationwide. Have you counted the number of dead police officers in Philadelphia? And militia numbers are reportedly down after the Oklahoma City bombing in 1995—seems it gave them a bad name. So why are militias getting so much attention from Missouri?

Well, it might just have something to do with the fact that, per square mile, the Ozarks have a richer history of right-wing extremism than, say, Oakland or Philadelphia. For instance, take the case of Timothy Thomas Coombs, a Patriot radical who in 1994 shot a Missouri state trooper with a rifle through the window of his home in a revenge assassination attempt (the trooper survived). Coombs to this day remains at large.

Right-wing extremists—not just militiamen, but their more virulent cousins, the white supremacists—are still a potent presence in Missouri. For 2009 alone, the ADL reported a variety of extremist activity in the state including paramilitary militia training, gatherings of the White Boy Society (a neo-Nazi biker group), and meetings and literature drops arranged by the National Socialist Movement (a neo-Nazi party).

Moreover, in recent years, contrary to Glenn Beck's assertion, there have been killings and assaults in Missouri (not to mention elsewhere) associated with the extremist Right: In 2002, a white supremacist named Kevin John stomped to death a man he thought was Jewish after an argument erupted in a St. Louis diner. In 2004, five men associated with white-supremacist groups were charged in a brutal, racially motivated assault outside a Springfield Denny's. In 2005, a white supremacist named Edward Hubbard, who worked at a printing shop in Liberty, stabbed his African American coworker to death with a screwdriver because of his race.

Somehow, all of these incidents were glibly erased from Glenn Beck's account of things—as they were for the rest of the mainstream pundits, including his Fox News fellows and prominent bloggers like Michelle Malkin, who similarly chimed in on the Missouri report, accusing the government of "smearing" conservatives. They were, however, just getting warmed up.

Conspicuously absent from Glenn Beck's denunciation of the Missouri State Highway Patrol report was any evidence of concern on his part for the very real problem it was intended to help address: the lethal threat to police officers posed by radicalized believers in far-right conspiracy theories. Beck and his fellow conservatives continued to blather away about the Missouri report for another week or so without ever once considering that there might be a serious, real-world purpose for this kind of intelligence reporting for law enforcement.

Then—just a little over a week after Beck's rant about Oakland—Richard Poplawski killed three police officers in Pittsburgh, and the very concerns raised by the Missouri report were made manifest. But because it happened in Pennsylvania and not Missouri, no one—particularly not anyone on the Right, and most notably not Glenn Beck—managed to make the connection. Outside of the liberal blogosphere, it was impossible to find anyone discussing how the Missouri report had foreshadowed what happened in Pittsburgh. Suddenly, though, the right-wing kvetching about the Missouri report subsided; the silence, however, was short-lived.

Moved to action in part by the Poplawski incident, the federal Department of Homeland Security (DHS) on April 7 released an "intelligence assessment" titled "Rightwing Extremism: Current Economic and Political Climate Fueling Resurgence in Radicalization and Recruitment." The assessment had been commissioned in 2008 by Bush administration officials and had just been completed. DHS officials, alarmed by the Pittsburgh shootings (which were specifically cited as "a recent example of the potential violence associated with a rise in right-wing extremism"), opted to hurriedly release it as a bulletin to "federal, state, local, and tribal counterterrorism and law enforcement officials." It later emerged that newly approved DHS chief Janet Napolitano had not reviewed the report before its release.

Just as the Missouri report had done, the DHS bulletin warned that conditions were ripe for a resurgence of right-wing extremism:

> Paralleling the current national climate, rightwing extremists during the 1990s exploited a variety of social issues and political themes to increase group visibility and recruit new members. Prominent among these themes were the militia movement's opposition to gun control efforts, criticism of free trade agreements (particularly those with Mexico), and highlighting perceived government infringement on civil liberties as well as white supremacists' longstanding exploitation of social issues such as abortion, inter-racial crimes, and same-sex marriage. During the 1990s, these issues contributed to the growth in the number of domestic rightwing terrorist and extremist groups and an increase in violent acts targeting government facilities, law enforcement officers, banks, and infrastructure sectors. . . .
>
> Historically, domestic rightwing extremists have feared, predicted, and anticipated a cataclysmic economic collapse in the United States. Prominent antigovernment conspiracy theorists have incorporated aspects of an impending economic collapse to intensify fear and paranoia among like-minded individuals and to attract recruits during times of economic uncertainty. Conspiracy theories involving declarations of martial law, impending civil strife or racial conflict, suspension of the U.S. Constitution, and the creation of citizen detention camps often incorporate aspects of a failed economy. Antigovernment conspiracy theories and "end times" prophecies could motivate extremist individuals and groups to stockpile food, ammunition, and weapons. These teachings also have been linked with the radicalization of domestic extremist individuals and groups in the past, such as violent Christian Identity organizations and extremist members of the militia movement.

The report's unambiguous language evidently reminded mainstream conservatives just how close they had grown to the radical fringe—and that freaked them out. Their immediate response was to deny any such proximity and be outraged that anyone would point it out.

A week later, a story in the *Washington Times* described certain aspects of the bulletin:

> A footnote attached to the report ... defines "rightwing extremism in the United States" as including not just racist or hate groups, but also groups that reject federal authority in favor of state or local authority.
>
> "It may include groups and individuals that are dedicated to a single issue, such as opposition to abortion or immigration," the warning says.

The howls of wounded indignation from the mainstream right were immediate. Pundit Michelle Malkin, one of the most widely read right-wing bloggers, promptly ran a post headlined "The Obama DHS Hit Job on Conservatives Is Real," calling it a "piece of crap report" that "is a sweeping indictment of conservatives."

This blog raised an immediate question: was Malkin saying that mainstream conservatives are now right-wing extremists?

The DHS report—which, like the Missouri report, was accurate in every jot and tittle of the facts—had carefully delineated that the subject of its report included "rightwing extremists," "domestic rightwing terrorist and extremist groups," "terrorist groups or lone wolf extremists capable of carrying out violent attacks," "white supremacists," and similar very real threats described in similar language.

There was nothing about conservatives. The word never appeared in the report. Nonetheless, over the next few weeks, all that you heard about this report was that it "smeared conservatives" as well as "our military veterans."

The supposed "smearing veterans" charge arose from a portion of the bulletin warning that returning veterans who have been radicalized, or were already right-wing extremists, pose a particular threat:

> DHS/I&A [Intelligence & Assessment] assesses that rightwing extremists will attempt to recruit and radicalize returning veterans in order to exploit their skills and knowledge derived from military training and combat. These skills and knowledge have the potential to boost the capabilities of extremists—including lone wolves or small terrorist cells—to carry out violence. The willingness of a small percentage of military personnel to join extremist groups during the 1990s because they were disgruntled, disillusioned, or suffering from the psychological effects of war is being replicated today.

Malkin complained in her post that the report was indulging in "anti-military bigotry." She was evidently unaware that the DHS report simply echoed an assessment made by the FBI a year before. In a July 2008 report titled "White Supremacist Recruitment of Military Personnel since 9/11," the FBI concluded that neo-Nazis and other white supremacists had successfully joined the ranks of American armed forces serving in Iraq—though it counted only about 200 of them—and that the hate groups from which they operated were also actively seeking to recruit military personnel already serving.

As the FBI report explained:

> Military experience—ranging from failure at basic training to success in special operations forces—is found throughout the white supremacist extremist movement. FBI reporting indicates extremist leaders have historically favored recruiting active and former military personnel for their knowledge of firearms, explosives, and tactical skills and their access to weapons and

intelligence in preparation for an anticipated war against the federal government, Jews, and people of color. . . .

The prestige which the extremist movement bestows upon members with military experience grants them the potential for influence beyond their numbers. Most extremist groups have some members with military experience, and those with military experience often hold positions of authority within the groups to which they belong. . . .

Military experience—often regardless of its length or type—distinguishes one within the extremist movement. While those with military backgrounds constitute a small percentage of white supremacist extremists, FBI investigations indicate they frequently have higher profiles within the movement, including recruitment and leadership roles.

The wording of the DHS bulletin was open to potential misinterpretation, since it tended to focus on the potential for recruitment of returning veterans and neglected the broader scope of the issue, including the presence of neo-Nazis already in the military. Indeed, the DHS bulletin was not without its flaws, but these were largely analytical and methodological. The bulletin's analyst authors drew incorrect conclusions about economic effects on racist recruitment based on old methodology. It also failed to distinguish between those blocs of the extremist Right dedicated to radical and violent overthrow of the "New World Order" and those whose activities were focused more on mainstreaming extremist beliefs, which are overlapping blocs but decidedly distinct.

Mainstream conservatives ignored these relatively minor flaws and instead created a loud and entirely fake controversy over issues drawn from an intentional misreading and distortion of the bulletin. What erupted over the next few weeks was a national chorus of conservative pundits—particularly at Fox News, but on CNN

(Lou Dobbs especially), MSNBC, and elsewhere as well—pouncing all over the story and running segment after segment devoted to exploring why the DHS wanted to demonize veterans and conservatives.

On Fox News, Bill O'Reilly put it this way:

> This is the bottom line on this: The federal government has changed from a conservative-oriented federal government under the Bush administration to a liberal-oriented federal government under Obama. . . .
>
> So, of course, these people, instead of saying, you know, we might have some Muslim problems, maybe there's a little cell somewhere talking to Pakistan and getting orders. No, it's the Glenn Beck guys, but we don't really have any evidence. But this is what's on their mind because that's the way they think.

On his nightly CNN program, Dobbs ran a poll:

> Our poll question tonight is: Do you think a person concerned about borders and ports that are unsecured, illegal immigration, Second Amendment rights or returning veterans from the wars in Iraq and Afghanistan is likely or even possibly probable, as the Department of Homeland Security suggests, to be a right-wing extremist? Yes or no. Cast your vote at LouDobbs.com. We'll have the results here later in the broadcast.

Even televangelist Pat Robertson got into the action. On the April 16 edition of *The 700 Club,* he and co-host Terry Meeuwsen had a lively discussion of the report in which he called for the public to crash the DHS phone lines. He added: "It shows somebody down in the bowels of that organization is either a convinced left-winger or somebody whose sexual orientation is somewhat in question."

Virtually every Fox anchor—from Glenn Beck to Bill O'Reilly

to Bret Baier to Sean Hannity to Greta Van Susteren—featured a segment discussing the issue, and the theme consistently was that the DHS was using its law-enforcement powers to try to intimidate conservative activists. Van Susteren featured Republican former senator Rick Santorum in a discussion in which they placed the blame firmly on Napolitano's shoulders, claiming: "It's her department—the people that she hired. I mean, these are people that she hired, that the Obama administration hired to write this. This isn't holdovers from the Bush administration that wrote this. These are her folks!"

There was one notable exception on Fox: On April 15, the day before Santorum made these false charges, Fox News anchor Shepard Smith featured a segment with investigative reporter Catherine Herridge, who reported that the issue of potential violence from right-wing extremists in response to Obama's election was initially raised by authorities during the Bush administration. Herridge concluded that nearly all of the claims made by angry conservatives—including that DHS was ignoring left-wing terrorism—were groundless:

> Smith: So if this bulletin from April 7 looks at the right-wing groups, is there a bulletin that looks at left-wing groups as well?
>
> Herridge: Yeah, we were able to obtain that bulletin as well. It came out in January, and didn't get—there it is—didn't get the same attention. It looked specifically at groups like the Earth Liberation Front, or ELF, groups that in the opinion of Homeland Security, in the future will try and attack economic targets and specifically use cyber-attacks, because they see that as sympatico, or in concert with some of their other beliefs. So there are two assessments. The one on the left, the one on the right is the one that's getting the attention because of the leak.... I would point out that both of these assessments, Shep,

were commissioned under the Bush administration. It takes some time to do them. They only came out after he left office.

This reportage, however, went completely ignored not just by the rest of the Fox News crew but also by their cohorts in the right-wing punditocracy. Soon there was a clamor for Napolitano's head, not just from Santorum but from Rush Limbaugh and a number of other prominent conservatives. Veterans' groups—particularly the American Legion—jumped aboard the outrage bandwagon and began demanding that Napolitano apologize.

Initially Napolitano defended the report for its factual accuracy and purpose, which was to help give law-enforcement officers the informational tools they needed to help survive in the field. However, the clamor and controversy finally grew so intense that she eventually met with the commander of the American Legion and offered an apology, at least for the wording of the section on veterans, which she understood had offended a crowd of veterans eager to misread it: "I apologize for that offense," she said. "It was certainly not intended."

Napolitano later told Fox News what she regretted most was the wording of the footnote discussing anti-government groups: "If there's one part of that report I would rewrite, in the word-smithing, Washington-ese that goes on after the fact, it would be that footnote."

This apology didn't satisfy the right-wing pundits, who continued to grouse that the DHS was "profiling conservatives as right-wing extremists." Nonetheless, the issue finally began to die down after Napolitano's mea culpa.

The up-is-down controversy diminished (if not demolished) the bulletin's overarching purpose: to help prepare law-enforcement officers for potential threats in the field. Despite the hysteria, those threats are all too real. As if to underscore this point, April was bookended by another shooting of police officers by an angry and paranoid man with a military background. This time it took place in Okaloosa County, Florida, and the shooter was a 28-year-old U.S. Army Reserve soldier named Joshua Cartwright—who also feared President Obama was going to take his guns away.

Cartwright was a big man with a history of violence. He was arrested in November 2008 for domestic battery after beating his wife, Elizabeth. Out on bond, he beat her again the morning of April 25, 2009—after an argument over a tube of Clearasil escalated into a dispute over the large collection of guns he had in the house, at the end of which he punched her to the floor and then left to go shooting with some friends at a local gun range. She drove herself to the hospital, where she filed a second domestic-abuse report.

The incident report described an out-of-control and continually angry husband who threatened his wife, kept guns and knives about the house, was "severely disturbed" about Barack Obama's election as president, and harbored paranoid beliefs that the U.S. government was conspiring against him.

Two sheriff's deputies—Burt Lopez and Warren "Skip" York, both 45-year-olds who had retired from the air force (Lopez had five children and York had a 10-year-old son)—went out to the Shoal River Sporting Clays and Shooting Center just west of Killingsworth Crossroads, where Cartwright was fond of going, to arrest him. They both wore armored vests. Cartwright was uncooperative from the start, even after they disarmed him, so they hit him with a Taser. However, Cartwright had hidden another gun somewhere on his person. When he got up from being hit by the Taser, he fired, hitting both deputies with multiple shots to places not protected by their vests, including the head. Both were dead on the scene.

Cartwright went tearing out of the gun range and headed east down Highway 90 in his pickup truck. Police caught up with him about 30 miles away in DeFuniak Springs, at the road's intersection with Highway 331, where deputies had laid down spikes in hopes that tactic would stop him. It did. Cartwright's tires blew out as he drove across them and then, rammed by a patrol car, the truck went careering into a borrow pit and landed on its roof. Cartwright managed to crawl out of the backside of the wrecked truck and began firing, using the bed as cover. The collected force of officers at the scene responded in kind—about 60 rounds of ammunition were fired, and when it was over, Cartwright was dead of multiple gunshot wounds.

It brought to mind one passage of that DHS bulletin in particular, which now sounded ominously prescient: "Lone wolves and small terrorist cells embracing violent rightwing extremist ideology are the most dangerous domestic terrorism threat in the United States."

Within a matter of weeks, that warning would prove to be profoundly prophetic.

FOUR

Bloodying the Shirt

Scott Roeder was like a lot of anti-abortion conservatives— including Bill O'Reilly—who obsessed over the activities of a 67-year-old Wichita, Kansas, abortion provider named Dr. George Tiller. Tiller was one of only a tiny handful of abortion providers in Kansas and the four states surrounding it, and he was one of the only providers of late-term abortions in the entire country. This made Tiller the focus of a great deal of anger on the part of abortion opponents, who frequently protested outside his clinic and named him "Tiller the Baby Killer."

Roeder, a 51-year-old who lived in the Kansas City suburb of Merriam, was frequently one of those protesters. On May 31, 2009, he shot Tiller in the head. Tiller died instantly.

Tiller was no stranger to violence. In 1993, an anti-abortion extremist named Rachelle "Shelley" Shannon shot him in both arms, but he survived. Before shooting Tiller, she had embarked on a cross-country arson spree against abortion clinics. Shannon, who was active in the extremist Army of God faction that believes the murder of abortion doctors is justifiable in defense of the unborn, was convicted of Tiller's shooting and the arsons and remains imprisoned.

Scott Roeder had been a lurker on the fringes of the far right for some time. In the 1990s, Roeder was an active "constitutionalist" in the Patriot movement who filed Montana Freemen-style "sovereign citizenship papers" and was arrested in 1996 for driving with a Freemen license plate. The belief system of "organic sovereigns" was first promoted in the 1970s by the far-right Posse Comitatus movement, itself imbued with the racist and anti-Semitic ideology known as Christian Identity. According to Posse doctrine, nonwhites are subhuman "mud people" and Jews are the descendants of Satan. Posse believers declared that white Christians could assert their "sovereign citizenship" if they renounced their ties with the "Zionist-controlled" federal government. They also could create "common law courts" comprised solely of fellow "sovereigns," whose rights trumped those of Fourteenth Amendment citizens—people of color and non-Christians.

As Leonard Zeskind observes:

> It was an arcane theory which promoters sometimes used to justify tax protest, embezzlement and larceny. But its central tenets placed it at the heart of the white nationalist movement, which contended that the United States was, or should be, a white Christian republic rather than a multi-racial democracy.

Roeder became especially obsessed with abortion and became involved with violent groups like the Army of God and its more mainstream cohort, Operation Rescue, some of whose members have also been associated with the killings of abortion providers. Roeder once met with David Leach, the editor of the Army of God's newsletter, *Prayer and Action News,* after Leach had met with Shannon in her jail cell. "I met him once, and he wrote to me a few times," Leach told the *Kansas City Star.* "I remember that he was sympathetic to our cause, but I don't remember any details."

Leach did remember Roeder's obsession with government conspiracies. He described how Roeder demonstrated a technique for removing the magnetic strip from a five-dollar bill. "He said it was to keep the government from tracking your money," Leach explained.

Roeder's interest in Shannon underscored his growing obsession with Tiller. He began posting at Internet forums suggesting action directed within Tiller's church. This post from May 19, 2007, is attributed to him on Operation Rescue's Web site:

> Bleass everyone for attending and praying in May to bring justice to Tiller and the closing of his death camp. Sometime soon, would it be feasible to organize as many people as possible to attend Tillers church (inside, not just outside) to have much more of a presence and possibly ask questions of the Pastor, Deacons, Elders and members while there? Doesn't seem like it would hurt anything but bring more attention to Tiller.

For several years, Kansas's evangelical-Republican attorney general, who opposed abortion rights of any kind, investigated and harassed Tiller. Finally, in 2009, his successor brought 19 misdemeanor charges against Tiller that related to violations of the state's ban on late-term abortions, and the doctor's case went to trial in March.

Scott Roeder sat in on the trial frequently and kept in touch with Operation Rescue organizer Cheryl Sullenger, who helped Roeder track the trial in court.

"He would call and say, 'When does court start? When's the next hearing?'" Sullenger told the *Kansas City Star*. "I was polite enough to give him the information. I had no reason not to. Who knew? Who knew, you know what I mean?"

After three weeks of a jury trial, on March 27 Tiller was acquitted. This infuriated the anti-abortion extremists who had pinned their hopes on the case shutting Tiller's clinic down, and it apparently made Roeder determined to act on his own. He began indulging in a number of acts of vandalism, including applying Super Glue to the clinic's doors. The manager of the clinic phoned authorities and reported that he had seen Roeder engaging in the act, which was a federal offense in violation of the Freedom of Access to Clinic Entrances (FACE) Act. No investigation was ever initiated. And Roeder decided to take it to the next step.

As Tiller was chatting with his fellow ushers in the foyer of Wichita's Reformation Lutheran Church—where he had been a longtime member—Roeder strolled in, pulled out a handgun, and shot Tiller once in the head. When two other ushers moved to stop him, he pointed the gun at them and then walked out the front door, got in his car, and drove back toward Merriam. Police caught up to him on Interstate 35 in Johnson County and arrested him. On the dashboard of Roeder's car was a note reading "Cheryl" and "Op Rescue," with Sullenger's phone number.

Tiller's death could have been avoided had the government simply enforced the law. As Rachel Maddow reported afterward on her MSNBC program, the federal government had the power to stop the terrorism and threats of violence to abortion clinics under the FACE Act—and miserably failed to do its job. It ignored the clinic manager's reports on Roeder's increasing vandalism, and it didn't take seriously the escalating nature of the threats.

In an interview with national radio/TV host Amy Goodman, Dr. Susan Robinson, an associate of Tiller's who flew to Wichita every month to perform abortions in Tiller's clinic said this:

> It is generally regarded amongst those who do clinic security, if local authorities are not responsive, if they don't show up or they don't vigilantly enforce the law, that it encourages the anti-abortion people to push it further and further. In Wichita, Dr. Tiller was constantly dealing with the same lack of enforcement.

Wichita prohibits placing signs on city property. But they allow the anti-abortion protesters to set up dozens of crosses and leave them all day. Dr. Tiller went to the city attorney over the crosses and complained that people block the clinic driveway. He told me that the city attorney said, "I would rather be sued by George Tiller than the anti-abortion folks."

As Daphne Eviatar reported in the *Colorado Independent,* the feds during the Bush years got into the habit of not enforcing the FACE Act:

> According to statistics provided by the Department of Justice, the Bush administration brought only about two criminal prosecutions per year in the entire country under the FACE Act, and never more than four in any single year. The Clinton administration, in contrast, prosecuted 17 defendants for violations of the FACE Act in 1997 alone, and an average of about 10 per year since the law was enacted in 1994. Those cases included one against a woman in 1996 who yelled through a bullhorn to a doctor, "Robert, remember Dr. Gunn. This could happen to you . . . ," referring to Dr. David Gunn, the first abortion doctor ever murdered, in 1993. In another case, a man who parked a Ryder truck outside a clinic shortly after the bombing of a federal building in Oklahoma City, where a Ryder truck had been used to carry explosives, was found to have threatened force. Stalking, arson and bomb threats are also illegal.

However, federal action in Wichita may not have been able to prevent the killing. What ultimately mattered most was the homicidal frenzy anti-abortion radicals had worked themselves into. Pundits of the mainstream media—in particular, Fox News's Bill O'Reilly—gave a big helping hand.

Bill O'Reilly, like Scott Roeder, had an unhealthy obsession with George Tiller. Beginning in 2005, he made reportage on Tiller a regular feature of his top-rated Fox News show, *The O'Reilly Factor.* He constructed a running narrative about Tiller that portrayed him as a genocidal monster, claiming variously that Tiller was willing to "kill babies" at any stage of development for his $5,000 fee, that he was so eager to perform late-term abortions he allowed women to claim "temporary depression" as a medical condition to qualify for them, and that he had over the years "killed 60,000 babies."

In 2006, O'Reilly and his ambush-crew specialist, Jesse Watters, went hard after Tiller, accusing him of wantonly murdering babies with late-term abortions. In a November 6 report titled "Killing Babies in America," O'Reilly intoned:

> For more than a year, "The Factor" has been investigating Dr. George Tiller of Kansas. For $5000, "Tiller the Baby Killer," as some call him, will perform a late-term abortion for just about any reason.

O'Reilly went on to describe how Tiller reportedly used the "mental health exception," concluding:

> So what we have here in Kansas is a doctor who will terminate a pregnancy at any time for a reason that is vague and undefined. Now I ask you, ladies and gentlemen, even if you are pro-choice, do you believe this is morally right?

On the same show, O'Reilly invited abortion-rights activist Amy Richards to appear—so he could blindside her with his "evidence." He ended up shouting at Richards, accusing her of coddling killers:

> I don't care what you think. We have incontrovertible evidence that this man is executing babies about to be born because the

woman is depressed . . . if you don't believe me, I don't care. . . .
You are OK with Dr. Tiller executing babies about to be born
because the mother says she's depressed.

A few days later, in his regular "Talking Points Memo" opening
segment, O'Reilly explained what it all meant:

> If we as a society allow an undefined mental health exception in
> late-term abortions, then babies can be killed for almost any rea-
> son. . . . This is the kind of stuff that happened in Mao's China
> and Hitler's Germany and Stalin's Soviet Union. . . . If we allow
> this, America will no longer be a noble nation. . . . If we allow
> Dr. George Tiller and his acolytes to continue, we can no longer
> pass judgment on any behavior by anybody.

In December 2007, O'Reilly tried to throw more gasoline on
his Tiller bonfire by interviewing a young woman who claimed
she was deeply traumatized by a late-term abortion at Tiller's
clinic. O'Reilly launched into crusader mode, and on January
6, 2008, he urged a massive protest at Tiller's clinic: "There
should be thousands of people protesting outside Tiller's abortion clinic in Wichita." In February, O'Reilly sent out another
of his ambush-TV crews (this time led by Porter Barry) to stalk
Tiller at his home and at the clinic. Tiller responded by calling
the police.

Where was O'Reilly getting his information? Operation Rescue.
The organization—which runs O'Reilly's column in its newsletter—reported that "O'Reilly's staff used the Tiller Report II, produced by Operation Rescue, to learn more about the infamous late
term abortionist."

The demonization of Tiller on O'Reilly's show was so constant
and so intense—and the calls for action to stop him were so incessant—that it almost would have been a miracle if no one had tried

to kill him. In one instance, on his radio show, O'Reilly even suggested, briefly, that someone should step outside the law:

> Now, Tiller's pumping all kinds of money into obviously the attorney general race. He wants the guy that's gonna let him off the hook to win. Those of you listening in Kansas, you ought to know that. You know, I don't—I'm not gonna tell you who to vote for. You guys know these guys better than I do, but I tell you what, anything Tiller wants, I'm voting the other way. And if I could get my hands on Tiller—well, you know. Can't be vigilantes. Can't do that. It's just a figure of speech.
>
> But despicable? Oh, my God. Oh, it doesn't get worse. Does it get worse? No.

O'Reilly had so closely associated himself with the Tiller story that, when Scott Roeder finally did get his hands on Tiller, the questions about O'Reilly's role in the killing were almost immediate.

Just as immediate were O'Reilly's heated denials. The day after the killing, he went on *The O'Reilly Factor* and attacked his critics:

> When I heard about Tiller's murder, I knew pro-abortion zealots and Fox News haters would attempt to blame us for the crime, and that's exactly what has happened. . . .
>
> Every single thing we said about Tiller was true, and my analysis was based on those facts. . . .
>
> Now, it's clear that the far left is exploiting—exploiting—the death of the doctor. Those vicious individuals want to stifle any criticism of people like Tiller. That—and hating Fox News—is the real agenda here. Finally, if these people are soooo compassionate—so very compassionate, so concerned for the rights and welfare of others—maybe they might have written something, one thing, about the 60,000 fetuses that will never become American citizens. Or am I wrong?

The next night, O'Reilly began claiming that when he called Tiller a "baby killer," he was only reporting "what groups were calling him." But PolitiFact, Media Matters, and other media critics with backfiles of what O'Reilly had actually said examined this claim and found it bogus. PolitiFact found 42 instances of O'Reilly mentioning Tiller by name, dating back to 2005, and in 24 of those instances, O'Reilly specifically referred to Tiller as a "baby killer."

The incoming fire enraged O'Reilly. He completely snapped when, on June 10, Salon.com's managing editor, Joan Walsh, went on MSNBC's *Hardball with Chris Matthews* and laid into him:

> When Bill O'Reilly goes on TV every night and calls Dr. Tiller a baby killer and a Nazi and a Mengele, and shows where he works, why do we put up with that? Why is that entertainment in our culture? It's demonizing a private citizen for doing a lawful job? Why are people doing that? Why is that acceptable? I would like to see a debate about that.

O'Reilly was infuriated and the next night mentioned that he had invited Walsh to come on his show and defend her position. So on June 12, Walsh appeared opposite O'Reilly, and the exchange was truly epic.

O'Reilly began by badgering Walsh with a classic when-did-you-stop-beating-your-wife line of questioning: "Do you feel that late-term fetuses deserve any protections at all, Ms. Walsh?"

Walsh responded tentatively, even as O'Reilly repeated the question, and finally gave the best answer she could come up with: "I believe the law should be what it is, Bill." Walsh's ambiguous answer annoyed O'Reilly, who kept pressing the issue. Finally, O'Reilly—still smarting from Walsh's critique on *Hardball*—lashed out:

O'Reilly: You know who has blood on their hands? You.

Walsh: That's ridiculous, Bill.

O'Reilly: You don't care about these babies—you're the zealot.

Walsh: You know, you're really, you're a piece of work, my friend. I don't have blood on my hands—you do. I didn't crusade for anything. I work for abortion reduction. I'm a pro-choice Catholic who believes in abortion reduction and working with young girls and giving them rights, giving them information.... Don't demonize me, my friend. You'll be sorry.

Walsh pointed out that in attacking Tiller as he had, O'Reilly had demonized someone who had previously been wounded by gunfire and whose clinic had been bombed.

O'Reilly: I'm sorry about that.... But my constitutional right says I can say what I say, you can say what you say, as vile as you say it, you can say it, and I would never condemn you for saying it. You are misguided, you have blood on your hands because you portrayed this man as a hero, when he killed late-term babies for casual reasons.

Walsh: And you routinely attack ... people on the left—Janeane Garofalo, Michael Moore—who you think their rhetoric leads potentially to acts of violence. It never has led to one act of violence. But you've already driven that crazy guy [Jim David Adkisson] in Knoxville last year who read your writings and then went and shot up a church and shot liberals, that's already happened once, and you don't feel any responsibility at all, now that it's happened a second time, Bill? Talk about blood on your hands.

O'Reilly: Miss Walsh, I appreciate you coming on the program. I think everybody knows exactly where you're coming from.

Of course, everybody already knew where Bill O'Reilly was coming from. The next night, he ran an edited version of the interview, minus the parts where Walsh scorched him, and invited his guests to run down Walsh when she wasn't there to defend herself.

Meanwhile, Scott Roeder—from his prison cell, awaiting trial—communicated through the press that more violence awaited pro-choice clinics: "I know there are many other similar events planned around the country as long as abortion remains legal," Roeder told an Associated Press reporter. When asked what he meant, he refused to elaborate further.

For some reason, Bill O'Reilly did not report that story.

The extent to which Scott Roeder was inspired by Bill O'Reilly's rhetoric remains an open question. There's no evidence—as there was in the case of Richard Poplawski's Glenn Beck video—that Roeder was particularly influenced by O'Reilly's rants. He almost certainly called Tiller a "baby killer" long before O'Reilly began bandying the phrase about, and he adopted the radical beliefs involving the "justifiability" of killing Tiller long before O'Reilly began his crusade.

Right-wing radicals like Roeder wear their extremism proudly and see mainstream-conservative figures like O'Reilly ultimately as sellouts unwilling to drink the *real* Kool-Aid. Still, if they do watch TV news (and they usually do), they largely watch Fox, sometimes exclusively. Whether Scott Roeder fits that description is unknown. What we do know is that he was an avid reader of the Operation Rescue newsletter that ran O'Reilly's columns, which were frequently about Tiller. Moreover, given the frequency with which O'Reilly railed against Tiller, combined with Roeder's own obsessive interest in all things Tiller, it's probable that Roeder would have been aware of O'Reilly's attacks.

Militant anti-abortion ideologues celebrate and cherish their own outsider status. The people committing these acts see themselves as terrorists and extremists. They embrace the notion that they are outside the mainstream, which in their view is hopelessly corrupt and sinful. They embrace their radicalism and are proud of it. They make wry jokes about it. To the far right, even Fox News is part of the "liberal media" unwilling to tell the "real" truth.

So when they see someone like Bill O'Reilly or Glenn Beck or Lou Dobbs repeating for a mass national audience things they believed were only understood by people like themselves, it has a powerfully validating effect and, as they see it, gives them permission to act. Just as hate-crime perpetrators believe they are acting on the secret wishes of their communities, violent extremists have a need to believe that they are acting heroically, on behalf of their nation or their "people." Mainstream validation tells them they are supported.

Their fellow right-wingers in the mainstream don't condone or share their behavioral extremism but do share their belief that abortion is murder and that Dr. Tiller was a "mass murderer." Unfortunately, they are much too busy covering up the fact that their shared rhetoric empowers and energizes the extremists. Their friends in the media are willing, even eager, accomplices in the cover-up.

A main form of denial is to redefine "terrorism" to exclude anti-abortion violence—to recast people like Scott Roeder as mere common criminals. In 2001 then Republican representative Porter Goss of Florida—before he resigned to become CIA director—made this view explicit: "The trouble is, 'terrorism' is a very broad word, and it lends itself to a lot of mischief for people who would abuse common sense," Goss said in a congressional hearing.

He then cited bombings of abortion clinics: "To me, that's not the kind of terrorism I'm talking about."

The blind spot continues to this day: When NBC News's Brian Williams interviewed John McCain and Sarah Palin in October 2008, he asked Palin: "Is an abortion clinic bomber a terrorist, under this definition?"

Instead of answering, Palin changed the subject:

> There's no question that Bill Ayers, via his own admittance, was one who sought to destroy our U.S. Capitol and our Pentagon—that is a domestic terrorist. There's no question there. Now, others who would want to engage in harming innocent Americans or facilities that—it would be unacceptable—I don't know if you would use the word "terrorist" there, but it's unacceptable, and it would not be condoned, of course, on our watch.

When Tiller was assassinated, she issued a statement of regret, but assiduously avoided referring to the act as terrorism.

Abortion is far from the only issue that inspires right-wing extremists to acts of terrorism. Additional inspirations include gun rights; taxes and federal monetary issues; disputes over land use, public resources, and the environment; education; school prayer; law-enforcement tactics; and other fears related to federal and state governance. Often, all of these issues coalesce into a big ball of conspiracy theories and paranoid fears about a looming one-world government.

One of the most significant and troubling manifestations of the extremism of the Patriot/militia movement of the 1990s was the sharp spike in threats against local law-enforcement officials. Practically a pandemic of threats against judges occurred in the interior West (particularly Montana and Nevada). Local, state, and federal judges all came under siege from a variety of spoken and written threats, in their offices and in their homes. The threats were a direct outgrowth of the Patriot movement's ardent adoption of the concept of "sovereign citizenship." In the 1990s the concept was promoted most notably by the Montana Freemen. When the movement faded in the early 2000s, so did the threats against judges.

In 2009, it became clear that the trend had returned. The U.S. Marshals Service reported in June that threats against federal judges and prosecutors had ballooned in recent years, rising from 500 in 2003 to 1,278 in 2008, and were on track to go even higher in 2009. The *Washington Post* reported:

> Worried federal officials blame disgruntled defendants whose anger is fueled by the Internet; terrorism and gang cases that bring more violent offenders into federal court; frustration at the economic crisis; and the rise of the "sovereign citizen" movement—a loose collection of tax protesters, white supremacists and others who don't respect federal authority.…
>
> Hundreds of threats cascaded into the chambers of John M. Roll, the chief U.S. district judge in Arizona, in February after he allowed a lawsuit filed by illegal immigrants against a rancher to go forward. "They cursed him out, threatened to kill his family, said they'd come and take care of him. They really wanted him dead," said a law enforcement official who heard the calls—which came from as far as Richmond and Baltimore—but spoke on condition of anonymity because no one has been charged.

Agitation over gun rights continued, even though the Obama administration made no attempts in 2009 to approach the issue. That, however, just seemed to make the extremist Right more paranoid because they believed the absence of discussion was proof that it was being planned in secret.

The gun-show crowd is more the Patriot contingent of far-right extremism: obsessed with guns and conspiracy theories, yet capable of paranoid bursts of extreme violence by lone-wolf actors.

Whatever agitation they began showing by the spring of 2009 was more than matched in intensity by their more violent cousins in the white-supremacist movement. *Newsweek*'s Eve Conant filed a report describing how many of them were working hard to mainstream themselves: "The haters are doing their best . . . to move out from the fringe and toward the mainstream—and they're boasting some success." At the same time, they couldn't fully suppress their underlying violent nature: Conant observed that a number of them on the Web call for armed revolution and refer to President Obama as "a dead man."

The real threat, as Conant reported, was not so much the visible, public racists, but rather the less flamboyant and more violent figures they inspire. Mark Potok, of the Southern Poverty Law Center, told Conant: "The lone-wolf idea is much scarier than the big-plot idea. Big plots don't succeed because these guys cannot keep their mouths shut."

When the Department of Homeland Security issued its law-enforcement bulletin on right-wing extremists (see chapter 3), the mainstream right's chief shrieking point was that somehow the bulletin had conflated them with the extremist right-wingers. The upshot of all the shrieking was that Homeland Security was labeling conservatives America's chief terrorist threat.

In fact, the actual report concludes this way:

> Lone wolves and small terrorist cells embracing violent right-wing extremist ideology are the most dangerous domestic terrorism threat in the United States. Information from law enforcement and nongovernmental organizations indicates lone wolves and small terrorist cells have shown intent—and, in some cases, the capability—to commit violent acts.

The lone-wolf concept was popularized in the late 1980s by an Aryan Nations leader named Louis Beam as an extension of his strategy of "leaderless resistance." Beam observed that the traditional top-down hierarchy favored by the racist Right was actually quite dangerous for insurgents, especially in "technologically advanced societies where electronic surveillance can often penetrate the structure, revealing its chain of command." In leaderless organizations, "individuals and groups operate independently of each other, and never report to a central headquarters or single leader for direction or instruction, as would those who belong to a typical pyramid organization." Rather than issue orders or pay operatives, the function of the organizations' mouthpieces is to inspire individuals or small, localized cells to take action on their own initiative.

A white supremacist named Alex Curtis even went so far as to develop a "point system" for lone wolves. The strategy was inspired by at least one lone-wolf shooter: Joseph Paul Franklin, a racist sniper who in the late 1970s and early 1980s killed as many as 20 people—mostly mixed-race couples—on a serial-murder spree and attempted to assassinate Vernon Jordan and Larry Flynt. William Pierce, former leader of the white-supremacist group National Alliance, dedicated his incendiary 1989 novel *Hunter* to Franklin; the novel was a follow-up to Pierce's 1978 book *The Turner Diaries,* the notorious domestic-terrorism blueprint that was found in Terry Nichols's home and apparently helped inspire his and Timothy McVeigh's terrorist act in Oklahoma City.

There has been no dearth of lone wolves (or small cells) in the years since Beam articulated this strategy for the radical right: Eric Rudolph, Timothy McVeigh and Terry Nichols, Buford Furrow, Benjamin Smith, James Kopp, and Jim David Adkisson among them. It all adds up to a long trail of "isolated incidents."

Scott Roeder's act made clear that the lone-wolf strategy was alive and well, and only a little over a week after he struck, so did James von Brunn.

Stephen Tyrone Johns was a 39-year-old gentle giant of a man employed as a guard at the United States Holocaust Memorial Museum, just a block off the National Mall in Washington, DC. Besides his intimidating size—he stood six feet six— he was well known at the museum as a friendly man. When, in the early-afternoon hours of June 10, 2009, he saw an elderly man seeming to struggle with something as he approached the museum's front door—behind which sat the security apparatus designed to keep weapons out, along with a phalanx of Johns's fellow security guards—Johns went to open the door for him.

The elderly man was 89-year-old James von Brunn, who had double-parked his car in the southbound lane of Raoul Wallenberg Way directly in front of the museum entrance. He got out of the car with a .22 rifle in one hand, held at his side to somewhat obscure it. Johns apparently did not see it until, as he held the door for him, von Brunn raised it and fired once point-blank, hitting Johns in the upper chest.

Because the Holocaust Memorial Museum is a frequent recipient of bomb and death threats, it is well guarded, though, until that day, there had never been an incident of violence in its 16-year history. Inside the door were a number of other guards, several of whom, upon hearing the gunshot, pulled out their weapons. As von Brunn came through the door, he raised the rifle again as if to fire, and they opened fire on him. He was hit by a bullet to the face, which knocked him backward through the door. Though he was badly injured, von Brunn survived. Stephen Johns did not.

When the smoke had cleared and the hundreds of people inside the museum had been safely escorted out, details began to emerge about the elderly man, now recovering from his wounds in a hospital bed, who had wreaked all this havoc—and most of all, why he had.

It was not the first time that James von Brunn had terrorized a building full of people in DC. In 1981, he had entered the Federal Reserve Building carrying a handgun, a knife, and a sawed-off shotgun inside his coat. He pulled out the handgun and stuck it in the stomach of a security guard, demanding that he be taken to see then Fed chairman Paul Volcker. He and the guard made it up to the second floor before a phalanx of security guards surrounded von Brunn and disarmed him. He was convicted in 1983 of burglary, assault, weapons charges, and attempted kidnapping, and he served six and a half years in prison for the crime before being released.

Here's how von Brunn described it on his Web site:

> In 1981 von Brunn attempted to place the treasonous Federal Reserve Board of Governors under legal, non-violent, citizens arrest. He was tried in a Washington, D.C. Superior Court; convicted by a Negro jury, Jew/Negro attorneys, and sentenced to prison for eleven years by a Jew judge. A Jew/Negro/White Court of Appeals denied his appeal. He served 6.5 years in federal prison.

James von Brunn was, like Scott Roeder, a longtime subscriber to Posse Comitatus beliefs, particularly the movement's contention that the Federal Reserve was operated by a conspiracy of Jewish bankers whose goal was to enslave the American people—which was why he had attempted to "arrest" Volcker. In the "autobiography" on his Web site, he described himself as a PT-boat captain in World War II who had become radicalized in the postwar years and had dedicated his life to promoting far-right ideology. What his writings consistently reveal is a man who was obsessed with the supposed persecution of white people at the hands of Jews. He denied that the Holocaust was a real event, and he believed that Jews secretly controlled America.

After the shooting at the Holocaust Museum, the ADL examined von Brunn's background and reported:

> As a result of his long history as an active white supremacist, von Brunn developed relationships with and connections to a variety of prominent white supremacists over the years, including Ben Klassen (whose portrait von Brunn painted), founder of the Creativity Movement; Willis Carto, a longstanding racist and anti-Semitic publisher and Holocaust denier; Tom Metzger, founder of White Aryan Resistance, and many others. One close connection was a retired Navy admiral and white supremacist, John G. Crommelin, who supported von Brunn for decades (and whom von Brunn also captured in portraiture).

Von Brunn's association with Carto in particular was a long-standing one; for years he had been a distributor of Carto's rabidly anti-Semitic newspaper, *The Spotlight,* and had worked for Carto's publishing company in those years as well. Eventually, as Carto's operations declined, von Brunn had tried his hand at forming a white-supremacist organization; in 2004, he called himself the "Supreme Archon" of the "Aryan Council" of the Holy Western Empire. You can get the flavor of von Brunn's beliefs from his description of his self-published online book *Kill the Best Gentiles*:

> Here are 350 pp of FACTS condensing libraries of information about the Talmud, Democracy, Marx, Genetics, Money, Aryans, Negroes, Khazars, The Holy Bible, Treason, Mass-media, Mendelism, Race, the "Holocaust" and a host of sup-

pressed "bigoted" subjects, all supported by quotations from many of history's greatest personages. Learn who is responsible for the millions of Aryan crosses covering the world's battlefields. Why our sons and daughters died bravely in vain. Learn why the "browning of America will alter everything in society from politics and education to industry, values and culture."

As the ADL explained, "von Brunn repeatedly touched on two subjects: the Federal Reserve, which he believed was controlled by Jewish bankers, and the Holocaust, which, like many Holocaust deniers, he believed never occurred. Central banks were, according to von Brunn, the 'biggest sleight-of-hand trick ever,' allowing Jews to buy anything, 'including the media, business, and government.'"

The belief that Jews controlled the media explained, for von Brunn, their ability to control the white population. A post at his Web site was headlined "Hitler's Worst Mistake: He Didn't Gas the Jews":

> Bit by bit Liberalism ascended. Bit by bit the Constitution was re-interpreted. Bit by bit government institutions and Congressmen fell into JEW hands—then U.S. diplomacy, businesses, resources and manpower came under JEW control.
>
> White men sat on their collective asses and did NOTHING—NOTHING BUT TALK. Never before in World history has a Nation so completely been conquered with absolutely NO physical resistance.

Von Brunn believed that President Obama represented the final step of the Jews' degradation of American government. He avidly subscribed to the "Birther" conspiracy theories, posting several pieces about Obama's supposed lack of citizenship as further proof of his illegitimacy as president and the conspiracy to put him in place. He also believed that Obama planned to confiscate his guns.

Perhaps most telling was the notebook he left behind in his car at the Holocaust Museum, which contained the following message:

> You want my weapons—this is how you'll get them. The Holocaust is a lie. Obama was created by Jews. Obama does what his Jew owners tell him to do. Jews captured America's money. Jews control the mass media. The 1st Amendment is abrogated—henceforth.

All of these collected facts revealed, without a hint of doubt, that von Brunn was a radical right-wing extremist. And yet, within mere hours of the shooting, right-wing pundits were going on the national airwaves and trying to claim that James von Brunn was not a right-winger at all. The day after the shooting, Glenn Beck told his viewers: "This is not the work of right-wing conservatives. This is the work of someone today who is racist, crazy, or most likely, both. Common sense tells you that there are very hateful people on the Right and the Left."

On his radio program, Rush Limbaugh declared that, if anything, von Brunn was a leftist:

> The facts of the case, however, are such that if we want to start assigning blame for this beyond this nutcase Jew-hater—and notice that very few people actually want to do that, they want to claim that this guy didn't have the ability to act on his own, he only could act if he was inspired by somebody—Well, who did he hate? He hated both Bushes. He hated neocons. He hated John McCain. He hated Republicans. He hated Jews as well. He believed in an "inside job" conspiracy of 9/11. This guy is a leftist, if anything. This guy's beliefs, this guy's hate, stems from influence that you find on the left.

This was, of course, absurd. Von Brunn hated the Bushes, neo-cons, McCain, and Republicans because they weren't far enough to the right. Notably lacking from Limbaugh's description was that Von Brunn also hated black people, and he especially hated Obama because he believed he was controlled by Jews. He also hated the Federal Reserve, taxes, the United Nations, and the federal government generically; he admired Hitler, urged the recriminalization of miscegenation, and promoted Holocaust denial—all beliefs traditionally associated with the far Right.

Nonetheless, his fellow conservative pundits soon echoed Limbaugh's nonsense. On his June 12 show, Glenn Beck hosted a discussion of the case with Jonah Goldberg and read a recitation of similar "evidence" that von Brunn was actually a leftist—or at least, not a right-winger. No, he was just "cuckoo for Cocoa Puffs."

Goldberg explained this in more detail in a column for the *National Review:*

> Never mind that von Brunn isn't a member of the far right. Nor is he a member of the far left, as some on the right are claiming. He's not a member of anything other than the crazy caucus. Von Brunn's True North is conspiratorial anti-Semitism and anti-Zionism. He's not a member of the Christian Right. In fact, he denounces Christianity—just as Hitler did—as a Jewish plot against paganism and Western vigor. Nor is he a capitalist. Again, just as Hitler did, he hails socialism as the solution to the West's problems.

Goldberg, in arguing thus, was continuing to pitch the historically fraudulent thesis he had successfully foisted upon the public in his book *Liberal Fascism: The Secret History of the American Left from Mussolini to the Politics of Meaning,* namely, that "properly understood, fascism is not a phenomenon of the right at all. Instead, it is, and always has been, a phenomenon of the left."

Beyond the ahistorical nature of this claim, there's also the reality of modern-day proto-fascists—groups like the Aryan Nations, Posse Comitatus, and a host of other white-supremacist organizations—which are, by any meaningful definition, clearly right-wing extremists. This reality tends to undermine, if not demolish, Goldberg's thesis about the nature of fascism. And it manifests itself most irrevocably when the likes of Scott Roeder and James von Brunn—clearly and identifiably right-wing extremist ideologues—make their bloodstained marks on the national landscape.

When we attempted to explore this issue with Goldberg in 2008, he dismissed the significance of such extremists:

> So, you want my short answer to why I don't discuss, say, the Posse Comitatus? Okay here it is: Who gives a rat's ass about the Posse Comitatus?
>
> I'm sure Neiwert's gorillas-in-the-mist reportage on these guys is top notch, and I'll take his word for it they're bad guys. But being bad guys alone doesn't in and of itself make them fascists. Indeed, from my limited understanding of what these guys believe, they are radical localists, who don't believe any government above the county level is legitimate. Do I really have to spell out why that's not exactly in keeping with hyper-statist ideology of Nazis and Italian Fascists? "Everything in Hazard County, nothing outside Hazard County," has a nice ring to it, but the Hegelian God-State it is not.

Characterizing the Posse Comitatus as mere "radical localists" is roughly as accurate as describing the Ku Klux Klan of the 1920s as a mere "fanboy cult" (something Goldberg also managed to do in his best-seller). By the summer of 2009—in the wake of Roeder's and von Brunn's rampages—blithely dismissing the impact of Posse Comitatus extremists on the national discourse no longer was really possible. So Goldberg reverted to arguing his claim that there was nothing particularly *right wing* about the kookery of people who subscribed to the beliefs of the Aryan Nations or the Posse Comitatus—they're just kooks, plain and simple.

This is palpable nonsense. What makes these people right-wing extremists is that not only do they adopt right-wing political positions, they take them to their most extreme logical (if that's the word for it) outcome:

- They not only oppose abortion but believe abortion providers should be killed.

- They not only believe that liberal elites control the media and financial institutions but that a conniving cabal of Jews is at the heart of this conspiracy to destroy America.

- They not only despise Big Government but believe it is part of a New World Order plot to enslave us all.

- They not only defend gun rights avidly but stockpile them out of fear that President Obama plans to send in U.N. troops to take them away from U.S. citizens.

- They not only oppose homosexuality as immoral but believe gays and lesbians deserve the death penalty.

- They not only oppose civil-rights advances for minorities but believe a "race war" is imminent, necessary, and desirable.

- They not only doubt the reality of global warming but believe it is a front for a massive conspiracy to enslave Americans and install a one-world government.

Accurately describing people like von Brunn and Roeder as right-wing extremists—and accurately warning law-enforcement officers about the rising likelihood of violence from far-right lone wolves—somehow amounts only to an attempt to "silence conservatives." Or as Beck put it in his exchange with Goldberg: "I contend this is not about us, who they're attacking, it is about stifling people, scaring them, keeping them, you know, on their couch."

Beck, on an earlier show, had similarly denounced the suggestion that James von Brunn was a right-winger, explaining that the problem was all the people who were getting provoked to anger by evil liberals:

> What they're missing is: The pot in America is boiling. And this is just yet another warning to all Americans of things to come. This guy is a lone gunman nutjob. . . . You're going to see a lot of nutjobs coming out of the woodwork now. . . . We are under attack in almost every shape and form in America. We need to look out for enemies foreign and domestic. . . . There is gonna be a witch hunt, I believe, in this country, and quite possibly all around the world. For two groups. First group: Jews. It happens every time. Second group, I think: Conservatives. . . .
>
> Meanwhile, the Department of Homeland Security reports about right-wing extremists. You remember that came out a few weeks ago? Left-wing bloggers and some in the media have blamed conservative hosts like me or Bill O'Reilly for just stirring the pot! I'm not stirring the pot. I'm pointing out the pot is boiling and there is trouble in America. Since when—have you ever heard of "don't blame the messenger"?

Disingenuous disclaimers notwithstanding, Glenn Beck clearly was stirring the pot. He was not alone—so were most of his cohorts at Fox News, as well as right-wing media figures like Rush Limbaugh and Lou Dobbs. Yet if they acknowledged that they were stirring the pot, they would have to change the very shticks that had made them all so successful in the first place.

It was much simpler, and more satisfying, to instead claim that they were being victimized by the liberal political-correctness police who wanted to somehow "silence" them. This tactic is in fact a time-tested, oft-favored rhetorical technique of the American Right: crying "bloody shirt."

Most of us are familiar with the dismissive charge raised in such situations—that liberals are "waving the bloody shirt"—that is, according to Wikipedia, "the demagogic practice of politicians referencing the blood of martyrs or heroes to inspire support or avoid criticism." American conservatives in particular make this charge with great regularity. It is, fundamentally, a way to turn their own foul behavior on its head and accuse those who would hold them accountable for it. That's what the phrase "waving the bloody shirt" has always meant since it was first coined in the wake of the Civil War.

As Stephen Budiansky explains in his book *The Bloody Shirt: Terror after the Civil War*, the phrase came about when a Northern-born schools superintendent named Allen Huggins was brutally beaten and whipped by night-riding Klansmen in the South for his refusal to cease efforts to "educate the negroes." When Congressman Benjamin F. Butler of Massachusetts railed against such outrages a few weeks later—specifically citing the Huggins case—the legend grew that Butler had waved Huggins's bloody shirt on the floor of the House to make his point, though there is no evidence he did so.

As Budiansky explains, "waving the bloody shirt" in short order became "the standard retort, the standard expression of dismissive Southern contempt whenever a Northern politician mentioned any of the thousands upon thousands of murders, whippings, mutilations, and rapes that were perpetrated against freedmen and women and white Republicans in the South in those years." Politicians, preachers, newspaper editors, and all stripes of defenders of the Southern oppression of African Americans used it to dismiss their critics. Budiansky adds:

To white conservative Southerners, the outrage was never the acts they committed, only the effrontery of having those acts held against them. The outrage was never the "manly" inflicting of "well-deserved" punishment on poltroons, only the craven and sniveling whines of the recipients of their wrath. And the outrage was never the violent defense of "honor" by the aristocrat, only the vulgar rabble-rousing by his social inferior....

The bloody shirt captured the inversion of truth that would characterize the distorted memories of Reconstruction that the nation would hold for generations after. The way it made a victim of the bully and a bully of the victim, turned the very blood of their African American victims into an affront against Southern white decency, turned the very act of Southern white violence into wounded Southern innocence; the way it suggested that the real story was never the atrocities white Southerners committed but only the attempt by their political enemies to make political hay out of it.

The longevity of this rhetorical sleight of hand is testament to its effectiveness: It may have taken root during Reconstruction, but it is still very much with us today, and favored not merely among those living in the South. As Budiansky notes, in the years since Reconstruction the phrase has "entered the standard American political lexicon, a synonym for any rabble-rousing demagoguery, any below-the-belt appeal aimed at stirring old enmities."

Its effectiveness was particularly evident in the ability of right-wing pundits to elude any real culpability for the extremist violence that began erupting in the spring of 2009. They proclaimed some version of "waving the bloody shirt"—and, almost as soon as the discussion of their responsibility for the all-too-truly bloodied shirts of George Tiller and Stephen Tyrone Johns began, it quietly ended.

It was such a handy maneuver that various forms of it—particularly to bolster their claim that people making the commonsense connection between incendiary right-wing rhetoric and explosive right-wing violence were somehow trying to "silence" or "suppress" conservatives—became the Right's favorite self-justification as their punditry descended into the abyss of abject wingnuttery.

The rhetorical device was their go-to way of defending their shiny new project for attacking the Obama administration—the Tea Parties. Which, naturally, was when the craziness reached depths previously unseen in American politics.

FIVE

Mad Hatters and March Hares

Beltway media elites were dumbfounded when, during the 2007 Republican primaries, a little-known congressman named Ron Paul from Texas, who identified himself more as a libertarian, scored a huge fund-raising bonanza. On a single day, he brought in $6 million. That's quite a haul for any leading candidate during a primary but a spectacular showing for someone deemed "unserious" by conventional wisdom due to his historical appeal to the far-right fringe.

Referred to in political circles as a "money bomb," Paul's fundraiser set a record for online donations at the time. Most of the money raised was via small donations, which shows the power of the Internet. Typically, candidates look for big donors to finance their campaigns, although there is a limit of $2,300 per individual. The Internet has shown the power of donations in the $10 to $25 range if they are contributed in significant numbers. In Ron Paul's case, the *Washington Times* reported that over 35,000 people donated to the Paul "money bomb." When those findings were reported, both the mainstream media and conservative circles took notice.

Ron Paul began drawing large crowds whenever he spoke and drew big ratings whenever he appeared on television, much to the consternation of Republican elites. Before the primaries started, Paul was adamant about his disdain for Bush's foreign policy, particularly the war in Iraq, which appealed to some on the left. His isolationist stance made him the rare Republican who believed attacking Iraq was a huge mistake. But for any candidate to win the Republican nomination, he or she had to support the Iraq and Afghanistan wars as well as pledge allegiance to the "fighting the terrorists over there" narrative coming from the Bush White House. Politicians who questioned this official line put themselves at risk of being attacked for their lack of patriotism. The attacks Paul endured, though, were worn like badges of honor.

The first Paul "money bomb" in 2007 occurred on November 5, Guy Fawkes Day. The second—more significant both monetarily and philosophically—occurred on December 16 because Paul supporters used the 234th anniversary of the Boston Tea Party as a rallying cry. Michael Levenson, reporting for the *Boston Globe,* noted that by 7 p.m., the campaign had collected a one-day record of $4.3 million in contributions from some 33,000 donors. By the end of the day, it had extended the haul to over $6 million. The December 16 fund-raiser also featured a march in the Boston snow, culminating with a protest that included tossing banners reading "tyranny" and "no taxation without representation" into boxes placed before an image of Boston Harbor.

Conservative organizers were watching this with keen interest because after eight years of conservative rule and with the country in bad shape, they were anticipating being swept out of office. The question for many of them was how to rebuild afterward. The "Boston Tea Party" protest carried out by the Ron Paul supporters provided the perfect model.

◇　◇　◇

The phrase *grass roots* describes activism that emanates from the ground up, from the homes of working families that are fed up with a certain political party or the state of the country and want to voice their opinions. However, *grass roots* can also be used deceptively to mask the powerful machinations of corporate wealth.

By pretending that their interests are the same as those of average working-class people who rent apartments, pay mortgages, hold two jobs, and pack school lunches for their kids, the multimillionaires who run American corporations have only one thing in mind: keeping the money flowing into their pockets. So they fund fake grassroots—or "astroturf"—operations that pretend to represent "ordinary Americans" but in reality are propaganda shops designed to support the interests of corporate wealth. The subterfuge is accomplished by encouraging people to believe that they are doing the right thing even though they are actively working against their own interests.

Ultra-wealthy interests like the Koch and Coors families fund astroturf organizations such as FreedomWorks to propagandize vulnerable Americans into believing that the fault for their tough economic times lies not with conservative governance (cutting taxes to corporations and the wealthiest Americans, demolishing regulations that protect the working class) but with minorities and welfare recipients—people, they are told, who are just lazy and don't want to work for themselves and whose laziness is enabled by liberal policies. It is, fundamentally, the practice of the politics of resentment, using cultural wedge issues to pry working-class people away from progressive politics.

Many of these interests had hopes that they could eke out another presidential victory in 2008 by nominating a relative moderate in John McCain. And going into the homestretch, things were looking good: McCain and his running mate, Sarah Palin, had ignited the Republican convention in St. Paul in late August and emerged with a lead in the polls. Then the roof caved in.

On September 23, 2008, Treasury Secretary Hank Paulson went before a skeptical Senate Banking Committee and asked that emergency funds to the tune of $700 billion be immediately pumped into the financial sectors or the entire global financial market would collapse and America would face another Great Depression. It was a stunning development for the already reeling presidency of George Bush, but what made it even stranger was that it happened so near to the end of the 2008 presidential campaign. The economic crisis proved to be the turning point in what had developed into a close race. John McCain decided to suspend his presidential campaign and return to Washington, though he admitted little understanding of economics (to underscore this, he had first responded to news of the crisis by insisting: "The fundamentals of the economy are sound") and could provide no real solutions. Many Americans saw his "suspension" as a political stunt and, soon after, Barack Obama—who had slipped behind McCain in the polls after the GOP convention—again soared ahead in the polls, eventually cruising to election.

Both liberals and conservatives were wary of the Bush administration's bailout proposals. For more than a year, homeowners had seen their mortgage payments double in the blink of an eye; then, unable to refinance due to plummeting housing values, they lost their homes to foreclosure. If American families had to pay the ultimate price for making a bad decision on financing a home due to the advice of lenders mired in credit default swaps or derivatives trading, why were Wall Street hucksters being bailed out with astronomical sums of money for their bad behavior? The public, both Left and Right, was furious.

After the House rejected the first attempt at a bailout on

September 29, 2008, the Senate convened on October 1 and passed HR 1424, a bill that had been expanded to include more stimulus proposals. On October 3, the House then passed the amended version of HR 1424, George Bush signed it into law immediately, and Wall Street received $700 billion through the newly created Troubled Assets Relief Program (TARP).

TARP funds came from American taxpayers, and the right-wing noise machine had always had success attracting support from them for their faux populist themes. Screaming about taxes is a nifty card to play because who really wants to pay taxes? Although the bailout was set in motion while Bush was in office, economists around the globe realized that after Obama was sworn in on January 20, 2009, a huge stimulus package would be needed to save the American economy from complete ruin. And so immediately after the inauguration, Congress set to work with the new president's team to craft a viable bill. Finally, on February 11, Congress reached a deal on a stimulus package.

At around the same time, Keli Carender, a Seattle schoolteacher and member of the Young Republicans, began a blog named Redistributing Knowledge, writing under the nom de plume "Liberty Belle." Carender wrote that conservatives needed to get busy and show real people what the GOP could do to solve the problems of the country, declaring: "We need something BOLD and DIFFERENT and REAL." Liberty Belle's second post put out a call to arms for conservatives across the land:

> There are tens of millions of us, if not more. I think if we chose a day to show the world, scary coworkers be damned, that we exist and we are just as passionate about the direction of our country, that we could maybe finally find each other.

On February 10, Liberty Belle announced she was going to hold a "porkulus protest" in Seattle the following Monday, February 16. She was aided by another member of the Young Republicans, Kirby Wilbur, who put her on his local Fox News Radio talk show. Conservative blogger Michelle Malkin saw an opportunity and jumped on Liberty Belle's blog posts; she told her readers to join the protests against Obama's "porkulus" bill and then issued a call for the same kind of protest to be held in Denver.

True grassroots activism doesn't come naturally to conservatives, and even with the efforts of conservative bloggers to organize additional rallies in Nashville and New York City, the "Tea Party" protests were a minor blip on the activist Richter scale. However, they were successful in persuading those well-funded conservative operatives to kick open the cash register and help spread the propaganda needed to underwrite a right-wing populist uprising. The trick was finding a way to appeal to working-class voters for whom the conservative brand had developed a foul odor, even though its hoary myths—that cutting taxes and deregulating everything in sight for the sake of "free enterprise" was the sure path to prosperity—were still alive and well. For conservatives to capture the imagination of the Republican base, they would need a way to hide the stench of their fouled governmental nest and bring those myths roaring back to life.

That problem was solved when Americans for Prosperity, a right-wing think tank funded by billionaire David Koch, joined in to provide much-needed resources and influence. A protest on the Colorado State Capitol steps was held on February 17, 2009, to coincide with Obama's signing of the stimulus bill at the Denver Museum of Nature and Science. Michelle Malkin, who had moved to the state the year before, arrived in Denver to help stage the protest, which was fully funded by Koch's group and by the Independence Institute, a conservative think tank funded by the

Coors family's Castle Rock Foundation. The protest drew a modest crowd of about 200 who screamed in unison: "No more pork!"

When President Obama arrived in Mesa, Arizona, on February 18 to give a talk at a local high school, he was met by 500 anti-tax protesters. "I'm out here to exercise my First Amendment rights while I still have them," Tim Guiney, 52, a Phoenix sales manager, told a reporter for the *East Valley Tribune*. "Everything that man stands for is the antithesis of what this country was founded on. He's a Marxist, fascist."

Meanwhile, as Michelle Malkin worked on her blog to get these fledgling protests off the ground, the spark that finally lit the fuse came from an unusual source, to say the least: a Wall Street insider and CNBC analyst named Rick Santelli.

Few Americans had heard of Santelli, a former trader and financial executive. CNBC's ratings are consistently low and, at the time, only people with a vested interest in the stock market were likely to know of him. But as President Obama was preparing his housing plan to help the millions of American homeowners in desperate shape, Santelli snapped in typical conservative fashion. On February 19, while discussing the Obama plan with CNBC host Joe Kernen in a broadcast from the trading pit of the Chicago Stock Exchange, he unleashed a rant that went viral when the video hit YouTube:

> Santelli: The government is promoting bad behavior. Because we certainly don't want to put stimulus forth and give people a whopping $8 or $10 in their check, and think that they ought to save it, and in terms of modifications . . . I'll tell you what, I have an idea. You know, the new administration's big on computers and technology— How about this, President and new administration? Why don't you put up a website to have people vote on the Internet as a referendum to see if we really want to subsidize

the losers' mortgages; or would we like to at least buy cars and buy houses in foreclosure and give them to people that might have a chance to actually prosper down the road, and reward people that could carry the water instead of drink the water?

Kernen: Hey, Rick . . . Oh, boy. They're like putty in your hands. Did you hear . . . ?

Santelli: No they're not, Joe. They're not like putty in our hands. This is America! How many of you people want to pay for your neighbor's mortgage that has an extra bathroom and can't pay their bills? Raise their hand. [Booing] President Obama, are you listening?

Trader: How 'bout we all stop paying our mortgage? It's a moral hazard.

Note that Santelli didn't blame his Wall Street cohorts or his CNBC colleagues who had ignored or lied about the state of the housing market. He didn't go after the bond-market rating companies that gave AAA ratings to toxic assets. He didn't look at Countrywide, the biggest mortgage corporation right in the middle of the chaos that was about to go bankrupt. Nope, he blamed *you*. The housing crash was the fault of the stupid American people who allowed themselves to be conned by mortgage brokers.

It made for wildly entertaining TV, especially for CNBC. It was like the Howard Beale character in the film *Network* telling his TV viewers to scream out "I'm as mad as hell and I'm not gonna take this anymore!" And then, having hooked the audience with anger, came the big pitch from Santelli:

We're thinking of having a Chicago Tea Party in July. All you capitalists that want to show up to Lake Michigan, I'm gonna start organizing.

As the video went viral, conservatives lapped it up. By the end of the day, OfficialChicagoTeaParty.com had gone online. Soon after, a Facebook page for the Tea Party was created, administered by people affiliated with Dick Armey's FreedomWorks and Americans for Prosperity.

CNBC immediately ran a commercial starring Santelli, and his rant was the talk of cable TV for a week or so. Some close observers thought there was something off about it. Barry Ritholtz, a blogger and Wall Street man who also is a regular guest on cable-news shows, voiced his misgivings:

> His rant somehow felt wrong. After we've pissed through over $7 trillion in Federal bailouts to banks, brokers, automakers, insurers, etc., this was a pittance, the least offensive of all the vast sums of wasted money spent on "losers" to use Santelli's phrase. It seemed like a whole lot of noise over "just" $75 billion, or 1% of the rest of the total ne'er-do-well bailout.

Nonetheless, within days of Santelli's rant, the "Chicago Tea Party" organized for February 27 had morphed into a "Nationwide Chicago Tea Party," with similar protests organized in some 40 cities across the country. TalkingPointsMemo.com (TPM) interviewed the man who had organized the event in Tampa, Florida, a local consultant named John Hendrix. He told TPM that he got the idea for the Tea Party from Tom Gaithens of Freedom-Works—one of the Right's premier astroturfing outfits—while in the same breath claiming that the protests were "completely spontaneous."

A major player involved in organizing and promoting the Tea Party protests was FreedomWorks' Dick Armey, the Republican former House majority leader from 1995 to 2002. Armey is credited as being the author of the notorious "Contract with America," the driving force behind the Republican takeover of the House of Representatives in 1994. Armey has always been a skillful manipulator of the press, and his talents were at the forefront during the 2000 presidential election, when he was responsible for many of the smear campaigns against Al Gore.

Armey didn't go quietly into the night when he retired from the House in 2002. He reentered the fray with the Koch Foundation-funded astroturf organization Citizens for a Sound Economy, later rebranded "FreedomWorks." FreedomWorks created a phony grassroots site titled AngryRenter.com in April 2008 to attack Obama's housing-bailout plans: "A third of the American public rents," spokesman Adam Brandon told CNN, echoing Rick Santelli. "They're saying 'I've been saving for a mortgage for years. I could have jumped in on a subprime loan too. Now I'm going to have to pay for a government bailout.'"

It was the business-friendly *Wall Street Journal* that exposed the Web site's astroturfing origins a few weeks later:

> Though it purports to be a spontaneous uprising, AngryRenter
> .com is a product of an inside-the-Beltway conservative-
> advocacy organization led by Dick Armey, the former House
> majority leader, and publishing magnate Steve Forbes, a fellow
> Republican. It's a fake grass-roots effort—what politicos call an
> AstroTurf campaign—that provides a window into the ways of
> Washington.

However, by then the Tea Parties had become the focus of FreedomWorks' operations. And they were soon to get a boost beyond their wildest imaginings: the full-fledged support of a cable news network—namely, Fox News.

On February 27, the day the "Nationwide Chicago Tea Party" occurred, Fox News host Greta Van Susteren described the protests on her show while showing footage from the Tampa event:

"Tea Party" protests are erupting across the country. Angry tax-payers, or at least some of them, are taking to the streets in the spirit of the Boston Tea Party. People are protesting President Obama's massive $787 billion stimulus bill, his $3.55 trillion budget and a federal government that has been ballooning by the day since the president took office.

That, as it turned out, was just the beginning. Within two weeks, Fox News would become the national propaganda organ of the Tea Party movement and, in the process, transform it from a low-level astroturf operation into a national phenomenon.

It costs advertisers thousands of dollars to air a single 30-second commercial on a few cable stations for a week, even in relatively cheap rural markets. To advertise nationally on Fox News—the ratings leader in cable news—costs hundreds of thousands of dollars, even millions if the ads air often enough and during prime-time programs.

So what Fox News offered the organizers of the Tea Parties—and the conservative movement opposing Obama's presidency—was something you couldn't measure monetarily. Not only did Fox air a steady onslaught of Tea Party promotional ads, it embraced the outright promotion of the events in its news broadcasts and on its "opinion shows." The channel's on-air personalities as well as its Web site took an active role, day after day and night after night, in promoting and urging the Fox audience to join in the Tea Party protests. Media Matters, a nonprofit organization that tracks the conservative media, documented 63 instances where Fox News anchors and guests openly promoted the Tea Parties and discussed them as a legitimate news event.

Initially, there was a lull; there was only passing mention of the

Tea Parties on Fox in the two weeks after Van Susteren's show. Then, on March 16, three Fox anchors—Glenn Beck, Bret Baier, and Bill O'Reilly—featured segments discussing the Tea Parties, again in glowing terms. O'Reilly told his audience:

> Big government spending protests are taking place all over the country. The latest in Cincinnati, where about 5,000 folks showed up, showed their displeasure with the Obama's administration money strategy. These gatherings are being dubbed tea parties.

Beck in particular most avidly embraced the Tea Parties, making them his own pet cause. Some of this had to do with the ease with which the Tea Party themes—an embrace of small-government philosophy, with an anti-tax and pro-gun fervor thrown in for emphasis—melded with the populist themes Beck was already exploring in depth on his show. On March 13, he had hosted a special one-hour program themed "You Are Not Alone" that was notable for some of Beck's most maudlin crying jags, including his oft-lampooned sob, "I just love my country—and I fear for it!" The show—like Beck's later Tea Party promotions—featured broadcasts from specially gathered audiences in locations around the country who wanted to join Beck's cause of "standing up to big government." Its purpose was to launch Beck's "9/12 Project"—named dually for Beck's wish to bring the country back to "where we all were on the day after 9/11" as well as for the "9 Principles and 12 Values" Beck espoused. These principles and values were drawn from the 1972 book written by far-right conspiracy theorist W. Cleon Skousen, *The 5,000-Year Leap,* which Beck promoted on his show and Web site.

After March 16—when Beck noted the Tea Parties mostly in passing—the Tea Party themes began to meld seamlessly with Beck's "9/12 Project." On March 18, Beck remarked: "People are starting to get angry. These tea parties are starting to really take off." On March 20, Beck began making the connection explicit.

Once again denouncing the Missouri law-enforcement report on right-wing extremism, he connected the "extremists" described therein to the Tea Partiers:

> But if you're concerned about the government, you're con-
> sidered dangerous now in America. More than 160,000
> Americans have already signed up to be part of our 9/12
> Project, "912project.com," since we launched it a week ago—
> 163,000 people have signed up. Who are these people? They're
> people just like you that are just concerned about our govern-
> ment and they're concerned about our country.
>
> You know, are they militia members? Yes. Yes, sure they are,
> along with all the other people that are now on the tea parties
> nationwide. There is one here in Orlando, Florida. Tomorrow is
> supposed to be huge.

Beck mentioned the Orlando Tea Party warmly on March 23 as well, and on March 24 he hosted two of the event's organizers, Lisa Feroli and Shelley Ferguson, saying: "I have been telling you for weeks that you've got to stand up. And a lot of people around the country are doing these tea party things. But please, make them about principles, not about the parties. Make them about the principles."

Beck continued promoting the Tea Party protests each night through the rest of March. On his April 2 program, he announced that he would be hosting a special Tea Party broadcast on April 15:

> Tax Day, two weeks away. All right. More Americans are
> fed up with the nonsense in Washington both left and right.
> They are holding tea parties on April 15th. In this show, I
> can now announce that we're going to have our program live
> from the only place in America where I think it really, really
> makes sense—the Alamo. Plant your flag, America. It's in San
> Antonio, Texas. We will see you there on Tax Day!

Beck was leading the way for the other Fox anchors. A few days later, on April 6, he announced that not only would he be hosting his San Antonio "Tax Day Tea Party" on the 15th, but Neil Cavuto, Sean Hannity, and Greta Van Susteren were planning similar broadcasts that day from respective Tea Parties in Sacramento, Atlanta, and Washington. Fox was flooding the airwaves with Tea Party protests.

Beck was prolific in promoting the Tea Parties. Seventeen times over the course of 21 shows between March 16 and April 14 he urgently implored his audiences to take part in the tax day protests. One of the more piquant episodes came when he hired motivational speaker and sometime actor Bob Basso to dress up in colonial costume and pretend to be Thomas Paine, who then embarked on a Tea Party-loving rant:

> The time for talk is over. Enough is enough. Your democracy has deteriorated to government of the government, by the government, and for the government. On April 15, that despicable arrogance will be soundly challenged for the whole world to see. Our friends will applaud it. Our enemies will fear it.
>
> In an unprecedented moment of citizen response not seen since December 7, 1941, millions of your fellow Americans will bring their anger and determination into the streets. . . .
>
> Your complacency will only aid and abet our national suicide. Remember, they wouldn't dare bomb Pearl Harbor, but they did. They wouldn't dare drive two planes into the World Trade Center, but they did. They wouldn't dare pilot a plane through the most sophisticated air defenses in the world and crash into the Pentagon, but they did. They wouldn't dare pass the largest spending bill in history, in open defiance of the will of the people, but they did!

Beck's fellow Fox hosts did their best to keep pace. Sean

Hannity featured segments on the Tea Parties a total of 13 times between March 12 and April 14, and Neil Cavuto's afternoon business-oriented show featured 10 segments devoted to the protests during that same period. Nor were the "opinion shows" the only ones to do so: Another 15 or so Tea Party promotional segments ran during those weeks on such "news" shows as *Fox & Friends, America's Newsroom,* and *Special Report with Bret Baier.*

Fairly typical was a March 23 broadcast in which *America's Newsroom* anchor Bill Hemmer directed people to a list of Tea Party events on FoxNews.com and promised to "add to [the list] when we get more information from the New American Tea Party." Likewise, on the March 25 *Special Report,* host Bret Baier said that the Tea Parties are "protests of wasteful government spending in general and of President Obama's stimulus package and his budget in particular." On an *America's Newsroom* broadcast on April 6, Fox contributor Andrea Tantaros described the protests: "People are fighting against Barack Obama's radical shift to turn us into Europe." Fox News also aired on-screen text stating that "Tea Parties Are Anti-Stimulus Demonstrations."

Despite the obvious anti-Obama bent of all these protests, Beck and other Fox hosts worked hard to present the Tea Parties as "nonpartisan," bringing on guests who were either disappointed Democrats or conservatives still angry with the Republican Party. Yet the nonstop drumbeat around the protests made clear that they were primarily in response to Obama administration policies.

The March 24 segment of *America's Newsroom* promoting the Tea Parties was a classic instance of this. In it, Hemmer interviewed a man named Lloyd Marcus, who was president of the National Association for the Advancement of Conservative People of Color, and he told Hemmer that he previously "was on a 40-city

'Stop Obama' tour." Marcus wrote a song about his views, which was posted on FoxNews.com:

> Mr. President!
> Your stimulus is sure to bust.
> It's just a socialistic scheme,
> The only thing it will do
> Is kill the American Dream.
>
> You wanna take from achievers
> Somehow you think that's fair.
> And redistribute to those folks
> Who won't get out of their easy chair.
> We're havin' a tea party across this land.
>
> If you love this country,
> Come on and join our band.
> We're standin' up for freedom and liberty,
> 'Cause patriots have shown us freedom ain't free.
>
> So when they call you a racist cause you disagree,
> It's just another of their dirty tricks to silence you and me.

Fox News's Web site was rich with Tea Party promotion, as were its affiliates like the new Fox Nation site, which tried to act as a sort of "information central" for the Tea Parties, with numerous links discussing and promoting the protests. One link, titled "Find a Tea Party," directed readers to a Google Maps page for "2009 Tea Parties." Another link to a YouTube video was headlined "The Trillion Dollar Tea Party Video," which featured Tampa Bay-area Tea Party organizers explaining why viewers should join their "local tea party." For those who couldn't personally be there, Fox News announced "a virtual tax day tea party" at FoxNation.com instead.

Sean Hannity's Web site at Fox featured a graphic with links to a message-board discussion: "This thread is for the sole purpose of getting the word out about organized Tea Party events around the country. If you know of a planned event, please post the information here." Hannity's producers wrote a blog post on his site proclaiming, "Get your Tea Party Tees at CAFE PRESS and wear them on April 15!" There were also "some helpful links" to AtlantaTeaParty.net and TaxDayTeaParty.com.

There were also promotional ads. In the 10 days leading up to the April 15 protests, Media Matters reported that Fox News aired 107 ads about them.

At times, Fox tried to deny that this deluge of glowingly sympathetic "reports" and barrage of commercials on the Tea Parties constituted promotion of the event. On the morning of the protests, *Fox & Friends* host Steve Doocy told his audience that "Fox is not sponsoring any of them, but we have been covering them." This was a peculiar (not to mention disingenuous) remark, considering that Fox had repeatedly run on-screen graphics describing the events at which its anchors were to appear as "FNC Tax Day Tea Parties."

Then the paranoia began kicking in. When the Department of Homeland Security (DHS) issued its bulletin on right-wing extremism in early April, among the ways that Fox hosts attacked it was by speculating that it was intended to intimidate the Tea Party protesters, who might fit the description of right-wing extremists contained therein. David Asman, filling in for Neil Cavuto on *Your World,* began an April 14 segment by announcing: "Speak out, get shut down. What some say the government is doing to silence its critics." He went on to describe the DHS report as "ignoring liberal groups" (even though the DHS had previously issued a similar bulletin about left-wing extremists) and invited comment from guest Andrea Tantaros, who described the DHS report as "an attempt to silence the right." Tantaros went on to assure Asman that it was "no coincidence this is happening right before these Tea Parties." Asman wondered if the government "was going to be sending spies to these Tea Parties."

In fact, the timing of the release of the DHS bulletin—commissioned the year before by the Bush administration—had nothing to do with the Tea Parties and everything to do with incidents like Richard Poplawski's murder of three police officers in Pittsburgh. But if there was some confusion among the Tea Party set over just who might fit the description of right-wing extremist, there was a reason for that.

The April 15 tax day protests wound up being the largest of all the Tea Party events in 2009, and the largest gathering was Sean Hannity's Atlanta Tea Party, where the crowd was estimated at between 7,000 and 15,000 people. It was difficult to come up with an official number of total participants because estimates varied widely from city to city. Writing at FiveThirtyEight.com, Nate Silver reported 311,460 protesters in 346 cities.

Fox News's role in driving these crowd sizes cannot be understated; without its open promotion of the Tea Parties, it's unlikely the movement would have attracted more than a quarter of these crowds in a much smaller number of cities. And as you might expect, on the day of the protests, Fox's coverage was full-throated.

Things started off swimmingly with Fox Business Network anchor Cody Willard reporting from a Tea Party in Boston. He told his interview subjects: "I'm on your side. I'm trying to take down the Fed." Willard became even more excited a little later, exclaiming: "Guys, when are we going to wake up and start fighting the fascism that seems to be permeating the country? The fascism—the definition of it is big business and government getting in bed together. That is what these people are fighting. We have about 700 people here. They are starting to rally!"

Glenn Beck's event in front of the Alamo in San Antonio was more of the same, only on a bigger stage. His star guests were gun-wielding rocker Ted Nugent, conservative actress Janine Turner, and libertarian comedian Penn Jillette. Beck also set aside time to interview a Houston man named Joe Horn, identified by a Fox News graphic as having "shot 2 illegals burglarizing home" while Beck lauded him for his heroic defense of American principles: "Joe, what kind of world are we living in that people don't understand you have a right to life, liberty, and the pursuit of happiness?" (In reality, Horn had shot in the back two unarmed men he caught burglarizing his neighbor's home, after telling a 911 operator, "I'm going to kill them.")

In Sacramento, Neil Cavuto tried to inflate the number who turned out for his rally. He told viewers: "They were expecting 5,000 here, it's got to be easily double, if not triple that." However, Daily Kos caught video of Cavuto chatting with a producer before going live on the air in which Cavuto had said: "There's gotta be 5,000" (not "double, if not triple" that number). The producer then told Cavuto he thought that 5,000 was the right number.

In Atlanta, Sean Hannity featured guests like "Joe the Plumber" Wurzelbacher and astroturfmeister Dick Armey of FreedomWorks. The night before, Armey had gone on Hannity's show and touted the "grassroots" nature of the event: "This is a bona fide American uprising of real people. Nobody is managing this. These are not paid political operatives. This is not a union-organized outfit. . . . It is not orchestrated by anybody." Hannity described the cheering crowd in Atlanta as coming out en masse to protest "skyrocketing taxes and socialism."

The majority of the Tea Party attendees were probably soccer moms and normal, law-abiding, tax-paying citizens, but the protests also attracted—and simultaneously empowered—right-wing extremists. The whole scene was the Ron Paul campaign writ large, with an angry and disaffected but otherwise normal core constituency being significantly dragged to the right by the extremist bloc who promoted the kind of rhetoric that became common throughout the Tea Party ranks.

The tax day protests often resembled nothing so much as a scene from Lewis Carroll, complete with mad hatters and March hares. The nutty extremism was already apparent in some of the signs that were carried:

MARXISM:

OBAMA EMBRACES IT

REAGAN DEFEATED IT

OBAMA = SOCIALIST

ANATOMY OF A LIBERAL FASCIST COUP

(NINETY YEARS IN THE MAKING)

[Sign with drill pointing to Al Gore's head]

DRILL HERE

DRILL NOW

DRILL AL!

STOP OBAMA'S

MARXIST AGENDA

SAVE THE AMERICAN DREAM

OBAMA—WHO GAVE YOU

PERMISSION TO STEAL

MY COUNTRY? NOT ME!

EVEN HITLER WAS ELECTED

— ONCE!

OBAMA'S SOCIALISM
CHAINS WE CAN BELIEVE IN

GOVERNMENT CONTROL OF
BUSINESS IS FASCISM

WHERE'S THE BIRTH CERTIFICATE?

The sign carriers weren't the only fringe cases the Tea Party talk stirred up. In Oklahoma that day, a 52-year-old man named Daniel Knight Hayden became so worked up he was arrested for posting a series of increasingly bizarre death threats and violent anti-government rants on Twitter.

Hayden's MySpace page was a breathtaking gallery of right-wing memes about the "New World Order," gun control as Nazi fascism, and Barack Obama's covert use of television hypnosis, among many others. In the week leading up to April 15, he began sending a series of tweets threatening to take violent action at the Oklahoma State Capitol, site of the Tea Party tax day protests in Oklahoma City. They began on April 11:

> You IGNORANT SLAVES! "You want to live forever?"
> —Conan

> START THE KILLING NOW! I am willing to be the FIRST DEATH!

> After I am killed on the Capitol Steps, like a REAL man, the rest of you will REMEMBER ME!!!

> I await the police!

> Send the cops around. I will cut their heads off the heads and throw the[m] on the State Capitol steps.

> Of course they will kill me BUT life is no longer worth living. NOT in Oklahoma!

On April 14, more threats, again directed at police:

> 2 of 2: Tomorrow at NOON at the Oklahoma Stae Capitol . . .
> BE THERE! We need warm bodies.

> 1 of 3: Maybe it's time to die. Let's see if I can video record the
> Highway Patrol at the entrance to the Oklahoma State Capitol.

On April 15 at 12:49 a.m., Hayden posted a final announcement on Twitter:

> Locked AND loaded for the Oklahoma State Capitol. Let's see
> what happens.

FBI agents came to his home and arrested him without incident a short time later.

The story was noteworthy because Hayden appears to have been the first person ever arrested for making threats on Twitter. Amid all the voluminous airspace that Fox News journalists devoted to "reporting" on the Tea Parties, they never managed to inform their audiences about the case.

For a while after the April 15 protests, the Tea Party movement began to lose its focus, largely because there weren't any significant events on the horizon around which to organize. The next patriotic holiday was July 4, and so many of them began planning for a fresh round of protests then.

As David Weigel reported at the *Washington Independent*, though:

> The collaboration between the official Republican establishment and the Tea Parties has not lasted into June. The RNC has no plans to get involved with any Tea Parties. A spokesman for Rep. John Boehner (R-Ohio), who jaunted around northern

California to attend several Tea Parties, said that his holiday plans were private but would probably not include Tea Parties. Gingrich will not attend any of the Tea Parties, although he recorded video messages for events in Birmingham and Nashville "at the request of the respective organizers," according to spokesman Dan Kotman.

Only Fox remained loyal, and even then, its interest level was significantly lower for the July 4 Tea Parties than it had been in April. Glenn Beck, on his June 15 show, hosted "a disenfranchised Democrat" followed by "a disenfranchised Republican" to promote the Tea Parties. Similarly, the Fox Nation Web site avidly promoted the July protests, but there were no Fox anchors doing live remotes from the parties this time.

In all, the July 4 events tended to be more localized. Organizers counted on local news coverage and on such right-wing Web sites as PajamasTV, which asked people who attended to send in videos from their rallies for an "American Tea Party" show on the site. The leadership vacuum became an opportunity for far-right extremists to step up and take rhetorical charge of the Tea Parties.

Even before the July protests, the ADL warned that extremists—notably "white supremacists and neo-Nazi hate groups"—were planning to make their presence felt at the gatherings. Its Web site described the attempts by the racist Right "to co-opt the anti-tax message of the events as a means to spread racism and anti-Semitism":

> On Stormfront, the most popular white supremacist Internet forum, members have discussed becoming local organizers of the "Tea Parties" and finding ways to involve themselves in the events. Many racists have voiced their intent to attend these rallies for the purpose of cultivating an "organized grassroots

White mass movement," with some suggesting that they would do so without openly identifying themselves as racists.

These warnings came largely true when the July 4 Tea Parties rolled around. Not only were the fringe elements out in force, distributing propaganda and recruiting, but the speakers at the rallies used rhetoric taken straight from the conspiracist far right, including the Birthers, militiamen, and theocratic Religious Right. The nuttiness went beyond the signs in places like Duval County, Florida, comparing Obama to Hitler. At Crooks and Liars we gathered video samples from YouTube and Tea Party sites, taken around the country, and were struck by the prominence of far-right beliefs.

In Broken Arrow, Oklahoma, a young Marine sergeant named Charles Dyer stood up to advocate an organization called the Oath Keepers, a national group of veterans who openly subscribe to Patriot-movement conspiracy theories regarding the New World Order policies they believe President Obama intends to implement. Dyer, however, made clear that non-veterans were welcome: "Even if you're not current or former military, you too can be an Oath Keeper and spread the message."

Dyer went on, reading a list of ten "orders that we refuse to obey":

1. We will NOT obey any order to disarm the American people.

2. We will NOT obey orders to conduct warrantless searches of the American people.

3. We will NOT obey orders to detain American citizens as "unlawful enemy combatants" or to subject them to military tribunal.

4. We will NOT obey orders to impose martial law or a "state of emergency" on a state.

5. We will NOT obey orders to invade and subjugate any state that asserts its sovereignty.

6. We will NOT obey any order to blockade American cities, thus turning them into giant concentration camps.

7. We will NOT obey any order to force American citizens into any form of detention camps under any pretext.

8. We will NOT obey orders to assist or support the use of any foreign troops on U.S. soil against the American people to "keep the peace" or to "maintain control."

9. We will NOT obey any orders to confiscate the property of the American people, including food and other essential supplies.

10. We will NOT obey any orders which infringe on the right of the people to free speech, to peaceably assemble, and to petition their government for a redress of grievances.

Dyer then warned that "urban warfare" drills were secretly being used to prepare American troops for rounding up and incarcerating American citizens. "The only logical reason for them to train going door to door in America, practicing disarming people, is to actually do that one day, here in America," he said.

In Cape Coral, Florida, a rotund former judge and military man named Mike Chanopolis, wearing an orange golf shirt, told the assembled Tea Party audience:

The Constitution and the United States was the first time ever, in 4,000 years of recorded history, that a nation actually decided to base its law, and its government, on Biblical principles. And that's why we have been so successful. The reason that we're not so successful is that we've drifted away from that. . . .

The problem that we have with this president is, he was never qualified constitutionally to take the office! Okay? He wasn't born in the United States. If he was, he would have showed us!

The conspiracist element was everywhere—and so was the diffusion of energy. The Tea Parties seemed to be grasping for an issue, which gave the extremists the opportunity to offer theirs— whether it was staving off the black helicopters that would haul Americans off to concentration camps or declaring Obama an "illegal alien." But these were issues that had no grounding in reality, and to attract mainstream coverage the Tea Parties needed a real, live, mainstream issue to which they could bring their anti-government fervor.

The answer: health-care reform.

Greta Van Susteren was not the most ardent of Fox anchors in supporting the Tea Parties, but she managed to play a critical role at key steps in the development of the idea. Her February 27 show was the first to introduce the Tea Party movement to Fox News viewers. Five months later, on her July 28 program, she helped turn the Tea Parties into an anti–health-care-reform movement by reporting on the first Tea Party invasion of a public health-care forum.

The Tea Party involvement had occurred the day before in St. Louis, when Democratic senator Claire McCaskill's staff had hastily assembled a town-hall forum to discuss health-care reform with local constituents. The senator herself hadn't appeared, but her staffers had found themselves confronted by local Tea Party followers who shouted at them and jeered when they were told the senator supported reform. Van Susteren brought on St. Louis radio talk-show host and Tea Party organizer Dana Loesch, who was present at the forum, to talk about the scene. Van Susteren asked Loesch if McCaskill's absence was the reason her cohorts "sort of—I don't know if hijacked is the right word, morphed maybe, morphed it into a Tea Party." Loesch explained that the forum had come about because of a Tea Party protest two weeks before at the senator's St. Louis offices that had ended with police being called. The senator then arranged the forum "along with Carl Bearden of Americans for Prosperity, and we at the Tea Party Coalition just kind of helped it out, and got some people together and got the word out."

Loesch also claimed: "It was open to everybody, because this health-care legislation is a concern, I think, to everyone, regardless of whether or not they're conservative or liberal or a member of any party."

This was manifest nonsense. As with the April 15 Tea Parties, the town-hall protest was primarily about stopping Barack Obama, the newly elected president, from enacting the very policies for which he had campaigned and had been elected to enact.

More disturbing, in reviewing video of the St. Louis event, was the way the Tea Partiers used their numbers to shout down their opposition and generally intimidate the town-hall nature of the forum. What was supposed to have been an open discussion of the issues instead became a pushy shoutfest.

Within days of the St. Louis forum, Tea Party protests were breaking out at other health-care town-hall forums around the country. Similar disruptions occurred in Florida, Virginia, New York, Iowa, and Maryland. And it turned out that, as Lee Fang at Think Progress reported, the disruptions were being carefully planned and orchestrated by teabaggers:

> The lobbyist-run groups Americans for Prosperity and Freedom-
> Works, which orchestrated the anti-Obama tea parties earlier
> this year, are now pursuing an aggressive strategy to create an
> image of mass public opposition to health care and clean energy
> reform. A leaked memo from Bob MacGuffie, a volunteer

with the FreedomWorks website Tea Party Patriots, details how members should be infiltrating town halls and harassing Democratic members of Congress.

Some of the advice being dispensed to Tea Partiers was gathered in a memo:

- Artificially Inflate Your Numbers: "Spread out in the hall and try to be in the front half. The objective is to put the Rep on the defensive with your questions and follow-up. The Rep should be made to feel that a majority, and if not, a significant portion of at least the audience, opposes the socialist agenda of Washington."

- Be Disruptive Early And Often: "You need to rock-the-boat early in the Rep's presentation. Watch for an opportunity to yell out and challenge the Rep's statements early."

- Try To "Rattle Him," Not Have An Intelligent Debate: "The goal is to rattle him, get him off his prepared script and agenda. If he says something outrageous, stand up and shout out and sit right back down. Look for these opportunities before he even takes questions."

Dick Armey of FreedomWorks and other Tea Party organizers later tried to downplay the significance of the memo, claiming that it was not widely read or distributed. However, it fully described (or prescribed) the behavior that subsequently erupted at Tea Parties around the country.

Chris Good at *The Atlantic* warned that a long, hot August filled with these kinds of events lay ahead:

Over August recess, conservative activist groups will mount a renewed effort to kill the dreaded ObamaCare. August will be a melee of grassroots (or Astroturfed) activity on both sides: members of Congress will be home in their districts, holding town-halls, taking feedback from constituents—in other words, they'll be more open to pressure from activist campaigns than at any other time during the year.

He was precisely right. On August 1, visiting with constituents at an Austin town-hall forum, Democratic representative Lloyd Doggett of Texas encountered a disruptive mob of Tea Party protesters. When Doggett was asked whether he would support a public-option health plan even if he found his constituents opposed it, Doggett replied that he would. That sent the crowd into a frenzied chant of "Just say no," and they refused to stop. Doggett finally gave up and was nearly overwhelmed as he moved through the crowd and into the parking lot.

Doggett later issued a statement reaffirming his commitment to health-care reform and denouncing the protest.

> This mob, sent by the local Republican and Libertarian parties, did not come just to be heard, but to deny others the right to be heard. And this appears to be part of a coordinated, nation-wide effort. What could be more appropriate for the "party of no" than having its stalwarts drowning out the voices of their neighbors by screaming "just say no!" Their fanatical insistence on repealing Social Security and Medicare is not just about halting health care reform but rolling back 75 years of progress. I am more committed than ever to win approval of legislation to offer more individual choice to access affordable health care. An effective public plan is essential to achieve that goal.

On August 6, a crowd of jeering Tea Party protesters descended on a town-hall meeting sponsored by Democratic representative Kathy Castor in Tampa, Florida, "banging on windows" until police and organizers were forced to end the event. The hall origi-nally scheduled for the forum held only 250 people, and several hundred protesters showed up. Many of them—particularly the hundreds who had arrived from outside Castor's district—were forced to remain outside, where they chanted anti-Obama slogans. Some of them pounded on windows, frustrated at being shut out.

It was even worse inside. Castor and State Representative Betty Reed were scarcely able to make it through their opening remarks because angry protesters began shouting at them and interrupting. Just outside the auditorium's main doors, scuffling broke out between a couple of the participants who were jammed into the hallway like sardines, so police closed off the meeting area. A man who could later be seen on video with a torn shirt was treated for minor injuries following the tussle. Things became so intense that police escorted Castor out of the building after an event organizer suggested she leave for her own safety.

It left an impression, but not a positive one. "They think they're exercising their right to free speech, but they're only exercising their right to disrupt civil discourse," George Guthrie, who drove from Largo to attend the meeting, told a local TV station.

The protesters' behavior fit the blueprint for action laid out early on: Disrupt, distract, and destroy any chance for an actual civil and informed conversation. In other words, demolish the entire purpose of a town-hall forum. As Paul Krugman put it in his *New York Times* column:

> Some commentators have tried to play down the mob aspect of these scenes, likening the campaign against health reform to the campaign against Social Security privatization back in 2005. But there's no comparison. I've gone through many news reports from 2005, and while anti-privatization activists were sometimes raucous and rude, I can't find any examples of congressmen shouted down, congressmen hanged in effigy, congressmen surrounded and followed by taunting crowds. And I can't find any counterpart to the death threats at least one congressman has received.

It would not have been a problem if, say, right-wingers had gone marching in the streets in protest of the health-care plans; that's their right as Americans. And no one minded the fact that they chose to participate in these forums. But town halls were never designed to be vehicles for protest. They have always been about enabling real democratic discourse in a civil setting. When someone's entire purpose in attending a town-hall forum is to chant and shout and protest and disrupt, that person isn't expressing opinions but actively shutting down the democratic process.

Some members of Congress found the disruptions threatening enough to speak out. Democratic representative Brian Baird of Washington announced that instead of appearing in person, where "extremists" would have "the chance to shout and make YouTube videos," he would hold "telephone town halls" instead. Baird said some of the threats his office was receiving made clear that if he personally appeared, he was likely to have a mass disruption rather than an actual discussion of health-care reform, so he was going to take another approach. He added that he feared "an ambush . . . What we're seeing right now is close to Brown Shirt tactics. I mean that very seriously."

The remarks caused something of a national uproar, especially among right-wing pundits, who claimed that Baird was smearing all the participants with such characterizations. However, Baird made clear shortly afterward that he and his office had been threatened by some of these teabaggers, who faxed death threats and made them by phone as well. One phone message from August 10 said: "You think Timothy McVeigh was bad, there is a Ryder Truck out there with your name on it."

The Tea Party movement was turning into a revival of the Patriot movement of the 1990s, with all of the violent rhetoric and behavior that accompanied it. A prime example was the video that circulated among Tea Party followers titled "The Coming Civil

War," a 10-minute rant advocating a secession if President Obama enacted his "socialist" agenda:

> The hard truth is, we are headed for a civil war. Nevertheless, rest assured, this will not be the Civil War of 1861. This war won't be fought with larger-than-life generals, unless nationwide anarchy ensues. . . .
>
> In spite of these dire predictions, there is still time to save America, if only the millions of Americans who cherish freedom will rise up individually and collectively and get involved in the hard work of preserving, protecting, and defending our Constitution, and giving aid and comfort to those organizations that are working valiantly on their behalf. If you want to prevent a civil war, then you had better rise up now and send a clear message to the President and the U.S. Congress. Tell them you are giving them fair warning. Tell them: "We the People of the United States and the Separate States, will declare independence from the U.S. Government under the 9th and 10th Amendments of the U.S. Constitution . . . if the madness in D.C. doesn't stop NOW!"

The rant came courtesy of Ron Ewart, a western Washington resident who runs an outfit called the National Association of Rural Landowners (NARLO), which was built from the bones of organizations left behind by right-wing agitator Aaron Russo (who made large sums selling a "documentary," *America: Freedom to Fascism,* touting Posse Comitatus-style tax theories). NARLO was not only a big Tea Party supporter, it was also a listed sponsor of the Glenn Beck-inspired "9/12 March on Washington" being planned for September 12.

The extremism began to include weapons. Outside an early-August health-care event in New Hampshire featuring President Obama, a Tea Party follower named William Kostric showed up with a sign declaring "IT IS TIME TO WATER THE TREE OF LIBERTY," an allusion to and inversion of Thomas Jefferson's famous remark: "The tree of liberty must be refreshed from time to time with the blood of patriots and tyrants" (see chapter 3). And strapped to his leg was a loaded handgun in a holster.

The next day, Kostric was invited on MSNBC's *Hardball with Chris Matthews*. Matthews laid into the man with some tough questions about just what he'd hoped to accomplish: "Why did you bring a gun to an event with the president? ... You're carrying a goddamn gun at a presidential event."

Kostric claimed that he intended no threat by suggesting that blood needed to be shed and that he was just exercising his right to bear arms under the Second Amendment. Why he felt he needed to exercise that right at a town-hall forum on health care, though, he could never really explain. Instead, he insisted: "I'm not advocating violence. Clearly, no violence took place today." Matthews asked him what he *was* advocating. Kostric answered: "Well, I'm advocating an informed society, an armed society, a polite society. That's all there is to it."

What Kostric apparently intended was for his fellow gun owners to stage similar demonstrations. Sure enough, following his cue, more guns showed up at an Obama health-care event—this time in Phoenix, Arizona.

President Obama was scheduled to fly into Phoenix on Monday morning, August 17, to lead a town-hall forum on health-care reform. On Sunday morning, with Obama's impending arrival in all local news, Pastor Steven Anderson of Faithful Word Baptist Church in nearby Tempe held forth from the pulpit with a sermon titled "I Hate Barack Obama." Anderson avowed his complete and utter hatred of the president and openly wished for his death—because of his support for abortion rights and the "lewdness" he supposedly has brought to American society.

His key motif, inspired by one of King David's imprecatory prayers against his enemies, was to compare Obama to a slug or snail and wish he could pour salt on him:

> But let me tell you something: I don't love Barack Obama. I don't respect Barack Obama. I don't obey Barack Obama. And I'd like Barack Obama to melt like a snail tonight. Because he needs to recompense, he needs to reap what he's sown. . . .
>
> Now, look, if somebody wants me, if somebody twisted my arm and tells me to pray for Barack Obama, this is what I'm going to pray, because this is the only prayer that applies to him: "Break his teeth, O God, in his mouth. You know, as a snail which melteth, let him pass away." Like the untimely birth of a woman, that he thinks—he calls it a woman's right to choose, you know, he thinks it's so wonderful. He ought to be aborted. It ought to be, "Abort Obama."

He went on to equate Obama with Hitler, Stalin, and Jeffrey Dahmer. Anderson's sermon also mangled Obama's personal history, buying wholly into the "Birther" mythology and using a bevy of racist stereotypes along the way. He added that people like Obama are "so wicked" that they become "animals" who are "not human" and "past feeling." That led to his open wish for Obama's death:

> Nope. I'm not gonna pray for his good. I'm going to pray that he dies and goes to hell. When I go to bed tonight, that's what I'm going to pray. And you say, "Are you just saying that?" No. When I go to bed tonight, Steven L. Anderson is going to pray for Barack Obama to die and go to hell.

You say, "Why would you do that?" That our country could be saved.

The next day, among the crowd of Tea Party protesters who gathered outside Obama's event in Phoenix were about a dozen people carrying guns, including assault-style AR-15s. One of them was a member of Pastor Anderson's flock who had been in church the day before.

The gun stunt was cooked up by Ernest Hancock, an online radio host who, in the 1990s, had been a vocal supporter of the Arizona Viper Militia, a radical anti-government group whose members had been arrested and eventually convicted on weapons and conspiracy charges in 1996. After the Tea Party protest, Hancock interviewed for his show the churchgoer with an AR-15 who identified himself only as "Chris." Later, Hancock went on CNN and told host Rick Sanchez that he had carefully concocted the weapons stunt. Hancock said that, days before the event, he had contacted the Phoenix Police Department to let them know it would be happening. He explained that he was motivated in part by the controversy surrounding William Kostric.

Sanchez also interviewed Joseph Petro, a 23-year veteran of the Secret Service. Petro explained that brandishing weapons wasn't so much a security problem for the president—the Secret Service keeps a security perimeter around him at all times with no guns allowed—but for fellow citizens, both their safety and their right to unintimidated public discourse could be compromised:

> Sanchez: And the point they're going to make is, we have got a right to come out here and show everybody that we are for the Constitution, which gives us the right to bear arms.
>
> Petro: It is probably also not against the law to bring a can of gasoline and a match into an event. But is that a good idea? No.

Having exposed weapons in public events—and it is not just presidential events—I would say this at any public event—is just not—particularly where people are disagreeing. It is just—it's really a formula for disaster.

These gun-toting protesters portrayed themselves as simple, honest defenders of their gun rights when they showed up at public events, especially those featuring the president. They adamantly denied that openly displaying their guns might discourage their fellow citizens from speaking out with a contrary view. They were eager to assure the public that they posed no threat whatsoever to either the president or his supporters and that they were just ordinary citizens standing up for their rights. This is beyond disingenuous. It doesn't take a genius to figure out that the vast majority of the people who attend a public debate will perceive someone with a gun as a threat—particularly if they have an opposing view.

If the gun toters' assurances sounded less than convincing at the time, they became laughable when it emerged that "Chris"—the AR-15-toting African American interviewed by Hancock—was a regular at Pastor Anderson's church who had sat through the "I Hate Barack Obama" sermon and lapped it up. His full name was Christopher Broughton, and he knew Hancock through their mutual work on the Ron Paul presidential campaign in Arizona. Broughton was interviewed by the *Phoenix New Times*'s Stephen Lemons and made clear that he fully shared his pastor's enthusiasm for Obama's death: "It would be good for the country if he were to go sooner than later," said Broughton. "However it happens, I'm going to be happy that it happens. I'm gonna be a happy man . . . I would rejoice." He promised, however, that he would not be the guy to actually pull the trigger.

Travel guru Arthur Frommer posted on his widely read blog that he would in the future avoid traveling to Arizona:

I will not personally travel in a state where civilians carry loaded weapons onto the sidewalks and as a means of political protest. I not only believe such practices are a threat to the future of our democracy, but I am firmly convinced that they would also · endanger my own personal safety there.

Despite this burst of threatening wingnuttery, right-wing talkers continued to insist that the Tea Partiers were wholesome moms and pops asserting their rights and that efforts to paint them as being riddled throughout with extremist radicals were merely attempts to silence them.

Lou Dobbs entertained a discussion with Democratic strategist Karen Finney and Errol Louis of New York City's *Daily News* on his August 13 CNN program, and they confronted Dobbs with the issue of gun-brandishing protesters, demanding to know: "You think it's appropriate to bring guns to town hall meetings?" Dobbs replied:

You are doing everything you can to absolutely distort an event that occurred that was absolutely benign. A man was making a point. He happens to live in a state in which guns are permitted to be carried. It's open carry. It's a constitutional right.

Now you not only want to constrain freedom of speech and freedom of expression, you want to attack the Second Amendment and distort it into something sinister when you're sitting here talking in language that I frankly, Errol, I think is highly irresponsible.

Mostly, the pundits—particularly those on Fox—carefully avoided even mentioning the existence of the extremists. When Bill O'Reilly, for example, reran footage of Representative Barney Frank of Massachusetts castigating a woman for carrying an Obama-as-Hitler sign at his town-hall meeting on health care, he omitted the fact that the woman was a member of the far-right

Lyndon LaRouche cult. All O'Reilly managed to mention was that the woman was "a political activist," which is akin to calling a great white shark a fish.

It became a regular joke among Fox anchors to ask their Tea Partier guests whether they were radicals or Klan members and the like. While far from everyone at these events was an extremist, it was becoming clear that the percentages of them were steadily rising.

The health-care focus gave fresh life to the Tea Party movement, but as members of Congress began returning from their August recess, there were fewer town halls for the Tea Partiers to disrupt. What they could look forward to next was Glenn Beck's big "9/12 March on Washington," planned for September 12.

Beck's event had been announced back in February, well before the Tea Parties had coalesced or become a Fox News cause célèbre. But in the intervening months, the "9/12 Project" had seamlessly become so identified with the Tea Parties that they were now basically indistinct. Tea Party organizers started marshaling their forces to make the march another big national media event, along the lines of the tax day protests.

In late August, ads started showing up on Fox News promoting the Tea Party Express: a 7,000-mile cross-country bus tour featuring Tea Party events in 34 cities, beginning in Sacramento on August 28 and culminating in Washington, DC, on September 12.

Early on, CNN gave the tour some free promotion too. An August 27 report from Tony Harris featured both a fluff report on the cool bus being used in the tour and an interview with Mark Williams, the chief spokesperson for Our Country Deserves

Better. It was a largely congenial segment in which Williams was permitted to flatly deceive the CNN audience about the bus tour's purpose and intent.

Harris asked Williams whether the entire thrust of the Tea Parties was to attack President Obama's policies—a reasonable query, since these "partiers" were nowhere to be found when George W. Bush was busting budgets and running up massive deficits in the name of tax cuts for the wealthy. Williams, though, pretended throughout the segment that they were purely a non-partisan outfit angry only about overtaxation.

The tour was sponsored by the Our Country Deserves Better political action committee (PAC), an offshoot of Move America Forward, the right-wing response to MoveOn. It's chaired by Howard Kaloogian, a former Republican congressional candidate from California. The PAC was founded in August 2008—before the election—specifically to oppose Barack Obama and his policies. In October 2008, spokesperson Williams campaigned against Obama by characterizing him as a "socialist" on a bus tour called the Stop Obama Express and publicly endorsed the Birther conspiracy theory. In July 2009, the same organization ran a series of ads comparing Obama to Adolf Hitler.

CNN was susceptible early on to the deceptive charms of the Tea Party Express, but its coverage paled in comparison to the reportage that subsequently emanated from Fox News—and particularly from "reporter" Griff Jenkins, who followed the tour from start to finish and filed nightly reports from the events. These reports aired in segments hosted by all the various Fox anchors (Sean Hannity, Greta Van Susteren, Neil Cavuto, Bill O'Reilly, the *Fox & Friends* crew).

Jenkins made clear that he was sympathetic to the Tea Party cause, but he did include in most of the segments feature interviews with attendees so as to create some semblance of journalistic reportage. However, Jenkins's role as a cheerleader was unmistakable, and a YouTube video that popped up a month later showed a female producer for Jenkins's show waving her arms to encourage the crowd to cheer at the appropriate moments.

Two days before the march, at a big rally in New York, Jenkins dropped all pretense in a report for Sean Hannity's show. Rather than include any interviews, Jenkins simply gathered the Tea Partiers behind him as props and launched into a rant about how these events were all about average Americans taking back America from an out-of-control federal government:

> This is the 30th stop, Sean. This group, like the 29 before, is what I describe as the America Washington forgot. I say that because that is the way they feel. They are white, black [but crowd shots featured only white faces], young, old, male, female, and they are upset with the size of government, they are upset about the bailouts. They are upset about taxes, and they are upset about czars, Sean. They see themselves, in my observation of more than 50,000 people, they see themselves as a part of an America that is rising up to reclaim itself from a government that has run amok—a government that has overreached itself.

Jenkins wasn't reporting; he was essentially being a Fox-paid propagandist for the Our Country Deserves Better PAC.

When September 12 finally arrived, the media were in full frenzy mode, with camera crews from Fox as well as CNN and MSNBC covering the event. District of Columbia authorities calculated that some 70,000 people showed up.

Afterward, Beck and his supporters—notably right-wing pundit Michelle Malkin—tried to claim that there had actually been as many as two million people at the event. On Monday after the march, Beck told his radio audience: "according to overseas reporting," it had been the "largest march on Washington ever." (He was citing a *Daily Mail* report that had already been corrected.) On *Fox & Friends* that day, he told Steve Doocy that the crowd had been estimated at "1.7 million" and adamantly denied that only 70,000 had showed. Some conservative bloggers ran a photo showing a huge crowd clogging the National Mall—but the photo was taken on a sunny day (it was overcast in DC the day of the march), and it lacked the presence of the National Museum of the American Indian, which had been built in 2004.

The 9/12 event itself was actually rather uneventful. There was the usual parade of speakers, ranging from Dick Armey to Republican representative Marsha Blackburn of Tennessee (and a number of her fellow GOP congressmen, including Tom Price of Georgia and Mike Pence of Indiana, plus Senator Jim DeMint of South Carolina) to anti–health-care-reform lobbyist Betsy McCaughey. Stephen Baldwin, representing his and talk-radio veteran Kevin McCullough's *Xtreme Radio* show, was the only celebrity of any note. Most of the speeches were standard rants about big government, too much taxation, and the evils of health-care reform.

Out on the mall, though, there were all kinds of far more colorful expressions in the form of signs made by the protesters. The Tea Parties' extremist underbelly was exposed for all to see. Some of the signs were simply in outrageously bad taste, including one of the most popular signs, referencing the recent death of Democratic senator Ted Kennedy: "Bury ObamaCare With Kennedy."

Others were openly racist, including one featuring a large picture of Obama as a witch doctor, complete with a bone through his nose. Its script read: "Obama Care [with the 'C' as a hammer and sickle]: Coming soon to a clinic near you."

There was, again, no shortage of extremism in the signs, as had been the case on tax day:

DO I "LOOK" LIKE I WANT TO "SERVE"
IN OBAMA'S NAZI YOUTH MILITIA?
ARREST OUR COMMUNIST, FASCIST, RACIST,
LYING, PRESIDENT **NOW** FOR TREASON!!

FLUORIDE IN THE WATER IS A COMMUNIST PLOT

KENYA BORN [with picture of Obama]

IF AL QAEDA WANTS TO DESTROY
THE AMERICA WE KNOW AND LOVE
THEY BETTER HURRY BECAUSE
OBAMA IS BEATING THEM TO IT

Another popular sign at the protests Photoshopped Obama's face to look like Heath Ledger's portrayal of the Joker in *The Dark Knight,* frequently with the single word "socialism" underneath. A variation on this theme appeared on one sign at the march—it showed an Obama-Joker portrait morphed to look like Hitler and read "Obamacare is Eugenics."

Journalist Max Blumenthal strolled the Mall with a camera and interviewed some of the sign carriers. A man with a sign declaring Obama and Nancy Pelosi to be Nazis told Blumenthal he thought Obama was the biggest Nazi around:

> Because I think he's trying to destroy the United States. Not only do I think he's trying, but I think he's gonna accomplish it. He's gonna do—I'm afraid he's gonna do what Hitler could never do, and that's destroy the United States of America.

A man carrying a copy of the aforementioned "If Al Qaeda..." sign told him that Obama was a bigger threat to the country than terrorists: "Why? He's trying to change the country from within. We can fight Al Qaeda. We can't kill Obama." A friend chimed in: "He's the enemy within, that's why."

Most of these sentiments echoed ideas that had been expressed openly on Fox News, particularly on Glenn Beck's program. Blumenthal asked one of the 9/12ers what it was about Glenn Beck that was "so great." "Everything that he does," she replied. "If it wasn't for Glenn Beck, I think all of us would still be in the dark. He's opened up our eyes to everything, really." The sign bearers were simply reiterating ideas that had been handed to them as part of their nightly news consumption.

As was made manifest in the 1990s when the men who led the militia movement (Bo Gritz, John Trochmann, Mark Koernke, Norm Olson) began spewing this kind of rhetoric, toxic talk can have a radicalizing effect on the people who believe it, with frequently violent consequences. But this time around we began hearing it from mainstream Fox News pundits, from former Republican senators, from all kinds of people who should know better.

Former U.S. senator Rick Santorum told a Fox anchor in April 2009 that President Obama is "contemptuous of American values." A few nights later, Sean Hannity was on the same tack, asking Republican National Committee chairman Michael Steele: "Is there anything that he likes about this country?" Over on Michael Savage's radio show, his fill-in—*Washington Times* commentator Jeffrey Kuhner—said to his audience, addressing Obama: "You are a traitor to your country."

There is a relationship between this kind of rhetoric and the even crazier talk that emanates from the radical right. Some of the radicals who hear this talk from the armchair right-wing pundits—who indulge this stuff because it's a useful way to cynically rouse the troops—take the irrationality even further, to its illogical extreme, and are perfectly capable of acting on it.

A week after the 9/12 protest, House Speaker Nancy Pelosi voiced a similar concern when talking about how the debate over health care had veered off in a disturbing direction. "I have concerns about some of the language that is being used because I saw ... I saw this myself in the late '70s in San Francisco," Pelosi told a press conference, tears forming in her eyes. "This kind of rhetoric is just, is really frightening and it created a climate in which we, violence took place and ... I wish that we would all, again, curb our enthusiasm in some of the statements that are made."

It became part of a larger right-wing effort, especially among cable-news pundits and bloggers, not only to refute the concerns raised about the ugliness of the discourse, but to attack those who voiced the concerns by saying they were trying to smear poor innocent Tea Partiers. Glenn Beck tried to explain that Pelosi's fears were misdirected, since the problem was mentally ill nutcases, not the inflammatory rhetoric that inspired them:

> Look—Timothy McVeigh—nutjob! Nutjob! On the fringe
> of the right! That, President Clinton tried to blame on Rush
> Limbaugh. It was ridiculous then, and it's ridiculous now.
> Harvey Milk—killed by a guy who was hepped up on Twinkies.
> It was ridiculous then—it's ridiculous now. The shooter—and
> Timothy McVeigh—crazy people! It's madness.

The essence of Beck's argument was a familiar one (and predictably, was often repeated among his fellow right-wing pundits and talkers): Pelosi was "waving the bloody shirt," and the perpetrators of the town-hall ugliness were now the victims of liberal demagoguery.

What this defensiveness was intended to cover was an on-the-ground reality: The Tea Party movement, at least among the recruits and the devoted followers, was being taken over by extremists, particularly those from the Patriot movement. It had become, wholly, a right-wing populist phenomenon.

SIX

Right-Wing Populism and the Politics of Resentment

What became readily apparent early in the rise of the Tea Party movement was the American political tradition it represented: right-wing populism in action—indeed, in the process of taking the reins of the leaderless conservative movement, and by extension, the Republican Party.

The takeover was apparent in the very first big Tea Party event—the April 15 "tax day" protests. In the Fox News broadcasts carried live throughout the day, there was a lot of talk about how "this wasn't about Republicans and Democrats," this was about "the people vs. politicians," "right and wrong," "socialism vs. capitalism," etc., etc. You also heard a lot of talk about the parasites who feed off the producers, with glimpses of the "Atlas Is Shrugging" and "Ayn Rand Was Right" signs at the rallies.

This was all populism—and despite the token Democrat (inevitably a conservative Democrat) trotted out for the cameras from time to time, it was distinctly right-wing populism. The daylong broadcast from Fox—self-evidently the nation's leading conservative mouthpiece and propaganda organ—was a clear signal of the movement's embrace of its populist wing.

A giveaway moment came during Sean Hannity's evening broadcast from Atlanta, when he brought in a live feed from the "Rick and Bubba Tea Party"—hosted by radio talk-show hosts

Rick Burgess and Bill "Bubba" Bussey of the *Rick and Bubba Show*, from Birmingham, Alabama:

> Hannity: And I'm going to tell you one other thing: When did we ever get to a point in America where, we're nearly at the point where fifty percent of Americans don't pay anything in taxes! Nothing!
>
> [Crowd boos]
>
> Rick: The numbers out are just astounding that, that, how much that the very top taxpayers actually pay. I feel like these taxpayers are disenfranchised. I want them to have a share of the burden just like they have a share of the vote.

In other words, the tax burden of the wealthiest Americans should be exactly the same as that of every other voter; those wealthy Americans are being unfairly burdened with higher taxes. These pundits were, if nothing else, being honest about just who the "taxpayers" they were defending might be.

You could find similar sentiments on the Right only the month before, in mid-March, when it was revealed that executives at the insurance giant American International Group (AIG) continued to pay themselves multimillion-dollar bonuses with federal bailout money. This spurred a loud round of protest, mostly from liberals and labor groups angry about the abuse of taxpayer dollars.

Rush Limbaugh defended the bonuses, telling his radio audience: "A lynch mob is expanding: the peasants with their pitchforks surrounding the corporate headquarters of AIG, demanding heads. Death threats are pouring in. All of this being ginned up by the Obama administration."

Glenn Beck had a similar rant on his Fox show:

> What I really, really don't like here is the idea that we are willing to give in to mob rule. And that's what this is: The mob in

Washington getting everybody all—I mean, the only thing they haven't said is, "Bring out the monster!" It's mob rule! They are attempting to void legally binding contracts.

This kind of obeisance to the captains of industry and their untrammeled right to make profits at the expense of everyone else is a phenomenon known as producerism, which is a hallmark of right-wing populism. It's accurately defined in Wikipedia:

> Producerism, sometimes referred to as "producer radicalism," is a syncretic ideology of populist economic nationalism that holds that the productive forces of society—the ordinary worker, the small businessman, and the entrepreneur—are being held back by parasitical elements at both the top and bottom of the social structure. . . .
>
> Producerism sees society's strength being "drained from both ends"—from the top by the machinations of globalized financial capital and the large, politically connected corporations that together conspire to restrict free enterprise, avoid taxes and destroy the fortunes of the honest businessman, and from the bottom by members of the underclass and illegal immigrants whose reliance on welfare and government benefits drains the strength of the nation. Consequently, nativist rhetoric is central to modern producerism. . . . Illegal immigrants are viewed as a threat to the prosperity of the middle class, a drain on social services, and as a vanguard of globalization that threatens to destroy national identities and sovereignty. Some advocates of producerism go further, taking a similar position on legal immigration.
>
> In the United States, producerists are distrustful of both major political parties. The Republican Party is rejected for its support of corrupt Big Business and the Democratic Party for its advocacy of the unproductive lazy waiting for their entitlement handouts.

Chip Berlet has written extensively about the long historical association of producerism with oppressive right-wing movements and regimes:

> Producerism begins in the U.S. with the Jacksonians, who wove together intra-elite factionalism and lower-class Whites' double-edged resentments. Producerism became a staple of repressive populist ideology.... Specifically, it championed the so-called producing classes (including White farmers, laborers, artisans, slaveowning planters, and "productive" capitalists) against "unproductive" bankers, speculators, and monopolists above—and people of color below. After the Jacksonian era, producerism was a central tenet of the anti-Chinese crusade in the late nineteenth century. In the 1920s industrial philosophy of Henry Ford, and Father Coughlin's fascist doctrine in the 1930s, producerism fused with antisemitic attacks against "parasitic" Jews.

The producerist narrative is why Henry Ford is such a seminal figure for American right-wing populists, both as a leader in the 1920s and 1930s and as a figure of reverence today. Ford was also the ostensible author of *The International Jew,* a 1920 conspiracist tome that inspired Hitler's paranoia, and Ford's capital later helped build the Nazi war machine in the 1930s, so he was (and not coincidentally) perhaps the ultimate American enabler of fascism. (Glenn Beck has on several occasions on his Fox News show referenced Ford as something of a holy figure for his efforts to resist Franklin Delano Roosevelt's New Deal in the 1930s.) In today's producerist context, Ayn Rand and *Atlas Shrugged*—a tendentious novel speculating on the disasters that would befall the world if its great industrial leaders suddenly chose to stop producing—are important pieces of their mythology.

Right-wing populism is essentially predicated on what today

we might call the psychology of celebrity worship: convincing working-class schlubs that they too can someday become rich and famous—because when they do, would they want to be taxed heavily? It's all about dangling that lottery carrot out there for the poor stiffs who were never any good at math to begin with and more than eager to delude themselves about their chances of hitting the jackpot.

The thing about right-wing populism is that it's manifestly self-defeating: Primarily those who stand to benefit from this ideology are the wealthy, which is why they so willingly underwrite it. It might more accurately be called "sucker populism."

Nonetheless, right-wing populists have long been part of the larger conservative ideology—though mostly relegated to its edges. Some of the more virulent expressions of this populism, including the Posse Comitatus movement, Willis Carto's Populist Party, and the Patriot/militia movement of the 1990s, have been largely relegated to fringe status. However, there have been periods in America's past when right-wing populism was politically ascendant though not thoroughly mainstream, such as the Ku Klux Klan revival from 1915 to 1930.

It seems to have vanished from American memory that this later Klan, built on a romanticized image of the original post–Civil War Klan, was—albeit briefly—a real political force: a nationwide organization with chapters in all 48 states that briefly became a powerhouse in a number of states, including Oregon, Indiana, Tennessee, Oklahoma, and Maine, where the Klan played a critical role in the 1924 election of Owen Brewster to the governorship. The Klan of this period was about much more than racism, which was an expression of its larger mission—enforcing, through violence, threats, and intimidation, "traditional values" and what it called "100 percent Americanism." And like all right-wing populist movements, it promoted a producerist narrative in which noble white people, the cream of creation, were being culturally assaulted by a conspiracy of elites and ignoble nonwhites.

This Klan crumbled in the late 1920s under the weight of internal political warfare and corruption, and many of its field organizers later turned up in William Dudley Pelley's overtly fascist Silver Shirts organization of the 1930s. After World War II, the Silver Shirts, the American Nazi Party, and others like them were fully relegated to fringe status. So, too, were subsequent attempts at reviving right-wing populism that cropped up in the latter half of the century, including Robert DePugh's vigilante/domestic-terrorist Minutemen in the 1960s, the Posse Comitatus and "constitutionalist" tax protesters in the 1970s and 1980s, and the Patriot/militia movement in the 1990s. As had occurred at least since the 1920s, this brand of populism was riddled with conspiracist paranoia, xenophobic white tribalism, and a propensity for extreme violence.

Yet beginning in the 1990s, as conservatives increasingly adopted far-right rhetoric, strands of populism—particularly its deep, visceral, and often irrational hatred of the federal government— became more and more embedded in mainstream-conservative dogma.

Right-wing populism surged to the fore in 2008, first with the insurgent Republican presidential campaign of Representative Ron Paul of Texas and then, late in the campaign, with the arrival of Alaska governor Sarah Palin, the GOP's vice-presidential nominee.

Paul's presidential candidacy began picking up significant traction early in the Republican primaries, in no small part because of his opposition to the Iraq war. Shortly after he announced his run in March 2007, he began using ingenious online fund-raising methods—particularly the "money bomb" (see chapter 5)—that quickly broke all kinds of records and earned him the GOP's top-fund-raiser spot for the critical fourth quarter of 2007. Yet Paul tended to be ignored by both the mainstream media and mainstream Republicans. Fox News actually snubbed him by declining to invite him to one of its televised Republican debates featuring the rest of the GOP field. The one exception: Glenn Beck invited Paul to appear on his CNN Headline News show for an entire hour, the first of many appearances on Beck's shows.

Ron Paul also drew some of his most vociferous support from a voting bloc whose presence in the Paul camp went almost completely ignored by that same mainstream media: the extremists of the radical right. It was striking to observe the unanimity with which the far right had been coalescing behind Paul's candidacy. The support, unlike that for either of the two chief populist presidential candidates preceding him (Patrick Buchanan in 2000 and Ross Perot in 1992 and 1996), was not merely avid, it was perfervid.

Virtually every far-right entity on the fringes of the American political scene—neo-Nazis, white supremacists, militias, constitutionalists, Minutemen, nativists, you name it—lined up behind Paul. Rather quietly and under the radar, Paul managed to unite nearly the entire radical right behind him, more so than any presidential candidate since George Wallace in 1968. White supremacists from a variety of organizations—the National Socialist Movement (a neo-Nazi party), the neo-Nazi group Stormfront, National Vanguard, White Aryan Resistance (WAR), Hammerskins—became outspoken and unapologetic supporters of Paul and came out to rally for him at a number of his campaign appearances. For example, at a Paul rally in August 2007 in New Jersey, a sizable number of Stormfronters showed up, and a quick search of Stormfront's site for "Ron Paul" back then gave you a clear idea just how involved they were: 789,000 links.

Paul's appeal to the extreme right was not so much by design as by nature: a natural outgrowth of who Ron Paul is. Much of his popular image is predicated on the idea that he is a "libertarian" Republican—and he was indeed the 1988 presidential candidate of the Libertarian Party. But a closer examination of Paul's brand of politics—as practiced both in Congress and in the policies and ideas he has championed—makes clear that he has a closer affinity to the John Birch Society than any genuinely libertarian entity. His ideological framework—fighting the "New World Order"; eliminating the Federal Reserve, the Internal Revenue Service, and most federal agencies; getting the United States out of the United Nations; ending all gun controls; reinstating the gold standard—comes straight out of the wingnuttiest elements of far-right populism. Thus, Paul's candidacy, though it ultimately fell short, reflected not just a resurgence of right-wing populism but a dramatic weaving of extremist beliefs into the national conversation.

Ron Paul may have opened the door for right-wing populism, but he scarcely could have anticipated the overnight political star who would waltz through it to great fanfare—Sarah Palin. Hers was a different, more mainstream-friendly brand of right-wing populism—and it was embraced by a significantly greater portion of the American electorate.

Palin had been a populist figure right from the start of her political career as a member of the Wasilla City Council and then as the city's mayor. Shortly after winning her first council term on a pro-tax liberal agenda, Palin flipped her political allegiance and formed an alliance with a local group of anti-tax, right-wing populists who became her initial political base. There followed a long association with one of the local leaders of the secessionist Alaskan

Independence Party, which was also a major conduit for Patriot/ militia organizing in the state in the 1990s. Palin channeled those associations during her first run for the governorship.

Shortly after John McCain announced her as his running mate, Palin's populism became open to national view. It was more than just the aggressive, McCarthyite attacks on Obama as a "radical" who "palled around with terrorists" and the paranoid bashing of "liberal elites"—most of all, there was the incessant suggestion that she and McCain represented "real Americans" and were all about standing up for "the people."

Palin was populist, yes, but indisputably right-wing, too: socially and fiscally conservative, business friendly, and hostile to progressive causes. The producerist narrative was a constant current in Palin's speeches, particularly when she would get the crowd chanting "Drill, baby, drill!"

In her singular debate with Joe Biden, Palin continually cast herself and McCain as essentially populist:

> One thing that Americans do at this time, also, though, is let's commit ourselves just every day American people, Joe Six Pack, hockey moms across the nation, I think we need to band together and say never again. Never will we be exploited and taken advantage of again by those who are managing our money and loaning us these dollars.

Palin's populism probably saved the Republicans from the ignominy of being on the wrong side of a national landslide. They did eventually lose because the standard corporate-style Republicanism that McCain represented had become profoundly unpopular by the end of the Bush era. Moreover, after the election, Palin continued to be unusually popular among American conservatives, whereas McCain became an object of frequent excoriation, particularly by the Glenn Beck conservatives, who began labeling him a "progressive Republican." When Palin abruptly stepped down as governor of Alaska in July 2009—before she had completed her first term in office—her defenders depicted it as a "smart move" that would enable her to focus on the national stage.

Even before the election, conservatives who cherished their movement's intellectual traditions raised doubts about Palin's populist direction. Former Bush speechwriter David Frum remarked, in the *National Post:*

> So this is the future of the Republican party you are looking at: a future in which national security has bumped down the list of priorities behind abortion politics, gender politics, and energy politics. Ms. Palin is a bold pick, and probably a shrewd one. It's not nearly so clear that she is a responsible pick, or a wise one.

After the election—when the results made clear that Palin hurt the Republican ticket more than she helped—neoconservative writer Mark Lilla described in the *Wall Street Journal* the problem Palin posed for the Right:

> So what happened? How, 30 years later, could younger conservative intellectuals promote a candidate like Sarah Palin, whose ignorance, provinciality and populist demagoguery represent everything older conservative thinkers once stood against?

Lilla went on to describe how right-wing thinkers like Irving Kristol had gradually relinquished the legacy of intellectual conservatism:

> By the mid-'80s, he was telling readers of this newspaper that the "common sense" of ordinary Americans on matters like crime and education had been betrayed by "our disoriented elites," which is why "so many people—and I include myself among them—who would ordinarily worry about a populist upsurge find themselves so sympathetic to this new populism."

Thus, over the ensuing years, "there grew up a new generation of conservative writers who cultivated none of their elders' intellectual virtues—indeed, who saw themselves as counter-intellectuals." The rise of right-wing talkers on radio and television meant that they had a large and popular audience "that eagerly absorbs their contempt for intellectual elites. They hoped to shape that audience, but the truth is that their audience has now shaped them."

Palin's defenders derided such critics as out-of-touch elitists. William Kristol (Irving Kristol's son) taunted the critics in the *Washington Post*: "The mainstream media and the Republican establishment... tend not only to dislike and disdain Palin, they also want to bury her chances now as a presidential possibility. What are they afraid of?"

Replied Frum, at the *National Journal*:

> That's easy to answer: They—we!—are afraid that Palin's distinctive combination of sex appeal, self-pity, and cultural resentment has a following in today's GOP. We are afraid that it is not utterly inconceivable that she could win the Republican presidential nomination in 2012, and we are afraid that if she did so she would lead the party to a 1964-style debacle, accompanied by unnecessary losses down the ballot.

The problem for Frum and his fellow "intellectual" conservatives went much deeper than the overt anti-elitism practiced by a growing contingent within the populist movement. The takeover of the movement by right-wing populists in the post-Obama era ultimately was the product of the kind of politics practiced by Republicans for nearly all of the preceding half century: the politics of resentment. If the Tea Party movement had any godfathers, they were Goldwater, Nixon, and Reagan.

Most conservatives—as well as political historians—date the birth of the modern conservative movement to the failed 1964 Republican presidential candidacy of Barry Goldwater. During that time, a political style predicated on using racial, cultural, ethnic, and economic resentments as wedge issues to woo voters first became a central component of Republican Party politics.

After Richard Nixon's narrow loss to John F. Kennedy in the 1960 presidential campaign, Republicans embarked on a conscious effort to recast their image in the South. Following the lead of Goldwater and his allies, the Republican National Committee began "Operation Dixie," a course of action that attempted to win over southern voters based on conservative states'-rights and segregationist policies and entailed recruiting candidates with that agenda to run as Republicans.

This was called the "Southern Strategy," and in the 1964 presidential campaign Goldwater pursued it avidly. The key to the strategy was the Democrats' open embrace of civil-rights legislation in Congress that year, which meant that they were finally shedding their old southern segregationist image. Conservative southern voters were thus effectively disenfranchised—and in politics, nature abhors a vacuum. So in the 1964 campaign, it was Republicans, not Democrats, who were defending and promoting segregationist policies, both in the presidential campaign and, even more strikingly, in southern congressional races.

Joseph Aistrup, in his book *The Southern Strategy Revisited: Republican Top-Down Advancement in the South,* described how it worked:

> The major goal of the Southern Strategy was to transform the Republicans' reputation as the party of Lincoln, Yankees, and carpetbaggers into the party that protects white interests. Thus, subtle segregationist threads are sewn in to the tapestry of the

Southern Strategy. As a response in part to the GOP's new image and the liberalizing changes in the national Democrats' party positions, the Southern Democrats evolved from a party that depended on race-baiting, white supremacists to a party that needs and depends on black support to win elections.

In tandem with the Southern Strategy issue orientation, a number of Republicans attempted to use subtle segregationist suggestions to win elections. Southern Republicans developed a set of policy positions that reinforced their racially conservative policy orientations. Republicans opposed forced busing, employment quotas, affirmative action and welfare programs; at the same time, they favored local control and tax exemptions for segregated private schools.

Goldwater's success in the South, and the strong showings made in 1964 by even more segregationist Republicans in the South, provided movement conservatives with evidence that this approach would reap rewards. However, within the Republican Party—historically the defenders of civil rights for minorities, and still the "Party of Lincoln"—the conservatives' strategy raised serious concerns. There was strong dissent within the Republican National Committee from such GOP heavyweights as former committee chairman Meade Alcorn and New York senator Jacob Javits, who argued strenuously that the party should not abandon its historic commitment to civil rights in return for the votes of southern segregationists. Kentucky senator John Sherman Cooper agreed, emphasizing that the strategy was fundamentally amoral: "But in the long run, such a position will destroy the Republican party, and worse, it will do a great wrong because it will be supporting the denial of the constitutional and human rights of our citizens."

Nonetheless, it became the official strategy of the Republican

Party in the 1968 campaign under Richard Nixon, who deliberately used phrases that echoed many southerners' complaints about desegregation and adopted many of the themes of George Wallace: attacking the busing issue, pounding at "law and order," and decrying welfare. As Aistrup described it:

> The key to deciphering the Southern Strategy and understanding its evolution is found by revealing how its policy rhetoric appeals to its target audience, Southern whites. Many of the public words and deeds of the Southern Strategy have hidden meanings to adherents. Seemingly ambiguous political language has important, specific connotations for various groups in society.

Unstated, but understood, was the racial tone of these lines of attack: Whites were being forced to pay the costs of liberal programs to help poor blacks. Nixon played to people's resentments, both racial and cultural, and it worked, not just in his successful 1968 campaign but especially in his landslide 1972 victory over George McGovern, when he expanded his message to include mainstream resentment of antiwar liberals and "hippie" culture.

The Republicans' politics of resentment broadened from advocating states' rights and opposing busing in the 1960s and 1970s to opposing large segments of the civil-rights policy agenda, including affirmative action and quotas in the 1980s. In this sense, the Southern Strategy became directed at a broad swath of American voters and not simply those in the South. As Aistrup explained it: "When a GOP presidential candidate's campaign strategy emphasizes racially conservative appeals, he identifies not only himself but his party as the one that protects white interests."

It was Ronald Reagan who refined the Southern Strategy along these lines in the 1980s. And with Reagan came a new generation of political operatives who parlayed the racial resentments underlying the strategy into a broader set of negative appeals that ultimately transformed the conservative movement into the travesty of conservatism it has become today.

◇ ◇ ◇

The "Reagan Revolution" really wasn't about Ronald Reagan. Reagan was the vehicle by which conservative activists were given the chance they needed to attack and marginalize liberal ideology and policies. Reagan was a figurehead who united the movement's members, but their ambition far outweighed his commitment to their radical practices.

Reagan's advisers to his 1980 presidential campaign knew that to be successful, he needed to tap into the Southern Strategy. Staffers felt that, just as Nixon had done, they could lure disaffected white southern Democrats to their side. Reagan was able to avoid the appearance of racism by subtly using "code words" (now known as "dog whistles"), such as "states' rights," to indicate sympathy with those still smarting from Lyndon Johnson's "betrayal." The strategy wound up working to perfection, attracting millions of conservatives voters who came to be known as "Reagan Democrats."

Reagan had a history of making such appeals, dating back to his first political speech in 1964. Titled "A Time for Choosing," it played into certain sectors' resentment of minorities, women, "cultural elites," and welfare parasites.

> Not too long ago, a judge called me here in Los Angeles. He told me of a young woman who'd come before him for a divorce. She had six children, was pregnant with her seventh. Under his questioning, she revealed her husband was a laborer earning 250 dollars a month. She wanted a divorce to get an 80 dollar raise. She's eligible for 330 dollars a month in the Aid to Dependent

Children Program. She got the idea from two women in her neighborhood who'd already done that very thing.

In 1966, Reagan attacked feminism in his typical coded fashion by referring to student protesters in Berkeley, California, as "bums" and claiming the students were "engaged in orgies so vile I cannot describe them to you." His speeches also featured frequent references to moral values and their supposed degradation in an attempt to attract older whites who detested the youthful "hippie" uprising over the Vietnam War. He continued to exploit the politics of resentment in his 1976 Republican presidential-primary campaign. In a speech in Fort Lauderdale, Florida, for example, Reagan claimed that employees at a supermarket were "outraged" by a "strapping young buck" purchasing T-bone steaks with food stamps. This was the blueprint from which conservative operatives worked for years to come: Make politics personal by painting your opponents as the embodiment of decaying cultural and moral values, and policy be damned.

Reagan made this kind of appeal the cornerstone of his successful 1980 presidential campaign: His first speech after securing the Republican nomination in August was held at the Neshoba County Fair in Philadelphia, Mississippi. The town was nationally notorious as the place where three civil-rights workers—Michael Schwerner, James Chaney, and Andrew Goodman—had been murdered in 1964. And Reagan made the speech a classic piece of Southern Strategy:

> I believe in states' rights; I believe in people doing as much as they can for themselves at the community level and at the private level. And I believe that we've distorted the balance of our government today by giving powers that were never intended in the Constitution to that federal establishment. And if I do

get the job I'm looking for, I'm going to devote myself to trying to reorder those priorities and to restore to the states and local communities those functions which properly belong there.

As columnist Bob Herbert, writing years later in the *New York Times,* explained it:

> Everybody watching the 1980 campaign knew what Reagan was signaling at the fair. Whites and blacks, Democrats and Republicans—they all knew. The news media knew. The race haters and the people appalled by racial hatred knew. And Reagan knew.
>
> He was tapping out the code. It was understood that when politicians started chirping about "states' rights" to white people in places like Neshoba County they were saying that when it comes down to you and the blacks, we're with you.

In 1981, political scientist Alexander P. Larris sat down for an interview with an anonymous Reagan strategist who outlined for him how the strategy worked:

> You start out in 1954 by saying, "Nigger, nigger, nigger." By 1968 you can't say "nigger"—that hurts you. Backfires. So you say stuff like forced busing, states' rights and all that stuff. You're getting so abstract now [that] you're talking about cutting taxes, and all these things you're talking about are totally economic things and a byproduct of them is [that] blacks get hurt worse than whites.
>
> And subconsciously maybe that is part of it. I'm not saying that. But I'm saying that if it is getting that abstract, and that coded, that we are doing away with the racial problem one way or the other. You follow me—because obviously sitting around saying, "We want to cut this," is much more abstract than even the busing thing, and a hell of a lot more abstract than "Nigger, nigger."

It later emerged that the strategist was a young South Carolinian and Strom Thurmond protégé named Lee Atwater, a former chief executive of the College Republicans who had worked on the Reagan campaign under political director Ed Rollins. Atwater had employed his dark arts in the 1980 congressional campaigns and as a consultant for incumbent South Carolina representative Floyd Spence in his campaign against Democratic challenger Tom Turnipseed. South Carolina voters were the subject of what came to be known as "push polling": Voters would receive a call from a pollster asking them to answer a few questions from a fake survey that would inform them, for instance, that Turnipseed was a member of the National Association for the Advancement of Colored People. Most polling is designed to gather hard data and relevant information about issues and candidates, but push polling is a dirty trick used to smear candidates through fake talking points woven into the "survey" that could lead a voter to change his or her mind.

In 1988, with Reagan heading out the door as president, Atwater was given the job of maintaining conservative hegemony by heading up the presidential campaign of Reagan's designated successor, then vice president George Herbert Walker Bush. With Bush trailing in the polls against Democratic nominee Michael Dukakis in mid-summer, Atwater devised a strategy born straight from the loins of the Southern Strategy: the Willie Horton smear.

In 1974, Horton, an African American, and two of his pals robbed and murdered a young gas station attendant in Lawrence, Massachusetts. The attendant was brutally stabbed 19 times. Horton was convicted of murder and sentenced to life in prison. Through a rehabilitation program begun in 1972, Horton was given a weekend furlough in 1986 and escaped. In 1987, he broke into a house, beat up a man, raped a woman twice, and was eventually caught and charged with the crime. As the 1988 presidential race was heating up, an aide of Atwater's, James Pinkerton, dug up the Horton story. They found that it tracked well in focus groups. Suddenly, an ad started running blaming Dukakis for having furloughed Horton, featuring images of the menacing-looking black man and whipping up racial fears.

The ad was not officially a product of the Bush campaign. Rather, the group sponsoring it—the National Security Political Action Committee—was an "independent" operation run by a conservative operative named Floyd Brown, who was surreptitiously receiving support from the conservative-movement attack machine, with guidance from Atwater and others inside the Bush campaign.

The Bush team disingenuously denied any responsibility for the Horton ad, but it worked. Soon after it began running, Dukakis slipped in the polls and was forced into a defensive position from which he never recovered, eventually losing the election in a landslide. Atwater was celebrated as a master campaign strategist and was hired to run the Republican National Committee. Before he died of a brain tumor in March 1991, he wrote several articles renouncing his former tactics and expressing his regrets. But over in the war rooms of the conservative movement, no such regrets were to be found; intent on continuing the strategies that had brought them so much success, they worked to find a successor to Atwater and found it in Karl Rove.

Rove was part of a cadre of GOP ideological leaders who had emerged from the leadership of the Nixon-era College Republicans of the 1970s—including conservative-movement guru Grover Norquist, Republican uber-lobbyist Jack Abramoff, and religious right icon Ralph Reed. Rove had been elected chief executive of the College Republicans in 1972, a skinny kid with lamb-chop sideburns, and he jumped into the job with relish, leading seminars that taught young right-wingers how to indulge in dirty campaign tactics. This led to a brief role in the Watergate affair, after the *Washington Post* reported on his seminars in a story headlined "GOP Party Probes Official as Teacher of Dirty Tricks." An investigation ordered by then Republican National Committee chairman George H. W. Bush in short order cleared him of wrongdoing. Rove remained associated with the Bush family thereafter. However, he ran into trouble again in 1992, working on Bush's unsuccessful reelection campaign, when he was fingered as the source of a leak about campaign chairman Robert Mosbacher and fired.

Rove had become a highly successful campaign consultant, helping dozens of Republicans around the country win elections, and he promptly resumed that work. His major ascension came in 1994 via the Bush family—this time working on the Texas gubernatorial campaign of George W. Bush, whom he had first met in November 1973. After Bush ousted incumbent Ann Richards, Rove helped him win reelection in 1998 and then was hired in 2000 to head up Bush's presidential campaign.

In that year's Republican primary, Bush's chief rival—Senator John McCain of Arizona—ran into the usual Rovean buzz saw of dirty tricks. The most notorious of these was a South Carolina push poll using racist innuendo intended to undermine McCain's support. The pollsters asked voters: "Would you be more or less likely to vote for John McCain . . . if you knew he had fathered an illegitimate black child?" This was no random slur. McCain was campaigning at the time with his dark-skinned daughter, Bridget, adopted from Bangladesh. It worked. Owing largely to the Rove-orchestrated whispering campaign, Bush prevailed in South Carolina and secured the Republican nomination.

Karl Rove became Bush's chief of staff in the White House and proceeded, over the next seven years, to turn his office into a center for dirty political tricks and partisan politicization of the nation's governmental operations. Rove orchestrated the smear of Bush critic Joe Wilson, who had attacked the White House for spreading false information about Iraq's ability to build weapons of mass destruction as a way to coax the nation into war, which eventually led to the outing of Wilson's wife, Valerie Plame, as a CIA agent. He also masterminded an effort to purge the Justice Department of U.S. attorneys who had failed to use their positions to bring fabricated "voter fraud" cases against Democrats in the 2004 election—which, true to form, was similarly littered with dirty tricks, most infamously the phony Swift Boat attacks on Democratic nominee John Kerry.

When Rove left the Bush White House in August 2007, he was immediately hired by Fox News as their Republican "political analyst." Once again behind the scenes, he was free to help orchestrate the Republican Party's message, this time over the airwaves—and he was surrounded by like-minded individuals eager to join in.

Their main order of business, once Republicans were out of office, was to get them back in, by any means necessary. For Fox News, that meant one thing: war on the new administration headed by President Barack Obama.

SEVEN

Fox's War on the White House

For most of the first nine months of the Obama administration, White House communications director Anita Dunn had managed to maintain a relatively low profile. There were only brief mentions of her speaking up periodically to defend the White House, but otherwise most of the TV-viewing public had never heard of her.

That all changed the morning of October 11, when Dunn went on the CNN Sunday talk show *Reliable Sources* with host Howard Kurtz, the *Washington Post*'s media writer, and proceeded not only to lambaste Fox News but announce that there was a reason the White House was not sending out administration officials—including the president—to appear on Fox's Sunday shows:

> Dunn: A week ago many conservative commentators had been rejoicing in the fact, celebrating in the fact that the United States didn't get the Olympics, one week later they seem to be somewhat bitter at the fact that an American President was awarded the Nobel peace prize. So I think people will draw their own conclusions about the reflexive negativity on the part of some commentators regardless of what happens. . . .
>
> Kurtz: You were quoted this week in *Time* magazine as saying of

Fox News, it's opinion journalism masquerading as news. What do you mean, "masquerading"?

Dunn: Well, you know, Howie, I think if we went back a year ago to the fall of 2008, to the campaign, that, you know, it was a time that this country was in two wars, that we'd had a financial collapse probably more significant than any financial collapse since the Great Depression. If you were a Fox News viewer in the fall election, what you would have seen would have been that the biggest story, the biggest threats facing America were a guy named Bill Ayers and something called Acorn, when the reality of it is that Fox News often operates almost as either the research arm or the communications arm of the Republican Party.

The month before, President Obama had appeared on five Sunday-morning talk shows, including Univision's *Al Punto*. However, he had rejected appearing on Fox News Sunday with Chris Wallace, a move that had inspired Wallace to call the Obama administration the "biggest bunch of crybabies I have dealt with in my 30 years in Washington." In her interview with Kurtz, Dunn revealed that Obama stayed away from Fox because of its reflexive and highly partisan opposition to nearly every policy he had undertaken. Dunn said that Obama would go on Fox sometime in the undefined future, but "he understands he's not going on, it really isn't a news network at this point, he's going to debate the opposition and that's fine." She also noted:

> When they want to treat us like they treat everyone else—but let's be realistic here, Howie. They are—they're widely viewed as, you know, part of the Republican Party. Take their talking points and put them on the air. Take their opposition research and put them on the air, and that's fine. But let's not pretend they're a news network the way CNN is.

Over at Fox News, it was as though someone had tossed a Baby Ruth into a swimming pool: The shrieking and hysteria in the mad scramble to respond were almost comical. The angry retort from Fox was immediate, loud, and absurdly hyperbolic. On Monday, nearly every Fox anchor ran a segment describing Dunn's "attack on Fox" and loudly wondering if the White House was trying to "silence its critics." By the end of the week, Anita Dunn was no longer a nonentity at Fox—in short order she became Fox's Public Enemy No. 1, the target of a smear campaign painting her as a "radical." The network described the story, complete with a permanent studio graphic, as the "White House's War on Fox."

Dunn's critique was occasioned in no small part by the response at Fox to the surprise announcement the Friday before that President Obama had won the 2009 Nobel Peace Prize—two weeks, as it happened, after his failed diplomatic attempt to win the 2016 Summer Olympics for Chicago. Rather than congratulate the president on the achievement as a fellow American, the Right exploded with dismay. Rush Limbaugh told his radio audience:

> This fully exposes, folks, the illusion that is Obama. This is a greater embarrassment than losing the Olympics bid was. . . . You are destroying your country as a superpower—keep it up, bud. These are the accomplishments they're looking for. He's basically emasculating this country and they love it. . . . It really is insidious. The intent of the committee is to neuter the United States of America. They've done it by rewarding a pacifist.

Republican National Committee chair Michael Steele kvetched: "It is unfortunate that the president's star power has outshined tireless advocates who have made real achievements working towards peace and human rights."

The Obama-bashing was rampant on Fox. Glenn Beck told his radio audience: "The Nobel Prize should be turned down by Barack Obama and given to the Tea Party goers and the 9/12 Project." *Fox & Friends'* Steve Doocy: "Barack Obama was in office only two weeks when he was nominated. What did he do?" Brian Kilmeade, also on *Fox & Friends:* "This arguably could be the third person to win the award for not being George Bush." Kilmeade also speculated that Obama had delayed his decision on increasing troop strength in Afghanistan to win the prize.

Nearly all of Fox's anchors spent the day of the announcement running down Obama's Nobel Prize. The chief exception came from Bill O'Reilly, who opined that, "deserved or not," "having a U.S. president honored with a peace prize is good for the country." But then he invited on Bernard Goldberg, who ran through their comparable records of nonaccomplishment and announced that he would win the prize next year.

The real corker, of course, came from Glenn Beck, who was able to figure out just what Obama's Nobel Peace Prize really meant:

> My first thought was, this is just so revealing on how this whole system works, you know what I mean? But the second is: It may be more revealing on how Europe and the rest of the world views Obama. He is dismantling the United States one piece at a time.

Sean Hannity devoted two whole segments to the subject, featuring guests Dick Morris and Mark Steyn, respectively. Hannity echoed Doocy, arguing that Obama had been in office only 12 days when he was nominated for the prize—a non sequitur, considering that final voting on the prize occurred the month before the announcement (and the nominations were announced February 27, five weeks after Obama took office). Morris saw an ominous cast to the prize: "There's a broader context to this. This is part of Europe's efforts to colonize the United States—to reverse the effects of the American Revolution."

Steyn had a similar take, suggesting that the award was all about eviscerating American global power. He listed aspects of Obama's policies that he thought weren't in the interests of global peace, including his policies in Afghanistan. Hannity chimed in: "I've often said that I think liberals define peace as the absence of conflict. I define peace, very simply, as the ability to defend yourself and destroy evil enemies." Perhaps he thought this qualified him for a Nobel Prize too.

And then, without a hint of irony, Hannity brought up Dunn's remarks:

> What do you make of Anita Dunn in the propaganda office, in the White House attacking the Fox News Channel? You know, I would think that, you know, with unemployment at 9.8 percent, a general asking for 40,000 troops, and you know, a lot of problems this country has, you'd think they would have, you know, a little bit more in terms of their priorities rather than attacking a news organization and creating an enemies list.

Beck had been even more shrill in his denunciation of Dunn that afternoon, claiming that "free speech [is] under attack" and that he planned to show viewers "how this administration is consolidating power, and how your right to speak out and your right to hear, simply opposing voices, people who are asking legitimate questions, are all under assault." He went on:

> What a bunch of warmongers we have—I mean, oh! They're in the White House, America is fighting Afghanistan, Osama bin Laden, Al Qaeda, the Taliban, and now, these people have taken

on another enemy—Fox News. I want to show you exactly where the enemy is.

Beck got out a map of Manhattan, circled the location of the Fox News studios, then surrounded it with toy tanks and fences, saying, "we've got the missiles pointed right at Fox." He added:

> This is something new. . . . There was that enemy list with Nixon, but I think the enemy list—I believe that whole thing, that was just who's not coming to state dinners. Could be wrong. I don't think that they've used White House resources, your tax dollars, to target the media before.

Of course, there was no "enemies list," though Fox anchors began continually flogging the idea that there was. Hannity, discussing the matter with former Bush White House press secretary Dana Perino the next night: "What you're saying is that if you disagree with this White House, that they have an enemies list, that they're promising retribution." This was a concoction of Fox's perfervid imagination, along with the "White House's War on Fox."

The Obama White House, in reality, did not "declare war on Fox News," as the network's favorite talking point claimed. Rather, it was self-evident to anyone watching cable news in 2009 that Fox had declared war on the Obama White House from the day of the president's inauguration—and it took the White House until October to finally decide to fire back.

The campaign to undermine Obama, primarily by attacking his legitimacy, began almost the moment Obama took his oath of office on January 20. When administering the oath, Chief Justice

John Roberts botched a portion of it; Obama paused, and when Roberts repeated it with the wording still wrong, Obama followed in kind. Shortly afterward, Chris Wallace told the Fox News audience that Obama might not have been legitimately sworn in:

> I have to say I'm not sure Barack Obama really is the President of the United States because the oath of office is set in the Constitution and I wasn't at all convinced that even after he tried to amend it that John Roberts ever got it out straight and that Barack Obama ever said the prescribed words. I suspect that everybody is going to forgive him and allow him to take over as president, but I'm not sure he actually said what's in the Constitution, there.

Because these things take on a life of their own among the conspiracists of the Right, there was a brief oath-taking ceremony early that evening with Justice Roberts properly repeating the words so there would be no lingering questions.

Meanwhile, the Fox "opinion" anchors swung into immediate action on Inauguration Day. Sean Hannity attacked the new administration for the cost of the inauguration:

> Barack Obama's inaugural bash is going to be the most expensive celebration in U.S. history. Its opulence stands in stark contrast to our faltering economy, yet those who expected frugality from George W. Bush four years ago are strangely silent this go-around.

Hannity added that "the cost of Obama's inaugural will dwarf past celebrations and make those of President Bush's look like budget bashes." In fact, as Eric Boehlert reported at Media Matters, the costs of the second Bush inaugural were roughly the same as those for Obama's.

Hannity had made plain his intentions even before the inauguration. At his Web site, he began organizing in December what he called "the conservative underground" and asking people to "join the resistance" to the Obama administration. At the site's discussion forum, one of his regulars posted an online poll asking respondents to answer: "What kind of revolution appeals most to you?" The possible answers: "A. Military Coup. B. Armed Rebellion. C. War for Secession."

Meanwhile, Glenn Beck also used the inauguration ceremonies as a platform to attack Obama—on racial grounds, no less. Beck was irritated by the benediction given by civil-rights icon Reverend Joseph Lowery, who called for people of all races to come together and heal the nation:

> Lord, in the memory of all the saints who from their labors rest, and in the joy of a new beginning, we ask you to help us work for that day when black will not be asked to get back, when brown can stick around—[laughter]—when yellow will be mellow—[laughter]—when the red man can get ahead, man—[laughter]—and when white will embrace what is right.

This was too much for the tender racial sensibilities of Glenn Beck:

> Good thing Barack Obama distanced himself from Jeremiah Wright. Is this how the post-racial Obama administration begins? I mean, I understand that he's an older gentleman, and that's fine, but, really? Someday brown can stick around, the yellow man can remain mellow? And white will embrace what's right? Can you imagine anyone else saying something like that? Even at the inauguration of a black president, it seems white America is being called racist.

All that, of course, was just the warm-up.

Back in early January, before his Fox show began airing, Glenn

Beck met with Fox News president Roger Ailes to talk over plans for his show. He later described it for the *Los Angeles Times:*

"I wanted to meet with Roger and tell him, 'You may not want to put me on the air. I believe we are in dire trouble, and I will never shut up,'" said the conservative radio host.

But before Beck could say anything, Ailes shared a message of his own: The country faced tough times, he said, and Fox News was one of the only news outlets willing to challenge the new administration.

"I see this as the Alamo," Ailes said, according to Beck. "If I just had somebody who was willing to sit on the other side of the camera until the last shot is fired, we'd be fine."

This was precisely how Fox proceeded to deal with the Obama administration—on a war footing.

It wasn't just Fox, of course; the entire right-wing punditocracy reacted in roughly the same way. As he had so often in the preceding years, Rush Limbaugh set much of the tone for the "resistance" on his radio program. Four days before the inauguration, Limbaugh told his audience, "I hope he fails."

Sean Hannity invited Limbaugh on his Fox News show the day after the inauguration to continue exploring this theme, and Limbaugh explained that he believed Obama wanted to "set the stage for everything being government owned, operated or provided":

> Why would I want that to succeed? I don't believe in that. I know that's not how this country is going to be great in the future, it's not what made this country great. So I shamelessly say no, I want him to fail if his agenda is a far-left collectivism, some people say socialism. As a conservative, heartfelt, why would I want socialism to succeed?

Limbaugh couldn't resist throwing in his usual ugly notes of sexual innuendo and race-baiting, too:

> We are being told that we have to hope he succeeds, that we have to bend over, grab the ankles, bend over forward, backward, whichever, because his father was black, because this is the first black president.

Limbaugh's mission—to make Obama fail—became Fox's mission too, and particularly Hannity's. His evening show became a nonstop litany of attacks on Obama's policies. Scouring through the 2009 archives of Hannity's Fox News show, one would be able to find only a single guest—Phil Donahue on March 19—brought on for an interview segment to say any positive thing about the president or even remotely defend him. The only "balance" to be found was on his regular "All American Panel" segment featuring three people talking about the day's issues—typically, one liberal or Democrat (invariably a moderate) stacked against two conservatives and Hannity himself; sometimes Hannity skipped the pretense and just brought on three right-wingers.

The "socialist" label became a recurring theme for Hannity, along with whatever other angle he could find to attack Obama. As with the rest of the Fox anchors—particularly Glenn Beck—whatever Obama did and said, Hannity was agin it. This was the constant, daily theme on his Fox show, but a few samples should suffice to give the flavor of it all.

On February 18, Hannity devoted most of his show to attacking Obama's stimulus package for the economy, calling it: "Day number twenty nine of 'Socialism You Can Believe In.' The new America . . . A liberal hijacking of the American way of life."

On March 30, Hannity invited on Fox political analyst Dick Morris to discuss the stimulus proposal and the recent auto-industry bailouts. At the outset, Hannity sneered at Obama's handling of the bailout by calling him "commander and CEO," saying that Obama is "on a mission to hijack capitalism in favor of collectivism . . . the Bolsheviks have already arrived." Morris not only agreed, but suggested that the militia-style black-helicopter folks of the 1990s were being proved right:

> Morris: But there is a big thing that's going to happen in London at this G-20—and they're hiding it, they're camouflaging it, they're not talking about it: Coordination of international regulation. What they are going to do is to put our Fed and our SEC under the control, in effect, of the IMF.
>
> Hannity: Oh come on. You don't think they'll do this.
>
> Morris: That's what was in the draft agenda. They call it coordination of regulation. What it really is, is putting the American economy under the control of international regulation. And those people who have been yelling, "Oh, the U.N. is going to take over, global government—"
>
> Hannity: Conspiracy theorists.
>
> Morris: They've been crazy. But now, they're right! It's happening!

On the April 3 edition of *Hannity,* the host played a truncated clip of President Obama saying in a speech earlier that day in Strasbourg, France:

> In America, there's a failure to appreciate Europe's leading role in the world. Instead of celebrating your dynamic union and seeking to partner with you to meet common challenges, there have been times where America's shown arrogance and been dismissive, even derisive.

Hannity commented, "And the liberal tradition of blame

America first, well, that's still alive," and later wondered, "Why is there this anti-Americanism in Europe?"

What Hannity didn't show his audience were Obama's remarks immediately after the truncated outtake, which made clear he wasn't "blaming America first":

> But in Europe, there is an anti-Americanism that is at once casual but can also be insidious. Instead of recognizing the good that America so often does in the world, there have been times where Europeans choose to blame America for much of what's bad. . . . On both sides of the Atlantic, these attitudes have become all too common. They are not wise. They do not represent the truth. They threaten to widen the divide across the Atlantic and leave us both more isolated. They fail to acknowledge the fundamental truth that America cannot confront the challenges of this century alone, but that Europe cannot confront them without America.

Hannity's April 29 broadcast, on Obama's 100th day in office, was simply nutty. It opened with a video montage of Obama's first 100 days accompanied by dramatically ominous music and grainy clips of Obama in various acts of supposed perfidy, such as bowing deeply to the king of Saudi Arabia. The lead segment featured an interview with Karl Rove, who talked about the "looming socialism" inherent in Obama's policies. Hannity then went to his "All American Panel" segment with Geraldo Rivera, Ed Beckel, and Cincinnati radio talker Bill Cunninghman, who even managed to make Hannity look calm and rational.

What really set Cunningham off was Beckel's declaration that "this was the greatest presidential 100 days since Franklin Roosevelt, bar none." Cunningham was outraged by this and proceeded to indulge in every anti-Obama smear he could concoct:

Sean, what we have here is this little boy who grew up in Jakarta, Indonesia, at the age of 6 to 10, rejected by his own father, rejected by his own mother, rejected by his stepfather, raised by his grandparents, bowing before the King of Saudi Arabia, kissing the behind of every European socialist, saying okay to people like Ahmadinejad—we have the most dishonest, the most disreputable 100 days in American history, and this guy actually believes it's good!

On his May 5 show, Hannity featured a special segment with stirring rhetoric (accompanied by stirring music) about the "Tree of Liberty," comparing pre–Revolutionary War fervor to that of today's Tea Party crowds. Hannity also seemed to suggest that an uprising against the government might be in order.

Hannity's May 16 show was similarly rich with inapt analogies. He opened his program comparing the Obama administration to the evil anti-Catholic plotters who were the chief villains of the new Tom Hanks movie, *Angels and Demons*—all this in the context of Obama's somewhat controversial appearance at Notre Dame's commencement that weekend. (Some Catholic conservatives objected because of Obama's liberal position on abortion.) Then his guest, anti-abortion radical Randall Terry, came on and tried some analogies of his own. First he suggested that Obama's Notre Dame appearance was like Pope Benedict appearing before Planned Parenthood. Then, at the end of the segment, Terry went one better—Obama is like Hitler:

> Can you imagine somebody saying, "Let's have one of the leaders of Germany come in—we don't really like what he did with that Jewish thing, but they build great roads, and they gave people hope, and they helped rebuild the economy." It's crazy.

Yes, it was crazy indeed.

◇ ◇ ◇

The deluge of nutty talking points, outrageous falsehoods and distortions, and deliberate misrepresentations on Sean Hannity's program was representative of what could be found elsewhere on Fox News, particularly on Glenn Beck's afternoon show. Indeed, there was some speculation that Hannity's effort to ratchet up the craziness was a direct result of the immediate ratings success that Beck enjoyed: Hannity appeared to be looking over his shoulder and realizing that if he were to compete with Beck, he was going to have to push the envelope too.

Beck, as seen in chapter 2, was blowing past whatever restraints in rhetoric may have previously existed at Fox. He particularly specialized in broadcasting ideas and talking points derived from right-wing extremists and repackaging them for mainstream consumption. There were FEMA concentration camps whose existence he couldn't disprove (until he did), and the looming certainty that Obama was planning to grab Americans' guns and wanted to "indoctrinate" schoolchildren. Obama's stimulus package, Beck warned viewers, "enslaves" Americans. Not only did he pick up and run with the "Obama is a socialist" ball, but he began zigging and zagging with it: Obama was taking us down the path not to socialism but to communism. A few weeks later, it was "the road to fascism," not communism. Even later, it was "Maoism" and "radical Marxism."

All of these themes coalesced in Fox's open promotion of the anti-Obama Tea Parties, as described in chapter 5. Nearly every component of Fox's news operations was engaged in encouraging organized opposition to the president's policies. Even as it unleashed some of the ugliest aspects of right-wing populism by promoting ideas drawn from its most extreme elements, Fox tried to pretend it was merely "reporting" on the Tea Party phenomenon. Anchors like Sean Hannity, Glenn Beck, and Neil Cavuto did not act as observers; they were cheerleaders and leaders (as Beck was in the "9/12 March on Washington").

And it had a real-world effect, if a modest and temporary one: Health-care reform—especially progressives' preferred model that included a public option—suffered badly in the polls in the month of August and into September, until President Obama began making more public appearances and speeches on its behalf. By mid-September, a number of pundits—including Bill O'Reilly and Hannity—were declaring the public option all but dead.

In terms of real political impact, however, the most successful of all of Fox's campaigns against Obama was its witch hunt—led primarily by Glenn Beck—to root out the "radicals" among the "czars" appointed by Obama to various advisory roles within his administration. It cost one of those "czars" his administration job and hung a cloud over the White House that did not begin to dissipate until Anita Dunn decided to fight back.

Initially, Beck made passing references in the spring and summer to Obama's "czars" as being indicative of his "liberal fascist" tendencies. In mid-summer, the pace picked up markedly, focusing on the administration's green-jobs adviser, Van Jones, an African American man named the year before as one of the nation's "100 Most Influential People." Beck picked up on a WorldNetDaily story published in April that described Jones as "an admitted radical communist and black nationalist leader."

The piece, by Aaron Klein—sensationally headlined "Will a 'Red' Help Blacks Go Green?"—was drawn largely from readily available online sources, particularly a 2005 profile in an Oakland alternative weekly. That article, written by reporter Eliza Strickland in the *East Bay Express,* explained Jones's evolution from a young black radical to an establishment player. One passage described how he had been arrested in 1992 during demonstrations in San Francisco after the Rodney King riots in Los Angeles.

Jones was in his first year out of Yale Law School and working as a legal observer for the Lawyers Committee for Human Rights in the Bay Area. Jones explained that as he was "observing the first large rally since the lifting of the city's state of emergency, he got swept up in mass arrests," then came to sympathize with the black radicals and communists who'd been arrested with him:

> I spent the next ten years of my life working with a lot of those people I met in jail, trying to be a revolutionary.... I was a rowdy nationalist on April 28th, and then the verdicts came down on April 29th [acquitting the police officers in the King trial]. By August, I was a communist.

The story then detailed how Jones left them behind to become an environmental activist:

> He took an objective look at the movement's effectiveness and decided that the changes he was seeking were actually getting farther away. Not only did the left need to be more unified, he decided, it might also benefit from a fundamental shift in tactics. "I realized that there are a lot of people who are capitalists—shudder, shudder—who are really committed to fairly significant change in the economy, and were having bigger impacts than me and a lot of my friends with our protest signs," he said.

In Klein's version, all this background took on a sinister cast: "Jones said he first became radicalized in the wake of the 1992 Rodney King riots, during which time he was arrested."

Beck brought the story to mainstream attention on July 23, when he told his Fox News audience about Jones: "This is a guy who is a self-avowed communist, and he is in the Obama administration ... this guy wasn't a radical, and then was arrested. He spent six months in jail, came out a communist."

This was false: Jones had been only briefly detained and then released (and was later awarded compensation for his detention). Beck repeated the lie on his August 11 show: "This is a convicted felon, a guy who spent, I think, six months in prison after the Rodney King beating." (Beck eventually corrected the falsehood—on December 4.)

Beck worked up an all-out campaign attacking Jones. On July 28, he invited an "expert" named Phil Kerpen to explore what Beck saw as a massive conspiracy to place a circle of "radical Marxists" around President Obama, which he diagrammed on a whiteboard. Kerpen was an "analyst" for Americans for Prosperity, one of the "astroturf" organizations that had helped organize the Tea Parties. He had been on Beck's show in late June to attack Obama's cap-and-trade environmental plans as a "watermelon"—"green on the outside and red on the inside"—at the end of which the two of them had shared a slice of the fruit. Kerpen returned to Beck's show on July 30 and again on August 4 to repeat the attacks on Jones.

Kerpen's Americans for Prosperity operation was nothing if not adaptable. In organizing the Tea Parties and their disruptions of the health-care town-hall forums, it had largely been at the behest of insurance and pharmaceutical companies, which stood to lose money if health-care reform passed. Now, in attacking President Obama's cap-and-trade program and its green-jobs work, they were acting on behalf of corporate interests opposed to the environmental agenda.

Beck's attacks on Jones became an obsession, airing segments about him again on August 11, August 13, and August. 21. At about the same time, a civil-rights group called Color of Change—on whose board Jones had once sat—launched a campaign to persuade advertisers to stop supporting Beck's show. Beck apparently took this is as a frontal assault, and on August 25 began a weeklong special series, "The New Republic: America's Future," that placed Van Jones in the center of Beck's whiteboard diagram charting the "radical leftists currently advising the president of the United States." At the end of the week, he asked his audience: "Do we want communists in the United States government as special advisers to the president?"

On his September 1 show, Beck featured another of his patented spooky-music video packages, this time focusing on Jones and the administration's other "czars." "He has 37 czars to oversee and advise him directly," said Beck. "Never before have there been so many executive posts that were not confirmed by Congress and who answered only to the president." This was, again, false—many of the "czars" Beck cited were appointees who went through congressional approval, and Beck neglected to inform his audience that George W. Bush had employed 36 so-called czars during his tenure.

For a while it seemed that this Beck obsession would eventually peter out, as had many others, because it had attracted relatively little traction outside of his show and the right-wing blogosphere. But on September 1, DefendGlenn.com—a site devoted to defending Beck in the face of the growing advertiser boycott of his show—released a video of Jones speaking in February at an energy conference in Berkeley. A woman in the audience asked Jones why, even though Republicans previously had had no such problems passing legislation with a smaller majority during the Bush years, President Obama and congressional Democrats were having so much trouble getting their bills passed.

"Well, the answer to that is, they're assholes," Jones said, to uproarious laughter. "That's a technical, political science term. And Barack Obama's not an asshole." He continued: "Now, I will say this. I can be an asshole, and some of us who are not

Barack Hussein Obama are going to have to start getting a little bit uppity."

The remarks were impolitic but hardly cause for Jones's removal. Glenn Beck, in broadcasting the video on his Fox News show, seemed to think otherwise. Jones apologized, saying the remarks "were clearly inappropriate." And the matter again appeared likely to subside.

But it didn't. Two days later, a *Washington Times* story reported that Jones, in January 2004, had signed a petition calling for an investigation of the 9/11 attacks. The petition was organized by 911Truth.org, a group of conspiracy theorists who believe that the Bush administration was complicit in the terrorist attacks. Among the items was a demand "for immediate public attention to unanswered questions that suggest that people within the current administration may indeed have deliberately allowed 9/11 to happen, perhaps as a pretext for war." Jones publicly renounced his involvement, saying: "I do not agree with this statement and it certainly does not reflect my views now or ever." It later emerged that the statement suggesting 9/11 had been "deliberately allowed" had been added retroactively by the petition organizers; other signers indicated that they, too, had signed a petition calling only for an independent investigation.

Nonetheless, the damage was done. Republicans in Congress began agitating for Jones's resignation. Representative Mike Pence of Indiana remarked that Jones's "extremist views and coarse rhetoric have no place in this administration or the public debate." Senator Kit Bond of Missouri demanded Congress investigate Jones's "fitness" for the position. Obama was working to revive his health-care reforms in Congress, with a major televised speech planned for the next Monday, and the furor over Jones was proving a distraction.

So late on Saturday, September 5, Jones announced he was stepping down:

On the eve of historic fights for health care and clean energy, opponents of reform have mounted a vicious smear campaign against me. They are using lies and distortions to distract and divide. I have been inundated with calls—from across the political spectrum—urging me to "stay and fight." But I came here to fight for others, not for myself. I cannot in good conscience ask my colleagues to expend precious time and energy defending or explaining my past. We need all hands on deck, fighting for the future.

The next day on ABC's *This Week with George Stephanopoulos*, White House press secretary Robert Gibbs explained: "What Van Jones decided was that the agenda of this president was bigger than any one individual." The president, Gibbs said, did not endorse Jones's past statements and actions and didn't want him to go, "but he thanks him for his service."

Fox, and particularly Glenn Beck, was quick to declare victory—and to make clear that it was only getting started. Beck, rather than gloating, went on his show and warned that Jones's resignation was actually an attempt by the White House to have Jones "swept out with the trash, and they haven't answered the questions" about all the other "radicals" in the administration. Beck told his audience: "I believe our Constitution is under attack by people with a very radical agenda and one that you don't see, that you have to search for. Barack Obama has said that he wants to fundamentally transform this country, um, boy, I don't. I want to work on some of the things that we kind of stink at, but I don't think we need fundamental transformation."

Sean Hannity took a similar tack on his show that night: "Van Jones signifies the radicalism of this administration, and he was appointed to his position precisely because of his radical beliefs." Hannity continued: "All right, we know the White House sought out Van Jones. Which begs the question, how many more like him are serving in our government? Is Van Jones just the tip of the iceberg?"

Beck appeared on *The O'Reilly Factor* that evening for a conversation about Jones. O'Reilly asked Beck if he believed Obama is "a closet Marxist," and Beck responded affirmatively:

O'Reilly: You believe Barack Obama wants a communist society?

Beck: If you look at the people he surrounded him with—socialists, Marxists, Van Jones, a self-avowed communist!—if you look at what the Democratic Party has—

O'Reilly: You're not sure yet. You're just going down the road.

Beck: I'm asking the questions I think Americans need to ask.

O'Reilly: Oh, absolutely.

The bus the White House threw Van Jones under, driven by Fox, wasn't just aimed at progressive appointees. As Beck made clear, it was directed ultimately at Obama himself. Fox and its anchors were intent on delegitimizing the Obama presidency, and it was equally clear that, beneath the veneer of just "asking questions," the Fox anchors were playing the old right-wing cards of resentment and racial division.

Though the timing made it seem otherwise, Color of Change did not organize its advertiser boycott of Beck in response to his attacks on Van Jones. Rather, what inspired the group—which is an Internet-organizing outfit devoted to strengthening "Black America's political voice"—was something Beck himself had said on an unrelated issue.

On July 28, Beck had made his regular weekly appearance on the morning *Fox & Friends* program. The topic of discussion had been President Obama's sit-down discussion with Harvard professor Henry Louis Gates and the Cambridge police officer who, in mid-July, had arrested Gates at his home, an incident that sparked national controversy. Obama had told reporters:

> Now, I don't know, not having been there and not seeing all the facts what role race played in that, but I think it's fair to say, number one, any of us would be pretty angry. Number two, that the Cambridge police acted stupidly in arresting somebody when there was already proof that they were in their own home and, number three, what I think we know separate and apart from this incident is that there is a long history in this country of African-Americans and Latinos being stopped by law enforcement disproportionately. And that's just a fact.

Beck interpreted these remarks as being unduly insensitive to white people, because he lambasted Obama on *Fox & Friends:*

> This president has exposed himself as a guy, over and over and over again, who has a deep-seated hatred for white people, or the white culture, I don't know what it is. But you can't sit in a pew with Jeremiah Wright for twenty years and not hear some of that stuff and not have it wash over you....
>
> This guy has a social justice—he is going to set all the wrongs of the past right.... I'm not saying that he doesn't like white people. I'm saying he has a problem—he has a—this guy is, I believe, a racist. Look at the things that he has been surrounded by. Let's look at his new green-jobs czar.

This rant happened to include one of Beck's first mentions of Van Jones, but that wasn't the problem: Rather, what was plain to one and all was that this was a classic case of race-baiting, with

Beck informing his largely white audience that their president bore a real racial animus toward them—the intent being to whip up racial fears about Obama.

This outraged not just minority groups but a broad swath of mainstream observers. Even Howard Kurtz, the *Washington Post* media writer who tended to wrist-slap conservatives for outrageous behavior, eviscerated Beck on his CNN program *Reliable Sources:* "The national outrage meter doesn't even seem to move very much, so accustomed have we become about incendiary rhetoric. My personal needle has hit the maximum." He later wondered: "How can you call the president a racist? Especially a president, ironically enough, who usually tries to avoid or neutralize racial issues, except in this case."

Fox officially tried to distance itself from Beck's remarks. Fox News senior vice president of programming Bill Shine told TVNewser.com that "Beck expressed a personal opinion which represented his own views, not those of the Fox News Channel." Beck, however, never apologized for the remarks or explained them. In September, though, when confronted about them in an interview by CBS's Katie Couric, he simply resorted to the "asking questions" dodge:

> Couric: Do you stand by your assertion that, in your view, President Obama is a racist?
>
> Beck: I believe that Americans should ask themselves tough questions. . . .
>
> Couric: Are you sorry you said that at all?
>
> Beck: Mmmm, I'm sorry for the way it was phrased. I think everybody has to—living in a sound-bite world, really a nasty place to live—um, and it is a serious question that I think needs serious discussion.

Couric persisted in exploring the remarks and read a question from a viewer, who wanted to know what Beck meant by "white culture" in his attack on Obama. Beck simply refused to answer: "Ummmmm, I don't know." When Couric asked again—"Can you explain what you mean by the white culture? Because some people say that sounds kind of racist"—Beck whined that he was just "asking" if Obama is a racist (he hadn't; he had asserted that he was) and therefore he shouldn't be a "target." Couric was not so easily put off and kept asking Beck to explain, and Beck simply responded with silence, except to comment that he was "not going to get into your soundbite gotcha game."

Before the interview with Couric, Beck's silence in the face of the mounting outrage had already spoken volumes about his thinking on the matter: That is, Beck really did believe Obama was a white-hating racist. By early September, before Jones's resignation, 57 advertisers had announced they had withdrawn their funding for Beck's program. Fox News officials pointed out that the boycott didn't affect their bottom line—the advertisers, after all, had simply shifted their ads to other Fox programs. Still, it clearly took a toll on Beck, and he had responded, first, by whining that liberals were trying to deny him his "freedom of speech" (without explaining to the audience exactly what he had said to provoke their wrath) and, second, by ratcheting up the rhetoric against Jones.

In doing so, it was clear that he was intent on substantiating his claims about Obama's supposed racism. On his August 27 show attacking Jones and Obama's "czars," for instance, he had featured a segment with former Democratic pollster Patrick Caddell and right-wing blogger Michelle Malkin to talk about the "army" of "thugs" that President Obama was planning to gather under the combined umbrellas of ACORN, the Service Employees

International Union (SEIU), Color of Change, and whatever other insidious "radicals" whose connections to the "czars" Beck believed he'd uncovered.

What did this "army" of "thugs" look like? Why, they were all black people, of course. One video clip showed a couple of threatening-looking Black Panthers standing outside a Philadelphia polling area; another showed black nationalist Louis Farrakhan praising Obama. The display culminated with unidentified military-clad marchers engaging in what appeared to be martial-arts drills.

This, as Beck explained, will be "Obama's SS." The segment made clear the arc of Beck's thesis: He was right to call President Obama an anti-white racist because he was at that very moment forming an army of militant black thugs to take over white neighborhoods and threaten white children and impose a liberal fascist state. Or something like that. It emerged a couple of weeks later that these mysterious "thugs" were a troupe of dancers, students at the Urban Community Leadership Academy in Kansas City, Missouri, practicing for what's known as a "step show."

Van Jones's remark that people like himself "are going to have to start getting a little bit uppity" particularly upset Beck. Even after Jones resigned, he dwelled on it. The Monday after the resignation, Beck replayed the video clip and said: "Yeah, he's gonna get a little bit uppity. Oh, I bet he is. I bet he is. . . . Is he making a threat there? I don't know."

Racial resentment—and particularly fear of nonwhite people—had been an undercurrent at Beck's Fox show since it had debuted in January. In May, Beck had helped cheerlead the ultimately unsuccessful opposition to the nomination of Sonia Sotomayor to the Supreme Court—the first such nomination for a Hispanic in the country's history.

When her nomination was announced, the Right in unison jumped all over a remark Sotomayor had made in a panel discussion at a Berkeley legal symposium: "I would hope that a wise Latina woman with the richness of her experiences would more often than not reach a better conclusion than a white male who hasn't lived that life." Media Matters observed: "In fact, when Sotomayor made that statement, she was specifically discussing the importance of judicial diversity in determining 'race and sex discrimination cases.'"

Rush Limbaugh opened up the assault on Sotomayor with a radio rant directed at what became known as "the wise Latina remarks":

> Here you have a racist.... You might want to soften that, you might want to say, "a reverse racist." And the libs of course say that minorities cannot be racists because they don't have the power to implement their racism. Well, those days are gone, because reverse racists certainly do have the power to implement their power. Obama is the greatest living example of a reverse racist, and now he's appointed one.

The talking point became widespread among right-wing pundits, including Lou Dobbs, Patrick Buchanan, Ann Coulter, Michael Savage, Newt Gingrich, and Charles Krauthammer. But Glenn Beck was equally quick to chime in and soon became one of the leading voices calling Sotomayor a "racist." He did so on at least four occasions, adding that she was "divisive" and "not that bright." He also dismissively referred to her as "Hispanic chick lady" while portraying her as an "affirmative action" selection. When her nomination went before the Senate, he continued to attack her as a "racist"—as did a number of U.S. senators—and for good measure, he invited on Wayne LaPierre of the National Rifle Association to warn that Sotomayor was a gun grabber as well.

The Sotomayor attacks, though, were just part of a constant barrage of racial resentment on Beck's program, all of it ultimately directed at President Obama. On other occasions, Beck commented that Obama had been elected because of his race, not his policies. He called Democratic health-care reform plans "the beginning of reparations." At other times, he claimed that Obama plans to "settle old racial scores through new social justice."

The race-baiting plumbed new depths in November when Beck played for his audience an audio track of black people turning out for welfare assistance funds, originally showcased by Rush Limbaugh. It was nothing more than a nakedly racist bit of ugly stereotyping on the part of the radio talker Ken Rogulski, who produced it. Rogulski had gone to a onetime handout of special welfare funds to residents of Detroit and cherry-picked through the interviews he collected to find one that best suited the stereotype he wanted—that of African Americans too lazy and ignorant to do anything more than line up for free money and fawn over Obama for giving it to them. This was the clip that was endlessly replayed:

Host: Why are you here?

Woman: To get some money.

Host: What kind of money?

Woman: Obama money.

Host: Where's it coming from?

Woman: Obama.

Host: And where did Obama get it?

Woman: I don't know. His stash? I don't know. I don't know where he got it from, but he's giving it to us to help us. We love him. That's why we voted for him. Obama! Obama!

If you listen to the woman making the "Obama money" remarks, it's clear that she was cracking wise on the humorless, stereotype-dependent white guy asking questions she didn't know the answers to. Rogulski—and Beck and Limbaugh, by extension—were the butt of a joke and didn't seem to know it.

Beck, of course, heard something else altogether:

> All right. These are the people who have been abused by the system. They've been taught they needed the government. They've been taught to be slaves, and their master is Washington! Both parties!

Even when Beck tried to play the role of racial reconciliator, he only exposed his reflexive reliance on racial stereotypes and their underlying mythology. A week later, he hosted an hourlong program featuring an audience of black conservatives and invited a number of them—including Beck regular Charles Payne and talk-show host Lisa Fritsch—onstage as part of a discussion panel, which gave him the opportunity to indulge in some real buffoonery:

> Beck: How many people here identify themselves as African Americans? [About a third raised their hands.] OK—Why?
>
> Payne: It's interchangeable.
>
> Beck: But wait, wait. Why not identify yourself as Americans?
>
> Fritsch: Well, people can look at you and tell you're black. You can't escape that.
>
> Beck: Yeah, but I don't identify myself as white, or a white American.

But then, only a few moments later, he did exactly that:

> Because one of the problems that I have—and I have to tell you, as a white guy, as a white guy, I'm just being real honest with

you, as a white guy, I think white people are uncomfortable sometimes saying, "You know what, Martin Luther King"— and then quoting Martin Luther King, because, it's almost as if society says—"No no no! That's our guy! Not your guy!" And it shouldn't be that way. And so Martin Luther King, wasn't the dream that we're all judged by the content of our character?

A little later, Beck played for his audience the "Obama money" audio and asked: "Where does this come from?" It all was classic Beck: wrapping racial ignorance and blind hypocrisy in the trappings of an "honest racial discussion" that only reinforced the hoary stereotypes of white nationalism. Beck was always careful to create a kind of plausible deniability around his race-baiting, and this was his chief means of doing that.

With Van Jones's political blood in the water, the Fox anchors and their crews—as they had promised in the wake of Jones's resignation—began fanning out, looking for more "czars" whose "radicalism" they could uncover. Indeed, two days before Jones stepped down, Glenn Beck had urged his followers on Twitter: "Find everything you can on Cass Sunstein, Mark Lloyd, and Carol Browner." Soon, there was a list of other names as well: Ron Bloom, Nancy-Ann DeParle, Ezekiel Emanuel, Kevin Jennings.

Sean Hannity got to work too. At a September 7 rally in West Virginia, as Think Progress reported, Hannity stirred up the crowd by promising them: "By the way, we got one—we got rid of one [czar], and my job starting tomorrow night is to get rid of every other one. I promise you that."

Megyn Kelly helped warm things up on the September 8 edition of Fox News's *America's Newsroom*:

Well, more of Obama's special advisers are now under scrutiny following the resignation of his green jobs czar. . . . And now, questions are being asked about his so-called science czar, John Holdren. Now, he is under fire for a textbook discussing population control policies like forced sterilization and mandatory abortion.

That evening, Hannity made it an all-out assault on Holdren, claiming that the White House science and technology adviser had "advocated compulsory abortion" and "spoke out in defense of compulsory abortion and sterilization." This was, as usual, brazenly false: Holdren had coauthored an environmental sciences book more than 30 years before that discussed "compulsory control of family size" as a potential consequence in nations where "milder methods" fail to curb expanding birth rates. He had never "advocated" for any kind of involuntary birth control.

Ron Bloom, a "manufacturing czar," came under attack from Hannity as one of the "radicals and lobbyists joining this administration," and Beck called him "another extreme socialist in our midst." Glenn Beck called "energy czar" Carol Browner a "socialist" based on Browner's involvement with Socialists International, which is actually an international federation of progressive parties—one that includes among its members the British and Israeli Labor parties. Hannity attacked health-reform "czar" Nancy-Ann DeParle (who actually was not a "czar" at all—she was awaiting congressional confirmation) as being a member of "Obama's shadow government" and someone who worked for health-care companies "targeted in serious federal investigations and accused of kickback schemes and other ethical violations."

Both Beck and *Fox & Friends'* Steve Doocy variously warned viewers that Mark Lloyd, the chief diversity officer at the Federal

Communications Commission, "has stated that the United States should model its media after Venezuela." Meanwhile, Megyn Kelly hosted a segment with insurance lobbyist Betsy McCaughey, who outlined how Ezekiel Emanuel (the brother of White House chief of staff Rahm Emanuel and a medical adviser on health-care reform) "has got some rather—some might call them radical proposals for revision to our health care system." As Media Matters documented, McCaughey had cropped and distorted his remarks to smear him as "Obama's Health Rationer-in-Chief."

But with Van Jones's scalp—and Glenn Beck's credit for it— hanging on the Fox News trophy wall, Sean Hannity soon made it evident that he wanted one too. So he selected for his own witch hunt the White House's safe-schools adviser, an openly gay man named Kevin Jennings.

Jennings had been singled out by James Dobson's Family Research Council, beginning in July, for an incident he had described in his 1994 book *One Teacher in Ten*, involving a sophomore who came to him for counseling about his sexual relationship with an older man in Boston. Wrote Jennings: "I listened, sympathized, and offered advice. He left my office with a smile on his face that I would see every time I saw him on the campus for the next two years, until he graduated." The Family Research Council seized on the incident as evidence that Jennings was a "radical homosexual activist" who had "worked tirelessly to bring the homosexual agenda into our nation's classrooms." Eventually, its attacks made their way to Fox News and Hannity's show.

On September 30, Hannity devoted two segments to Jennings, including another "All American Panel" with Juan Williams as the token "liberal":

> We have the safe schools czar, a guy by the name of Kevin
> Jennings, OK? And he writes this book, and he gives infor-

mation to a 15-year-old—ABC News and Jake Tapper write
about this tonight—a 15-year-old sophomore, and his advice
to him when he's having a gay relationship is, you know, "Did
you use a condom?" He knew it was an older adult. Now, as the
Washington Times said, at the very least, statutory rape occurred.
And he didn't report it. Now he's saying that he made a mistake.
Only because it's been reported on. My question is, where's the
vetting process? Why was he even put in this position? . . .
    You know, Juan, I want him fired! I think he's inappropriate!
Anybody who has that kind of judgment does not belong to be
the safe school czar!

A couple of days later, Media Matters produced a driver's
license establishing that the young man in question was in fact
16 years old at the time of the incident in question—which, in
Massachusetts, is the legal age of consent. Jennings wouldn't have
found any authorities interested in any report he might have ten-
dered to them had he been so inclined, since no laws were violated.

On October 5, Fox News's Web site quietly ran a correction to
its original story. But Hannity refused to admit that there was no
basis for his claim that Jennings had violated the law by failing to
report a "statutory rape" and kept hammering away.

Over the next week and a half, Hannity ran a total of 12 segments devoted to attacking Jennings. Finally, it became apparent
that his charges were gaining little traction—grounded, as they
were, in fact-devoid gay-baiting smears. Then, on October 16,
Democratic strategist Alicia Menendez called him out on an "All
American Panel" segment for conducting a "witch hunt" that had
produced a resolution signed by more than 50 Republican congressmen calling for Jennings to resign: "I think that's so interesting that we have elected officials who are taking their cues from
cable news." This point produced an angry outburst of crosstalk

from her fellow panelists, but it may have been even more telling than it appeared, since Hannity afterward largely dropped his pursuit of Jennings.

Sean Hannity was far from alone in spreading the smears of Kevin Jennings. Bill O'Reilly (who quickly concluded the charges were groundless) and Glenn Beck both ran segments discussing Jennings. And Fox's ostensible "news" operations were ready to offer plenty of assistance.

On *America's Newsroom,* co-host Bill Hemmer told viewers that Jennings knew of a "statutory rape" case involving a student but "never reported it." *Special Report with Bret Baier* twice reported the Jennings smears as fact.

This was just standard operating procedure for Fox's daytime news shows, which regularly took their cues from stories drummed up in the afternoons and evenings by their "opinion" talkers. Some examples:

- On March 24, Marsha MacCallum on *Live Desk* joined in furthering the then popular theme that President Obama's programs were "socialist" by lauding her guest, Representative Michele Bachmann of Minnesota, when Bachmann claimed that Obama's proposals are a "lurch toward socialism." Said MacCallum: "I think you're absolutely right about that."

- After Glenn Beck and Sean Hannity attacked Sonia Sotomayor as a racist, Megyn Kelly on *America's Newsroom* told viewers that Sotomayor's "wise Latina" remark "sounds to a lot of people like reverse racism, basically. Like she's saying that Latina judges are obviously better than white male judges, and that that's her assumption, and people get worried about putting a person like that on the U.S. Supreme Court." Kelly later added, "I've looked at the entire speech that she was offering to see if that was taken out of context, and I have to tell you . . . it wasn't."

- After Sean Hannity and other "opinion" talkers described President Obama's trip to France as part of an "apology tour," Jon Scott on *Happening Now* asked if "the president's upcoming trip [to Europe and the Middle East will] be what conservatives might call another apology tour." Both Scott and his co-host, Jane Skinner, showed viewers a set of clips from Obama's remarks in an April 3 speech in France, carefully cropped to falsely suggest that Obama had criticized only the United States—just as Hannity had done two months before.

- James Rosen attacked Cass Sunstein, the nominee to be the White House regulatory overseer, in a September 9 story on *Special Report:* "Rats could attack us in the sewer and court systems if all of Cass Sunstein's writings became law. The Harvard Law professor . . . argued in 2004 that animals represented by human beings should be able to sue human beings and has even questioned whether humans can legally expel rats from our homes if doing so causes the rat's distress." The report came directly on the heels of a Glenn Beck segment making the same charges—albeit in a more incendiary fashion. Beck said that Sunstein was "a man that believes that you should not be able to remove rats from your home if it causes them any pain." What Sunstein had actually written was: "At the very least, people should kill rats in a way that minimizes distress and suffering. . . . If human beings are at risk of illness and disease from mosquitoes and rats, they have a strong justification, perhaps even one of self-defense, for eliminating or relocating them."

Similarly, as seen in chapter 5, these daytime news shows played an integral role in promoting the anti-Obama Tea Parties. *America's Newsroom, Fox & Friends, Live Desk,* and *Happening*

Now all avidly promoted Tea Party information on-air and online. The programs regularly hosted Tea Party organizers and posted protest dates and locations on-screen. Their Web sites all provided Tea Party information and directions as well.

If the news shows constantly blurred the line between opinion and news, at other times they obliterated the line between news and partisan propaganda. As Media Matters reported:

> During the February 10 edition of *Happening Now*, co-host Jon Scott purported to "take a look back" at how the economic recovery plan "grew, and grew, and grew." In doing so, Scott referenced seven dates, as on-screen graphics cited various news sources from those time periods—all of which came directly from a Senate Republican Communications Center press release. A Fox News on-screen graphic even reproduced a typo contained in the Republican press release. The following day, Scott apologized—for running the typo.

This wasn't the only occasion when news pieces simply transcribed Republican talking points. *Happening Now* aired two April 1 segments featuring seven "FOXfact[s]" that purportedly detailed the House Republican budget proposal. The "FOXfact[s]" were lifted directly from an op-ed by Republican representative Paul Ryan of Wisconsin that had appeared in that day's *Wall Street Journal*. On *America's Newsroom*, host Bill Hemmer reported on four "interesting" projects being funded by the just-passed economic stimulus package as part of keeping track of "stimulus money" using Fox's independent researchers. However, Hemmer had lifted the graphics, on-screen text, and all four of the projects directly from Representative Eric Cantor's Republican-whip Web site.

Fox fobbed off this kind of outright propagandizing on the public every day as "news" reportage, mixed in with the predictable menu of car chases and stories about missing college students. It amounted to a mountainous barrage of misinformation posing as news. The compiled record stood as stark evidence putting the lie to Fox News's claim, after Anita Dunn called it on the carpet, that its news reportage was distinct from and untainted by its "opinion" shows. Not only was the content of those "opinion" shows wildly incendiary and consistently (not to mention irresponsibly) afactual, but its "news" shows were carefully programmed to retransmit those fraudulent claims in the guise of straight information.

Anita Dunn had pointed out the problem publicly and exposed Fox News to a serious examination of its operations. Which meant, of course, that she was now in the network's crosshairs.

For most of the week after Anita Dunn made her critique, Fox's anchors and reporters were content to complain variously about the "White House's War on Fox" as an attempt to silence its critics, create an "enemies list," or threaten news networks to play nice. On the October 11 *O'Reilly Factor,* Bill O'Reilly vehemently denied that Fox's coverage was biased:

> Finally, Ms. Dunn is seeing the world through the prism of the other media, like NBC News and CNN. By all accounts, those networks favored Barack Obama over John McCain, and NBC actually promoted the president's candidacy and continues to give him excellent coverage.
>
> So by that measure, Fox News is indeed troublesome to the White House. But our hard news coverage is fair and balanced. Again, if somebody doesn't believe that, let's see the evidence because bloviating walks.

A mountain of such evidence was available, but since O'Reilly routinely dismisses his critics as being from the "far left," it never saw the light of day on his show. Instead, the chief theme at Fox was to cast itself as the victim of Nixonian thugs in the Obama White House, honest brokers of the news being attacked for innocently doing their job. But then, on Glenn Beck's October 15 show, things took another twist.

Beck opened the show ranting again about how the White House was riddled with "radical Marxists" who want to transform America into a communist state. It was all a warm-up for the video he had in hand for his audience—footage of Anita Dunn speaking at a high-school commencement ceremony earlier that year:

> The third lesson and tip actually comes from two of my favorite political philosophers: Mao Tse-tung and Mother Teresa—not often coupled with each other, but the two people I turn to most to basically deliver a simple point which is you're going to make choices; you're going to challenge; you're going to say why not; you're going to figure out how to do things that have never been done before. But here's the deal: These are your choices. They are no one else's.
>
> In 1947, when Mao Tse-tung was being challenged within his own party on his plan to basically take China over, the Nationalist Chinese helped the cities, they had the army, they had the Air Force, they had everything on their side. And people said, "How can you win? How can you do this? How can you do this? Against all the odds against you?" And Mao Tse-tung said, "You fight your war and I'll fight mine," and think about that for a second. You don't have to accept the definition of how to do things, and you don't have to follow other people's choices and paths. OK? It is about your choices and your paths. You fight your own war. You lay out your own path. You figure out what's right for you. You don't let external definition define how good you are internally. You fight your war, you let them fight theirs. Everybody has their own path.

And then Mother Teresa—who, upon receiving a letter from a fairly affluent young person who asked her whether she could come over and help with that organization in Calcutta, responded very simply: "Go find your own Calcutta." OK? Go find your own Calcutta. Find your own path. Go find the thing that is unique to you. The challenge is actually yours, not somebody else's challenge.

This video apparently blew Beck's mind, because it produced one of his patented weepfests, accompanied by a loopy rant about how "life was simple" in the golden days of America. The rant rambled into a weird metaphor comparing the nation to teenagers who innocently get stuck at a party and have to come home to Mom and Dad and face the music. His implication was, apparently, that the nation now faced dire consequences for having elected Barack Obama and his gang of Mao-quoting Marxist radicals—we've been bad teenagers, letting these evil radicals into the government. It was obvious that Beck believed that because Dunn had quoted Mao, she too was a Marxist radical.

There were a couple of problems with this thesis: The context of the entire video makes clear that this was a fairly innocuous speech promoting the usual "you are your own person" themes common to such ceremonies. Moreover, Republicans, including George W. Bush, have abundantly quoted Chairman Mao. Dunn never said she subscribed to communist ideology; she just said—with what should have been fairly self-evident irony—that she found Mao's writings useful for making her point. (Dunn later responded: "The use of the phrase 'favorite political philosophers' was intended as irony, but clearly the effort fell flat—at least with a certain Fox commentator whose sense of irony may be missing.")

So on October 19, Beck changed the game again. This time,

while repeating the attack on Dunn as a "Maoist radical," he truncated the clip so that only this was played: "Two of my favorite political philosophers: Mao Tse-tung and Mother Teresa—not often coupled with each other, but the two people that I turn to most..."

Not content to play it once, he ran the same snippet again. Twice he described Dunn as saying that Mao was one of the philosophers "she turns to most." The unedited sentence in the video made clear that she was explaining she found their words handy to make a universal and fairly banal point about being true to one's self. That's all. No Mao worship. Sean Hannity also played the truncated clip and similarly claimed that it was proof Dunn "worships Mao."

Outright dishonesty apparently wasn't enough, though. Beck continued rampaging against the White House by resorting to violent analogies. On his October 23 show, he brought out a wooden Spalding bat and waved it about as a prop to make a crude and ugly charge: that the White House, in calling out Fox and limiting the availability of administration officials for Fox's programs, was a bunch of Al Capone-like thugs. Beck played clips from the Kevin Costner/Robert DeNiro film *The Untouchables*, including one of DeNiro, as Al Capone, bashing in the head of one of his underlings with a baseball bat similar to the one Beck had in his hand. Beck also affected a tough-guy gangster voice to depict the administration as a bunch of petty thugs who threaten their opponents:

> You can all sit around the table, like those people did, and then you can say which one's gonna get whacked? You can sit there and you can live in fear. Or you can stand up and say "Enough of your bat!" I warn ya, that means that some people are gonna get whacked.... You gotta take a stand, even though you know,

in the end, you pull out a knife and they're gonna pull out a gun. The question we have to ask ourselves, what is it we truly believe in? What do we believe in? Who are we? Are we the guy who sits around the table in fear? Or are we the guy who stands up and says, "Hey! What the hell are we all doing? He's one guy! There's more of us than there is of him!" But I warn you, you have to ask yourself, if you stand up, what are you willing to do? Sure, you might get whacked, but let me tell you something, if you spend too much time in the bed with the mob, if you spend too much time at that table, you're gonna get whacked eventually anyway.

Two days later, Chris Wallace essentially repeated the performance on the supposedly bias-free *Fox News Sunday*. He replayed one of Beck's clips from *The Untouchables* and similarly characterized the Obama White House as a gang of thugs:

> I want to turn to one last thing, and that is the latest chapter in the Obama White House's war on Fox News and what some people are calling the administration's Chicago way of doing business. ·
>
> [Plays *Untouchables* clip with Sean Connery speaking: "He pulls a knife, you pull a gun. He sends one of yours to the hospital, you send one of his to the morgue. That's the Chicago way."]
>
> Dana, the latest chapter in the Chicago way was that the administration made an effort this week to use the White House pool—that's the—all the five major networks—to try to exclude Fox from interviewing pay czar Ken Feinberg.

The Feinberg charge was just another fake Fox controversy. It emerged that Fox hadn't been excluded—it had simply failed to make the request to join other pool reporters in the interview.

When pool crew members noticed that Fox wasn't on the list, they notified Anita Dunn, who made sure that Major Garrett, Fox's chief White House correspondent, was among the interviewers. Garrett himself confirmed that Fox was not excluded.

One thing was glaringly obvious about the *Untouchables/Feinberg* episode: It was another living, breathing repudiation of Fox's claim that its "news" shows (particularly Wallace's Sunday show) were completely separate operations from its "opinion" shows—and a classic example of the symbiotic relationship between "news" and "opinion" at Fox.

There was a problem, though: Even though Fox's manifestly propagandistic broadcasts both before and after Dunn's critique proved her point, no one inside the Beltway Village—and remarkably, almost none of its practicing journalists—seemed to notice. They had, instead, closed ranks and taken Fox's side.

Journalism is largely a self-policed profession, one in which standards are maintained by both internal editing and peer competition, with fellow professionals playing the role of calling out their peers for violating those standards. But that standard-keeping aspect completely failed when it came to Fox News—even after the White House had presented journalists with a golden opportunity to seriously scrutinize it.

Fox News had amassed a record, even before 2009, of failing to live up to basic standards of factual accuracy, genuine fairness and balance, and journalistic responsibility. After Obama's election, it seemed to abandon any pretense whatever of meeting those standards—running false "facts," deceptively edited videos, and outright ideological promotions while seriously mainstreaming extremist ideas from the radical right. As Media Matters put it in its exhaustive report on the relationship between Fox's news and opinion shows:

> It is Fox News that has been waging a partisan political war against the White House since Inauguration Day, and while doing so, revealing both its disdain for journalistic standards and its all-consuming political agenda—qualities that differentiate Fox News from any credible news organization.

Instead of dealing forthrightly with the problem, the Beltway Village circled its wagons around Fox for having been horribly attacked by the White House. Fox, unsurprisingly, ran a stream of guests willing to come on and denounce the White House as being misguided for choosing to defend itself.

The consummate example of this came from Sally Quinn, the classic Beltway Village insider (Quinn is the wife of former *Washington Post* editor Ben Bradlee and a pedigreed Washington society matron), who went on Bill O'Reilly's October 24 show to tut-tut the foolish Obama White House:

> Everybody is talking about it. And from what I can gather, certainly among my colleagues and other politicians, everybody thinks that it's Dumb and Dumber—what the White House is doing. Um, I've talked to one or two people who are sort of trying to figure out—they had a theory about why the White House was doing this, and maybe it made sense on some level, but most people think that it's just absolutely crazy! I am baffled by it. Particularly having gone through Watergate at the *Washington Post,* and having the Nixon people turn against the *Post,* it never pays. It just doesn't make any sense at all to take on a news organization and single a news organization out.

ABC News's Sunday talk show *This Week with George Stephanopoulos* featured similar sentiments from right-wing pundits George Will and Laura Ingraham. Will said:

Look, no president in the history of this republic has less reason
to complain about his treatment in the press than President
Obama. Liberals have academic, they have a mainstream media,
they have Hollywood. They're all for diversity and everything
but thought. And out here is this one channel, Fox, and they're
all up in arms because in the words of Ms. Dunn of the White
House, it is opinion journalism masquerading as news, which
some of us would say describes the "New York Times" and certainly MSNBC.

Ingraham, meanwhile, took a cue from Glenn Beck and suggested that the White House was more concerned with Fox than it
was with our enemies abroad.

About the only realistic note sounded by any Villager came
from *Time*'s Joe Klein, who wrote a column agreeing that there
was a problem with Fox but concluding that the White House was
stupid to try to take it on:

> Let me be precise here: Fox News peddles a fair amount of hate-
> ful crap. Some of it borders on sedition. Much of it is flat out
> untrue.
>
> But I don't understand why the White House would give such
> poisonous helium balloons as Glenn Beck and Sean Hannity the
> opportunity for still greater spasms of self-inflation by declaring
> war on Fox.
>
> If the problem is that stories bloated far beyond their actual
> importance—ACORN's corruption, Van Jones's radical past—
> are in danger of leaching out of the Fox hothouse into the general
> media, then perhaps the Administration should be a bit more
> diligent about whom it hires and whom it funds.
>
> If the problem is broader—that Fox News spreads seditious
> lies to its demographic sliver of an audience—the Administra-
> tion should probably be stoic: the wingnuts will always be
> with us. The best antidote to their garbage is elegant, intelligent

governance. The next-best antidote is occasional engagement: I thought Obama came away from his O'Reilly and Chris Wallace interviews much the better for it. (Though you don't want to sit down with a thug like Hannity or a weirdo like Beck.)

There were plenty of opportunities to examine the problem seriously. In late October, the Pew Research Center reported poll results indicating that Americans viewed Fox far and away as the most ideological network on television. The poll found that nearly half of Americans think of Fox as "mostly conservative," compared to only 36 percent who thought MSNBC was "mostly liberal," the next-highest ideological score. A previous Pew poll, conducted in April, had found that Fox was the runaway winner when people were asked which network had been too critical of President Obama. Yet neither poll was ever mentioned on any network, particularly not Fox, or discussed by any of the many pundits weighing in on the "White House War on Fox."

Instead, the controversy bubbled along for a few more weeks and gradually died away. Eventually, Anita Dunn left the White House, though not under pressure: She had announced her pending departure in April. And eventually, President Obama did sit down, in late November, for an interview with Fox's Major Garrett—though not on *Fox News Sunday*. And Fox News, just as it had done before, continued to run wild-eyed conspiracy theories and a stream of falsehoods masquerading as facts about the Obama administration, on both its opinion shows and its news shows. In other words, nothing really changed.

Fox News's employees received the ultimate confirmation that they were doing exactly what their bosses wanted them to do when Rupert Murdoch—the owner of Fox's parent company, News Corp., and probably the most powerful media mogul in history—submitted to an interview with Sky News Australia's David Speers in mid-November (News Corp. is a major shareholder in SkyNews).

Murdoch sneered at Anita Dunn's critique of Fox as "the communications arm of the Republican Party" as "nonsense, everybody knows that's nonsense." He claimed that "they admit that publicly that our reporting of the White House and that our reporters in the White House are absolutely fair. And we have said it publicly, and privately, 'You tell us whenever we make a mistake and we will correct it.' It's a matter of fact." Murdoch added:

> We do have, it's perfectly true, a couple of commentary shows in the evenings which tend to be strongly critical. One—that comes at 5 at night—is new and has just become unbelievably popular. But it's sort of a libertarian viewpoint this guy takes. It's just don't trust the government, don't trust me, just trust yourself, pure libertarianism, right? Um, and it's struck a nerve. So, um, no, we're fine.
>
> And otherwise, you see other shows, to criticize—we have on Republicans, and we have on Democrats. And we have them debate. The other networks only have Democrats. Or something to the left of them.

Murdoch's comments were either delusion or prevarication: Other networks feature a multitude of Republicans on their shows, but Fox features not a single liberal host or anchor and its Republican guests outnumber its Democratic guests, according to Media Matters, by a roughly three-to-one margin. Moreover, the pile of uncorrected falsehoods at Fox is so long it would take Fox a week simply to run them all if it wanted to catch up. Fox almost never corrects its errors, and when it does, it buries them (like the Kevin Jennings smear) on its Web site.

Nonetheless, Speers did not contest these claims but did point out that part of the problem was how far Glenn Beck—that special five o'clock "libertarian"—was pushing his rhetoric:

> Speers: Glenn Beck, who you mentioned, has called Barack Obama a racist, and he helped organize a protest against him, and others on Fox have likened him [Obama] to Stalin. Is that defensible?

> Murdoch: No, no, no, not Stalin, I don't think, ah, not one of our people. On the racist thing, that caused a grilling. But he [Obama] did make a very racist comment—ahh—about, you know, blacks and whites and so on, and which he said in his campaign he would be completely above. And um, that was something which perhaps shouldn't have been said about the President, but if you actually assess what he was talking about, he was right.

A few days later, a News Corp. spokesperson responding to the resulting uproar told Politico that Murdoch "does not at all, for a minute, think the president is a racist." And when a Media Matters reporter with a video camera asked Murdoch (while rushing through a hallway) to explain which comment Obama had made that was "very racist," Murdoch simply declaimed: "I denied that absolutely."

But by then it didn't matter. Murdoch had in any event confirmed two things: The path Glenn Beck and the rest of the Fox fearmongers were taking was exactly what the boss wanted. And Fox News had officially abdicated its responsibilities as a news organization.

EIGHT

The Brakes Fail

Naturally, a number of conservative Republicans—especially those from the nonpopulist, business-oriented wing of the party—were somewhat alarmed by the prospects of watching the bus they were riding in career over the cliff and into the abyss of right-wing populism and its attendant madness. However, none of them was in the driver's seat.

Early on in the Republicans' post-Obama descent into madness, there had been a few voices of dissent raised from the back of the bus. After Rush Limbaugh said that he hoped Obama would fail, there emerged a brief discussion among the pundit class about the reach and depth of Limbaugh's influence. President Obama, in a meeting with congressional conservatives, had remarked: "You can't just listen to Rush Limbaugh and get things done." A number of liberals contended that Limbaugh had become the de facto leader of the otherwise leaderless Republican Party.

Some congressional Republicans objected to this characterization of things. Representative John Boehner of Ohio, in an interview with right-wing radio host Hugh Hewitt, denied that his ideas came from Limbaugh: "I like Rush, but, he's a talk show host, and I'm in the policy-making business."

Limbaugh responded by blasting him as weak: "He's [Obama is] obviously more frightened of me than he is Mitch McConnell.

He is more frightened of me than he is of, say, John Boehner, which doesn't say much about our party."

Representative Phil Gingrey of Georgia came to Boehner's defense in these remarks to *Politico*:

> I mean, it's easy if you're Sean Hannity or Rush Limbaugh or even sometimes Newt Gingrich to stand back and throw bricks. You don't have to try to do what's best for your people and your party. You know you're just on these talk shows and you're living well and plus you stir up a bit of controversy and gin the base and that sort of thing.

The next morning, Gingrey issued a retraction, declaring that he saw "eye to eye with Rush," and that afternoon was on Limbaugh's show, abjectly apologizing:

> Rush, thank you so much. I thank you for the opportunity, of course this is not exactly the way I wanted to come on.... Mainly, I want to express to you and all your listeners my very sincere regret for those comments I made yesterday to *Politico*.... I clearly ended up putting my foot in my mouth on some of those comments.... I regret those stupid comments.

Even those Republicans who were somewhere near the front of the bus were not immune. A similar fate befell the new Republican National Committee (RNC) chairman—Michael Steele, the GOP's first-ever African American party chair—when, in early March, he had similarly questioned Limbaugh's leadership role. In a CNN sit-down with D. L. Hughley, Steele had grown combative when Hughley called Limbaugh "the de facto leader of the Republican Party." Steele vehemently denied this, asserting: "I'm the de facto leader of the Republican Party." Then he went on: "Let's put it into context here. Rush Limbaugh is an entertainer. Rush Limbaugh, his whole thing is entertainment. Yes, it's incendiary. Yes, it's ugly."

The next day, Limbaugh launched a brutal verbal assault on Michael Steele:

> I'm not in charge of the Republican Party, and I don't want to be. I would be embarrassed to say that I'm in charge of the Republican Party in a sad-sack state that it's in. If I were chairman of the Republican Party, given the state that it's in, I would quit.... Republicans and conservatives are sick and tired of being talked down to, they're sick and tired of being lectured to. And until you show some understanding and respect for who they are, you're gonna have a tough time rebuilding your party.

Steele, too, abjectly apologized, telling Politico in a telephone interview: "My intent was not to go after Rush—I have enormous respect for Rush Limbaugh.... I was maybe a little bit inarticulate.... There was no attempt on my part to diminish his voice or his leadership." Meanwhile, there were whispers from anonymous "Republican advisers to Congress" that unless Steele shut his trap, there would be a special session of the RNC to remove him. Steele said no more about Limbaugh, other than to praise him.

Some Republicans even began claiming that the White House was trying to create a distraction by using Limbaugh as a wedge issue. Senator John Cornyn of Texas circulated a petition demanding the White House "come clean" about its "conspiracy" to smear Limbaugh: "President Obama owes the American people an explanation. His staff should apologize to the American people for supporting these tactics and diverting attention to the hard work that needs to be done to get America's economy back on track."

The Obama-bashing populist rhetoric generated by Limbaugh, and adopted ardently by Fox News's opinion makers, was a product of the conservative movement's longtime embrace of the politics of resentment. The rhetoric, in turn, gave birth to the Tea Parties. By mid-April it was self-evident that the conservative movement in general and the Republican Party in particular were fully in the thrall of the movement's nascent populist bloc, as could be seen by the numbers of Republicans, both in Congress and on television, who vigorously supported the Tea Parties and what they represented. GOP congresspeople were featured prominently as speakers at the tax day Tea Parties as well as at Glenn Beck's "9/12 March on Washington."

But by early October, it became obvious to Republican Party leaders that, while the Tea Partiers could be relied on to incessantly attack President Obama, that did not necessarily mean they were loyal Republicans. Many of them leaned toward libertarianism, and others identified with far-right Patriot-movement beliefs, often under the flag of the Constitution Party. A serious rift between the Tea Partiers and Republican leadership began to develop.

One of the key disputes arose in Florida, where moderate GOP governor Charlie Crist's party-backed bid for the state's U.S. Senate seat ran into a challenge from an ardent conservative, Marco Rubio, widely supported by the Tea Party crowd. Similarly, in Colorado, Connecticut, and California, Tea Party activists began lining up behind challengers to GOP establishment-backed Senate candidates. In the race among Republicans to challenge incumbent Democratic senator Barbara Boxer of California, a conservative state legislator named Chuck DeVore, embraced by the Tea Partiers, was running neck and neck in the polls with former Hewlett-Packard CEO Carly Fiorina, who, like Crist, had been endorsed by the National Republican Senatorial Committee.

Tea Party organizers told Politico's Alex Isenstadt that "their resistance to Republican Party-backed primary candidates has much to do with what they perceive as the GOP's stubborn insistence on embracing candidates who don't abide by a small government, anti-tax conservative philosophy." Isenstadt reported:

"We will be a headache for anyone who believes the Constitution of the United States . . . isn't to be protected," said Dick Armey, chairman of the anti-tax and limited government advocacy group FreedomWorks, which helped plan and promote the Tea Parties, town hall protests and the September "Taxpayer March" in Washington. "If you can't take it seriously, we will look for places of other employment for you.

"We're not a partisan organization, and I think many Republicans are disappointed we are not," added Armey, a former GOP congressman.

Incumbent Republicans, too, were finding the Tea Party crowds more than a handful. Senator Lindsey Graham of South Carolina went home to Greenville in mid-October and held what he assumed was going to be an amicable town-hall forum filled with friendly fellow conservatives. It turned out that not even Graham met this crowd's right-wing purity test—particularly because Graham had had the temerity to announce that he was working cooperatively with Democratic senator John Kerry of Massachusetts (widely reviled on the right for his 2004 presidential candidacy) on comprehensive climate and clean-energy legislation.

A video of the event captured the flavor of the interrogation that ensued:

> Q: Senator, good evening, I'm a 21-year Navy vet, 17 years in the private sector, um, a huge strong supporter on health care and supporting military property. The question I have is: Why is it necessary to get in bed with people like John Kerry? Why don't *you* do something?
>
> [Loud cheers, boos]
>
> Q: I'd like you to get together with Senator [Jim] DeMint [Graham's South Carolina colleague in the Senate], and get the

EPA, and the Department of Agriculture, and the Department of Energy, and the EPA on the sidelines, and let the private sector go at the energy market. That's going to solve a whole bunch of problems related to that, and I'm having a real difficult time with your concept of principled compromise. And I'd like you to explain that.

Graham: How many members are there in the United States Senate?

[Crowd answers: "100"]

Graham: How many Republicans are there?

[Crowd answers: "40"]

Voice from the crowd: How many non-compromisers are in the Senate?

Graham began trying to explain that it made more sense for him to have a voice in the legislation by working with people like Kerry than to have no voice at all, but someone began shouting over him: "You and Obama are guilty of treason—Article One, Section Nine!"

It was a middle-aged man in a yellow "Don't Tread on Me" shirt popular with the Tea Party crowd. He kept shouting: "You're a traitor, Lindsey Graham! You betrayed this nation! You betrayed the state! . . . Read Article One, Section Nine!" (This section of the Constitution relates to limitations on the power of Congress.) The man eventually settled down, but throughout the rest of the town-hall forum that evening, Graham was periodically interrupted by similar shouts. Another questioner snidely asked him: "When are you going to announce that you're switching parties?" Some members of the crowd began shouting out Ron Paul's name as "a real conservative!" While Graham defended his Republican credentials, someone shouted: "You're a country-club Republican!"

Local Republicans were also angry with Graham over his vote in favor of confirming Sonia Sotomayor to the U.S. Supreme Court (Graham was one of only nine Republicans to do so, and he was the sole Republican vote for her on the Judiciary Committee). The Charleston County Republican Party got together and drafted a list of grievances, at the end of which they voted by a wide margin to censure Mr. Graham in harsh terms. The list included charges that Graham had called opponents of immigration law change "bigots," had voted for the Wall Street bailout, had held the GOP "hostage" by participating in bipartisan maneuvers, and had in general "tarnished the ideals of freedom."

The censure was largely engineered by acolytes of Senator DeMint, who was quietly organizing conservatives in South Carolina to resist moderating moves like Graham's, even though he and Graham remained on personally amicable terms. Graham managed to defuse two other local censure resolutions, but the grumbling was getting loud.

"I believe in the Constitution 100 percent—Mr. Graham does not," Terry Hutchinson, an auto mechanic in Rock Hill, told the *New York Times*'s Shaila Dewan outside the York town hall. "He voted for Sotomayor, that's the first thing. She is a liberal, she is a racist, and you support her? Wrong, absolutely wrong."

Dewan also interviewed the author of the censure resolution, J. Warren Sloane, vice chair of the Charleston County Republican Party. Sloane told her that independent voters like the Tea Partiers were turned off by such "mushy" Republicans: "Lindsey Graham paints himself as a martyr who is going against what his constituents feel because he knows what's best for the country.... We're a little bit tired of the martyr shtick."

Around the country, Republican officeholders were discovering that in helping unleash the Tea Parties, they had loosed a beast that was looking hungrily in their direction.

◇ ◇ ◇

With Jim DeMint's help, the Tea Party movement immediately went to work trying to translate its energy into real political gains. What the group wound up demonstrating, instead, was its own severe limitations.

The battleground chosen was a November 3 special election to replace Republican representative John McHugh, who had resigned his seat to accept President Obama's appointment as secretary of the army. McHugh's seat, in New York's 23rd Congressional District—the state's northernmost district, where the largest populations are in towns like Potsdam and Watertown—had been held for all the previous century by Republicans.

The local GOP establishment nominated Dede Scozzafava, a distinguished state lawmaker, and the Democrats nominated Bill Owens, a Plattsburgh attorney who was registered as an independent at the time. Meanwhile, the Conservative Party nominated Doug Hoffman, an accountant who lived in Lake Placid—outside the 23rd District—who had sought the GOP nomination and lost to Scozzafava.

Initially, polling showed a likely easy win for Scozzafava, who was favored in a late-September poll with 35 percent support to Owens's 28 percent and Hoffman's 16 percent. Scozzafava still showed 30 percent support in mid-October, though Owens had passed her—largely because Hoffman was beginning to siphon off her support. But then came the barrage from the Republican Party's right flank, and it all turned around in a two-week period.

First to weigh in was the Club for Growth, a corporate-backed political action committee with a history of helping far-right candidates, which threw its support behind Hoffman and began pouring money into his coffers. Then Hoffman picked up an endorsement from Jim DeMint, and Republican representatives Tom Cole of Oklahoma and Dana Rohrabacher of California likewise threw their support to Hoffman.

But the tsunami for Hoffman came on October 21 and 22, a two-day span in which he won the public embrace of both Glenn Beck and Sarah Palin. On the 21st, Hoffman appeared on Beck's radio show and enjoyed a sympathetic interview, near the end of which Hoffman informed Beck that he was "a member of the 9/12 group." Beck replied: "God bless you." Hoffman was invited to appear on more of Beck's radio programs and then made the first of several appearances on Beck's Fox News show on October 26. It was a mutual admiration society; Hoffman later told an interviewer that "Beck is my mentor."

Meanwhile, on the 22nd, Sarah Palin had posted an effusive endorsement of Hoffman on her Facebook page:

> Doug Hoffman stands for the principles that all Republicans
> should share: smaller government, lower taxes, strong national
> defense, and a commitment to individual liberty.... Republicans
> and conservatives around the country are sending an important
> message to the Republican establishment in their outstanding
> grassroots support for Doug Hoffman: no more politics as usual.

This set off a gold rush of support for Hoffman, with endorsements shortly arriving from former GOP presidential candidate Steve Forbes, former Pennsylvania senator Rick Santorum, and current Minnesota governor Tim Pawlenty.

Scozzafava did draw the support of establishment Republicans, notably former House Speaker Newt Gingrich, who harkened back to his own "Contract with America" glory days in endorsing her:

The special election for the 23rd Congressional District is an important test leading up to the mid-term 2010 elections. Our best chance to put responsible and principled leaders in Washington starts here, with Dede Scozzafava. . . . The Republican Revolution in 1994 started very much like what we see today. Like then, our country is reeling from misguided liberal policies, high taxes and out-of-control spending. This special election in New York's 23rd Congressional District could be the first election of the new Republican Revolution, but we need the momentum to get it started.

But Gingrich was shouted down by right-wing talkers like Beck and Rush Limbaugh, who attacked him for supporting Scozzafava. Meanwhile, right-wing bloggers—particularly Michelle Malkin and PowerLine—began chiming in, accusing Scozzafava of being a "RINO" (Republican in name only) and castigating her for a "liberal" legislative record.

The combined effect of all this negative attention was to drive Scozzafava's support so far south that, by the end of October, she was looking at less than 20 percent support in the polls, while Hoffman and Owens were neck and neck at 35 and 36 percent, respectively. On Saturday, October 31, four days before the polls opened, Scozzafava announced that she was dropping out, suspending her campaign, and releasing her supporters. Two days later, she announced that she was endorsing Bill Owens, the Democrat, and urged her supporters to vote for him.

When November 3 came around, it appeared that Scozzafava's supporters largely split their votes, so her endorsement wound up being relatively meaningless. The end result was that Bill Owens won the seat, defeating Hoffman by what looked to be a 49 percent to 45 percent margin on election day—at which point Hoffman conceded. After late ballots arrived several weeks later, the final tally had shrunk to 48.7 percent for Owens and 46.4 percent for Hoffman.

The initial response from the Tea Party crowd was a kind of denial. At the popular right-wing blog RedState, editor Erick Erickson announced:

> This is a huge win for conservatives. . . . I have said all along that the goal of activists must be to defeat Scozzafava. Doug Hoffman winning would just be gravy. A Hoffman win is not in the cards, but we did exactly what we set out to do—crush the establishment backed GOP candidate.

Glenn Beck's denial was so severe that on November 16, nearly two full weeks after the election, he convinced Doug Hoffman to come on his show and officially "unconcede," based on a highly hopeful reading of the late returns. A week later, when the math became insurmountable, Hoffman conceded again. But Beck, for some reason, never mentioned that to his audience.

The disappointed conservatives knew whom to blame: Newt Gingrich, of course. Right-wing bloggers attacked Gingrich for endorsing Scozzafava. Michelle Malkin said "no thanks" to the possibility of a Gingrich 2012 presidential run because he was the "most prominent GOP endorser of [the] radical leftist NY-23 congressional candidate." At RedState.com, Erickson wrote (before removing the post) that Gingrich "stands athwart history and pees on the legacy of 1994." But more important was that Rush Limbaugh blamed Gingrich for the defeat, telling his radio audience: "We cannot forget how this whole thing happened in the first place. There was not a primary. The right message here would indict the way party bosses, Republican Party bosses and these big thinkers like Newt screwed the whole thing up from the get go."

So Gingrich, the night after the election, went on Sean Hannity's Fox News show and did what all Republicans do when they are attacked by Rush Limbaugh. He abjectly apologized:

I think the nomination was a mistake. I wish that we had gotten involved earlier. And if we had, I would have done everything I could to make sure she had not been picked. And she clearly proved in the last few days that she was in no way a loyal Republican.

If real-world results count for anything, the Tea Partiers' first foray into politics was an abject failure. The right-wing populist coalition—Palin, Limbaugh, Beck, the astroturfers, and their hectoring crowd of supporters—had put their collective resources behind a politician who didn't even live in the district he wanted to represent, and yet the movement's members continued to claim that they represented "ordinary voters." In the end it cost the GOP a seat in a district that hadn't elected a Democratic politician in over 100 years.

Gingrich's excuse—that the local Republican establishment had not listened carefully enough to the demands of "conservative activists" (to wit, the Tea Party crowd)—soon became a centerpiece of the Tea Partiers' denial-driven analysis of what had happened in New York's 23rd District race. Three weeks after the election, a resolution began circulating among RNC members that proposed a sort of purity test for would-be conservative candidates. Titled "Resolution on Reagan's Unity Principle for Support of Candidates" (the text explained: "President Ronald Reagan believed... that someone who agreed with him 8 out of 10 times was his friend, not his opponent"), it listed 10 "conservative principles" it wanted potential candidates to sign and promise to abide by:

1. Smaller government, smaller national debt, lower deficits and lower taxes by opposing bills like Obama's "stimulus" bill;

2. Market-based health care reform and oppose Obama-style government run healthcare;

3. Market-based energy reforms by opposing cap and trade legislation;

4. Workers' right to secret ballot by opposing card check;

5. Legal immigration and assimilation into American society by opposing amnesty for illegal immigrants;

6. Victory in Iraq and Afghanistan by supporting military-recommended troop surges;

7. Containment of Iran and North Korea, particularly effective action to eliminate their nuclear weapons threat;

8. Retention of the Defense of Marriage Act;

9. Protecting the lives of vulnerable persons by opposing health care rationing and denial of health care and government funding of abortion; and

10. The right to keep and bear arms by opposing government restrictions on gun ownership

If any potential candidate disagreed with three or more of the "principles," and was therefore unwilling to sign the purity pledge, the organizers of the resolution wanted the RNC to withhold financial aid and endorsements.

The author of the purity test was RNC member Jim Bopp Jr. (Bopp's day job was acting as general counsel to the anti-abortion group National Right to Life), who said the resolution would be presented at the RNC's winter meeting in January. "The goal of the resolution is to take a position... towards reclaiming the Republican Party's conservative bona fides," Bopp told MSNBC's Domenico Montanaro. (In April, Bopp had drafted another RNC resolution demanding that Republicans rebrand the Democratic Party as the "Democrat Socialist Party.")

What the purity test represented, in realpolitik terms, was a demand from the Tea Partiers (whom the Republican establishment had believed it could unleash on the public and yet still contain) to local Republican Party apparatuses to hand over control of their candidate-selection process. All outward signs were that the establishment felt compelled to give it to them—which, if it came to pass, would mean that the inmates were now running the conservative asylum.

When President Obama gave his speech on health-care reform to Congress on September 9, he was rudely interrupted midway through by a member of Jim DeMint's clique of South Carolina arch-conservatives, Representative Joe Wilson. Obama had just reassured Congress that his health-care-reform package would not provide benefits to illegal immigrants, when Wilson shouted from the House floor: "You lie!"

It was an unprecedented breach of protocol and, more than that, a flagrant show of disrespect. It was unheard of for a member of Congress to interrupt a president addressing them—but then, President Obama was inspiring all kinds of unheard-of behavior from the increasingly rabid Right by then, and overt shows of disrespect had become yet another way of undermining his legitimacy.

There was an immediate outcry, with a number of Republicans as well as Democrats demanding that Wilson apologize. In short order, he did, issuing an official statement:

> This evening I let my emotions get the best of me when listening to the President's remarks regarding the coverage of illegal immigrants in the health care bill. While I disagree with the President's statement, my comments were inappropriate and regrettable. I extend sincere apologies to the President for this lack of civility.

Obama accepted Wilson's apology, but House Democrats wanted him to apologize on the floor of the House. Wilson refused, saying, "I believe one apology is sufficient." So on September 15, the House voted a "resolution of disapproval" chiding Wilson for his behavior.

Among the Tea Party crowd, Joe Wilson immediately became a martyr to "political correctness." Erick Erickson at RedState declared him a "great American hero" and opened up a fundraising campaign for his reelection. "I'm With Joe Wilson" became a popular slogan on T-shirts worn at Tea Parties. At the "9/12 March on Washington" there were frequent references to Wilson among the signs, such as "Joe was Right" and "Stand with Joe." Some signs simply read "Joe 2012."

"There are a lot of folks out there in the country that feel the president is lying, and that's why he has become something of a folk hero," Adam Brandon of FreedomWorks told Politico.

But many observers understood that there was a decided racial undercurrent at work—not just in Wilson's outburst, but in the increasingly nasty tone of the debate over health-care reform that it represented. Former president Jimmy Carter told *NBC Nightly News*:

> I think an overwhelming portion of the intensely demonstrated animosity toward President Barack Obama is based on the fact that he is a black man, that he's African-American. I live in the South, and I've seen the South come a long way, and I've seen the rest of the country that shares the South's attitude toward minority groups at that time, particularly African-Americans.

Carter's comments set off their own mini-furor. Michael Steele at the RNC denied that race was a factor at all: "President Carter is flat-out wrong," Steele said in a statement. "This isn't about race. It is about policy." Meanwhile, on all the cable shows, the question suddenly was about Jimmy Carter's remarks instead of Joe Wilson's. Carter—who was clearly singling out the racist fringe driving the nasty rhetoric—was regularly characterized, especially on Fox, as having "accused vocal opponents of the President's policies of being racist." On Fox's *Special Report with Bret Baier,* "All Star" panelist Charles Krauthammer weighed in:

> The accusation of racism is a sign of desperation by people who know they are losing the national debate and they want to hurl the ultimate charge in American politics. This is dealing from the bottom of the deck and I agree that it is a disgusting tactic. It's done as a way to end debate. The minute you call somebody a racist the debate is over, you don't continue. Accusations of racism are the last refuge of the liberal scoundrel.

Evidently, Krauthammer had conveniently forgotten that only a couple of months before, Fox's Glenn Beck had openly accused President Obama of being a racist. So had longtime Fox anchor Brit Hume, who thought Carter's remarks would hurt Obama:

> Baier: So does this work? What does this do to debate when it's thrown out there?
>
> Hume: Well, I think over time, it cheapens the charge. And I think in this instance . . . this is going to infuriate the people of good will who are resisting President Obama and not in any way because of his race but because of his policies. And my guess is, it has real backfire potential, which diminishes to some extent the consensus on race in America.

Another former president from the South, Bill Clinton, chimed in, remarking that it wasn't all about race, but was part of a larger animus: "Some of the extreme right who oppose him on health care also are racially prejudiced. And if you listen to some of the— look at some of the signs, or listen to some of the rhetoric, there's no question that that's true," Clinton told ABC's Robin Roberts on *Good Morning America.* "But I believe, if he were not an African-

American, all the people who are against him on health care would still be against him—because they were all against me, too."

Karl Rove appeared on Sean Hannity's show to decry such sentiments as reflective of nasty personal politics—and managed to do so without a hint of irony:

> Look his [Clinton's] comment was like Jimmy Carter—irrational and unbelievably partisan. This is the kind of stuff that he said routinely during the 1990s about his political opponents, denigrating them personally, questioning their motivations.
>
> Why can't he just accept the fact that people disagree with President Obama's health care plan as they disagreed with his health care plan, because they represent a spirit of liberalism and a government control and government domination of a very personal decision that ought to be left between a doctor and his patient as to the decision for our health?

As it happened, research was available strongly suggesting that there was a powerful connection between opposition to health-care reform and voters with racist attitudes about Obama. Marc J. Hetherington and Jonathan D. Weiler described the data in writing for the *Washington Post*:

> As evidence of the link between health care and racial attitudes, we analyzed survey data gathered in late 2008. The survey asked people whether they favored a government run health insurance plan, a system like we have now, or something in between. It also asked four questions about how people feel about blacks.
>
> Taken together the four items form a measure of what scholars call racial resentment. We find an extraordinarily strong correlation between racial resentment of blacks and opposition to health care reform.
>
> Among whites with above average racial resentment, only 19 percent favored fundamental health care reforms and 57 percent favored the present system. Among those who have below aver-

age racial resentment, more than twice as many (45 percent) favored government run health care and less than half as many (25 percent) favored the status quo.

No such relationship between racial attitudes and opinions on health care existed in the mid-1990s during the Clinton effort.

It would be silly to assert that all, or even most, opposition to President Obama, including his plans for health care reform, is motivated by the color of his skin. But our research suggests that a key to understanding people's feelings about partisan politics runs far deeper than the mere pros and cons of actual policy proposals. It is also about a collision of worldviews.

This is correlative, of course; the data don't indicate a cause-and-effect relationship. Rather, as Hetherington and Weiler explained, both sets of attitudes—racial bigotry and opposition to health-care reform—arise out of a common right-wing authoritarian worldview. The people who hold racist attitudes almost always also hold the virulent anti-government attitudes that ultimately fuel their opposition to policies like health-care reform—but not everyone who hates the government is racist, and certainly not everyone opposed to health-care reform is racist. At the same time, you can bet that someone who voted against Obama because he is a black man will also be violently opposed to health-care reform.

When people remark that "the Republican Party is the home of racists," they're not arguing that every conservative Republican is a racist, but practicing racists consistently self-identify as conservatives, and many are in fact Republicans (or sometimes even farther to the right). There are always exceptions, of course, but the known pattern is clear enough.

The Republican Right likes to argue that these kinds of observations conflate all members of a subgroup (in this case, racists) with the larger group in which it subsists (that is, Republicans). Thus, drawing attention to right-wing extremists for law-enforcement purposes, as the Department of Homeland Security did, is transformed by them into an attempt to categorize ordinary conservatives as terrorist threats. Or pointing out that some Tea Partiers engage in threatening Brownshirt-type behavior means you're smearing all of them as Nazis. Or pointing out that there is a nasty racial tone to the vitriolic protests against health care means you're trying to paint the opposition to health care as racist.

All of which means, of course, that you can never draw attention to racism or extremism in mainstream discourse—at least when it comes from the Right—because doing so means you're painting all those innocent conservatives who can't find the wherewithal to drive out the racist elements from their movement as racists too.

The early silencing of voices of dissent from within the ranks of conservatives had something of a chilling effect for most of the spring and summer, but by fall—as it became clear that the Tea Parties represented a real (and unhealthy) transformation of both movement conservatism and ultimately the Republican Party—a few of them began speaking out.

After Glenn Beck was featured in a fluffy *Time* cover story in November that somehow managed to overlook his history of extremist rhetoric and factual falsehoods, former Bush speechwriter Peter Wehner wrote about his concerns in *Commentary:*

> I understand that a political movement is a mansion with many rooms; the people who occupy them are involved in intellectual and policy work, in politics, and in polemics. Different people take on different roles. And certainly some of the things Beck has done on his program are fine and appropriate. But the role Glenn Beck is playing is harmful in its totality. My hunch is

that he is a comet blazing across the media sky right now—and will soon flame out. Whether he does or not, he isn't the face or disposition that should represent modern-day conservatism. At a time when we should aim for intellectual depth, for tough-minded and reasoned arguments, for good cheer and calm purpose, rather than erratic behavior, he is not the kind of figure conservatives should embrace or cheer on.

Joe Scarborough, a former Republican congressman, was even more damning in his MSNBC talk show, *Morning Joe:*

> But when you preach this kind of hatred, and say that an African American president hates all white people—stay with me—hates all white people, you are playing with fire. And bad things can happen. And if they do happen, not only is Glenn Beck responsible, but conservatives who don't—call—him—out—are responsible.

New York Times columnist David Brooks, a moderate Republican, pointed out on NBC's weekend *Chris Matthews* show: "What Rush and Glenn Beck are doing is race-baiting. 100 percent. That's race-baiting." He compared Beck and Limbaugh to Father Charles Coughlin, the 1930s FDR hater, who was also a demagoging anti-Semite:

> The one danger—the main danger of all this, the Glenn and the Rush and all that—they're not going to take over the country. But they are taking over the Republican Party. And so if the Republican Party is sane, they will say no to these people. But every single elected leader in the Republican Party is afraid to take on Rush and Glenn Beck.

Peter Wallsten, the Washington Bureau chief of the *Los Angeles Times*, filed a September 14 report describing some of the growing angst within the GOP establishment, particularly from members of its traditional pro-business bloc, many of whom were finding themselves in the same crosshairs of the Tea Party's populists as were Democrats:

> Amid a rebirth of conservative activism that could help Republicans win elections next year, some party insiders now fear that extreme rhetoric and conspiracy theories coming from the angry reaches of the conservative base are undermining the GOP's broader credibility and casting it as the party of the paranoid.
>
> Such insiders point to theories running rampant on the Internet, such as the idea that Barack Obama was born in Kenya and is thus ineligible to be president, or that he is a communist, or that his allies want to set up Nazi-like detention camps for political opponents. Those theories, the insiders say, have stoked the GOP base and have created a "purist" climate in which a figure such as Rep. Joe Wilson (R-S.C.) is lionized for his "You lie!" outburst last week when Obama addressed Congress.
>
> They are "wild accusations and the paranoid delusions coming from the fever swamps," said David Frum, a conservative author and speechwriter for President George W. Bush who is among the more vocal critics of the party base and of the conservative talk show hosts helping to fan the unrest.
>
> "Like all conservatives, I am concerned about this administration's accumulation of economic power," Frum said. "Still, you have to be aware that there's a line where legitimate concerns begin to collapse into paranoid fantasy."

Frum was one of several establishment Republicans who began raising voices of concern about the influence of far-right extremists, represented primarily by the Tea Parties and such leading populist figures as Glenn Beck and Sarah Palin, as well as the populist-right media, such as the popular webzine WorldNetDaily (WND).

WND had a long and colorful history of openly promoting

ideas from the extremist Right, particularly in the 1990s, when it embraced the Patriot/militia movement and its conspiracy theories. WND had been especially keen on the looming "Y2K Apocalypse" theory of 1999, which had thousands of true believers stocking up on rice and beans in anticipation of the collapse of society after all its computers went on the fritz on January 1, 2000. It didn't pan out that way, but that had no discernible effect on either the conspiracy theorists or WND, which simply moved on to new ground and kept chugging out the conspiracies. In 2009, its favorite was the "Birther" conspiracy theory.

By then, WND had become so influential—not just with the Tea Party fringe, but among Beltway Republicans—that it was in many ways setting the conservative fringe agenda. Its articles provided grist for conservative bloggers, and Fox News pundits cited its stories on the air. A story by David Weigel in the *Washington Independent* described how deeply influential WND had become, embodied by the resignation of Van Jones: WND had been the first to attack Jones with Aaron Klein's April 12 report, and that story proved to be the main wellspring for Glenn Beck's subsequent attacks on Jones. Weigel continued:

> WorldNetDaily's Web traffic, revenue, and influence are impressive. It frequently leads the pack in conservative online media. According to James R. Whelan, the Florida-based marketer who runs WorldNetDaily's ad operations, the site has already surpassed $1 million in ad revenue for 2009. It has a mailing list of more than 355,000 e-mail addresses, which has been built up through tools like daily polls on the site, and has been rented (through third-party vendors) by the Republican National Committee.

Some conservatives, though, decided to draw a line after WND's Jerome Corsi reported to his readers in February on a nefarious

scheme to pass legislation that would allow the Obama administration to begin rounding up and incarcerating conservatives:

> The proposed bill, which has received little mainstream media
> attention, appears designed to create the type of detention cen-
> ter that those concerned about use of the military in domestic
> affairs fear could be used as concentration camps for political
> dissidents, such as occurred in Nazi Germany.

In reality, the legislation—authored by Democratic representative Alcee Hastings of Florida—simply ordered the Department of
Homeland Security to prepare national emergency centers in the
event of natural disasters such as hurricanes and earthquakes. The
centers would provide temporary housing and medical facilities in
national emergencies and would be able to train first responders.
Corsi, of course, failed to mention any of this.

When the concentration-camp theory began circulating among
the Tea Party crowd—particularly among the Oath Keepers and
their fellow militiamen—it also bubbled up into the mainstream
press, as it did on Glenn Beck's show and in news reports. The
spread of the falsehood eventually spurred conservative blogger
Jon Henke, at TheNextRight, to urge his fellow conservatives to
disassociate themselves from WND in every way possible: "No
respectable organization should support the kind of fringe idiocy
that WND peddles. Those who do are not respectable." He urged
conservatives to organize a boycott of the webzine.

However, Henke continued to contend that the continuum
between far-right extremists like the WND crowd and mainstream conservatives remained limited in nature. That claim was
massively undercut by Terry Krepel's follow-up reporting for
Media Matters, which noted that "one of the organizations that
has rented WND's mailing list is . . . the Republican National

Committee." Henke then called upon the RNC to disassociate itself from WND, but they politely declined.

The RNC most likely declined to break from WND because the transmission belt—the repackaging of extremist ideas and agendas for mainstream consumption—had become the be-all and end-all of Republicans' political strategy, the natural outcome of practicing the politics of resentment. The idea, much as it had been for Clinton in the 1990s, was to delegitimize Obama's presidency by whipping up the far right with unhinging conspiracy theories that spread into the mainstream as well. Having undermined the president, "mainstream" Republicans could then exploit the weakness in precisely the way the Tea Parties nearly derailed the health-care debate: by so profoundly muddying the waters that rational discourse—not to mention forward progress—is nearly impossible. It's a deeply cynical, and dangerous, strategy, but after years of conditioning, it was the only option that conservatives could see or understand.

People like Henke—and Scarborough, and Brooks, and Frum—all recognized that there was a problem, but all of them were in denial about the extent to which the extremist influence had permeated their movement. None of them quite grasped the dimensions of what they were up against.

As David Weigel explained:

> Conservatives differ from liberals . . . in that their Web 1.0 sites like WND and FreeRepublic survived and kept their readers in the George W. Bush era, whereas liberals mostly "shop" at interactive blogs like Daily Kos and news sites like the Huffington Post. The conspiracist on the right has had stomping grounds at FreeRepublic and WND, while the radical on the far left is banned from sites like Daily Kos if he/she posts a conspiracy theory.

Certainly, the things Glenn Beck said throughout 2009 were nutty, irresponsible, and intemperate and reflected poorly on the American Right generally. That's probably because Beck is in reality a genuine far-right extremist who is gradually coming out of the closet about that—and as he does, he's lapping up the ratings. But Beck was far from the only "mainstream" figure dragging movement conservatism ever farther into the swamps of right-wing extremism.

On the October 13 edition of *Hannity*, the program devoted two whole segments, nearly 30 minutes in all, to promoting Jerome Corsi's new conspiracy tome, *America for Sale: Fighting the New World Order*. As Corsi explained to Hannity: "I'm showing that Barack Obama is a globalist, and the attack on American sovereignty—the giving away of the United States—has never been greater than under Barack Obama."

Corsi's book, as the title suggests, differed very little in ideas and overall thesis from the kinds of black-helicopter texts you could buy at tables set up at militia meetings in the 1990s; it was simply updated with more recent events cast in a conspiratorial light. It included Corsi's WND reportage on a supposed plan to dissolve the United States and create a new "North American Union."

In the 1990s, these kinds of theories tended to circulate at a slow crawl, mostly through Patriot-movement gatherings. In 2009, they were being broadcast to audiences of millions and given approval by a mainstream television network.

So in that summer and fall of 2009, when civil-rights monitors reported a fresh and unsettling new wave of 1990s-style militias springing up, it may have surprised those who weren't paying attention. But for those who were, it would have been a surprise if they hadn't.

NINE

The Only Thing We Have to Fear

The American Right's descent into madness, embodied in its takeover by right-wing populists, was more than a problem just for serious conservatives who understood that it would ultimately prove to be their destruction. The very nature of the insanity that was being unleashed posed a larger problem for the nation at large—namely, the implicit threat of violence and extremist unrest, represented most vividly by the revival of the militia movement.

In August 2009, the Southern Poverty Law Center published a disturbing and sobering report—confirming, in fact, something we had been reporting at Crooks and Liars for several months:

> They're back. Almost a decade after largely disappearing from public view, right-wing militias, ideologically driven tax defiers and sovereign citizens are appearing in large numbers around the country. "Paper terrorism"—the use of property liens and citizens' "courts" to harass enemies—is on the rise. And once-popular militia conspiracy theories are making the rounds again, this time accompanied by nativist theories about secret Mexican plans to "reconquer" the American Southwest. One law enforcement agency has found 50 new militia training groups—one of them made up of present and former police offi-

cers and soldiers. Authorities around the country are reporting a worrying uptick in Patriot activities and propaganda. "This is the most significant growth we've seen in 10 to 12 years," says one. "All it's lacking is a spark. I think it's only a matter of time before you see threats and violence."

A key difference this time is that the federal government—the entity that almost the entire radical right views as its primary enemy—is headed by a black man. That, coupled with high levels of non-white immigration and a decline in the percentage of whites overall in America, has helped to racialize the Patriot movement, which in the past was not primarily motivated by race hate. One result has been a remarkable rash of domestic terror incidents since the presidential campaign, most of them related to anger over the election of Barack Obama. At the same time, ostensibly mainstream politicians and media pundits have helped to spread Patriot and related propaganda, from conspiracy theories about a secret network of U.S. concentration camps to wholly unsubstantiated claims about the president's country of birth.

A few months later, in mid-November, the ADL released a similar report, examining not just the rise of the militias but a larger phenomenon it described in its title: "Rage Grows in America: Anti-Government Conspiracies":

> Since the election of Barack Obama as president, a current of anti-government hostility has swept across the United States, creating a climate of fervor and activism with manifestations ranging from incivility in public forums to acts of intimidation and violence.
>
> What characterizes this anti-government hostility is a shared belief that Obama and his administration actually pose a threat to the future of the United States. Some accuse Obama of plotting to bring socialism to the United States, while others claim

he will bring about Nazism or fascism. All believe that Obama and his administration will trample on individual freedoms and civil liberties, due to some sinister agenda, and they see his economic and social policies as manifestations of this agenda. In particular anti-government activists used the issue of health care reform as a rallying point, accusing Obama and his administration of dark designs ranging from "socialized medicine" to "death panels," even when the Obama administration had not come out with a specific health care reform plan. Some even compared the Obama administration's intentions to Nazi eugenics programs.

Some of these assertions are motivated by prejudice, but more common is an intense strain of anti-government distrust and anger, colored by a streak of paranoia and belief in conspiracies. These sentiments are present both in mainstream and "grass-roots" movements as well as in extreme anti-government movements such as a resurgent militia movement. Ultimately, this anti-government anger, if it continues to grow in intensity and scope, may result in an increase in anti-government extremists and the potential for a rise of violent anti-government acts.

Significantly, the report explored how this rage is being fed to a remarkable extent by mainstream media pundits on the Right, particularly Glenn Beck:

> Though much of the impetus for anti-government sentiment has come from a variety of grass-roots and extremist groups, segments of the mainstream media have played a surprisingly active role in generating such sentiment. Though a number of media figures and commentators have taken part, the media personality who has played the most active role has been radio and television host Glenn Beck, who ... has acted as a "fearmonger-in-chief," raising anxiety about and distrust towards the government.

It devoted an entire section to discussing Beck's role:

> The most important mainstream media figure who has repeat-
> edly helped to stoke the fires of anti-government anger is
> right-wing media host Glenn Beck, who has a TV show on
> FOX News and a popular syndicated radio show. While other
> conservative media hosts, such as Rush Limbaugh and Sean
> Hannity, routinely attack Obama and his administration,
> typically on partisan grounds, they have usually dismissed or
> refused to give a platform to the conspiracy theorists and anti-
> government extremists. This has not been the case with Glenn
> Beck. Beck and his guests have made a habit of demonizing
> President Obama and promoting conspiracy theories about his
> administration.
>
> On a number of his TV and radio programs, Beck has even
> gone so far as to make comparisons between Hitler and Obama
> and to promote the idea that the president is dangerous.

As if intent on proving the ADL correct, Beck went on his Fox
show the very afternoon the report was issued and warned his
viewers of Obama's plans to impose a New World Order as part of
his plan to "fundamentally transform" America:

> On the scale of insane things, I want to show what we skipped
> past. Ready? Look at this. Put it up here. [Graphic displays a
> list: "Recession/Depression/Great Depression/Collapse of the
> Dollar/Global Currency/One World Government/New World
> Order"] We're in a recession now. People argue over whether
> we're even in a recession! We're in a deep recession. I think we're
> on the edge of a depression because of what we're doing.
>
> OK, so, we have skipped a deep recession and skipped depres-
> sion—even the Great Depression—we went right to the collapse
> of the dollar. Then he went right to global currency. One world
> government! And a New World Order! [Slaps] Like that!

The ADL report inspired a Tim Rutten column about Beck in the *Los Angeles Times*. Rutten compared Beck to Father Charles Coughlin (a right-wing populist extremist, anti-Semite, and popular radio host in the 1930s and early 1940s) and wondered why Fox was giving him such a long leash:

> It's hard to imagine any contemporary cable system dropping Fox News simply because Beck is an offensively dangerous demagogue—not with his ratings at least. His new foray into politics, though, presents Rupert Murdoch's network with a profound challenge. Is it willing to become the platform for an extremist political campaign, or will it draw a line as even the authoritarian Catholic Church of the 1940s did?

Beck was giving real succor to some of the country's worst anti-Semites by promoting their ideas; his fearmongering echoed theirs so closely that it rapidly became an important recruiting tool for them. Alexander Zaitchik explored this connection for Salon.com, reporting on the warm regard in which many white supremacists held Beck, illustrated by this post from UtashaNY culled from the Stormfront.org discussion forums:

> UstashaNY offered up an analogy to substance abuse, with Beck as the soft-stuff hook:
>
> > Beck, Dobbs etc. are like gateway drugs. If it wakes up one person to learn something about whats really going on and that person does the research, looks deeper and deeper into WHO and WHAT is behind all of this, then its a win for the movement. NOBODY in the msm is reporting the stuff Beck does, let him keep talking. It will wake people up, believe me. . . . He is more of a help to us then you may think. Until we have a REAL voice in the msm, guys like him and Dobbs are a stepping stone right into our laps. Its only a matter of time.

Beck never mentioned the ADL report on his Fox News show, but MSNBC's Keith Olbermann invited Arianna Huffington on *Countdown* to discuss it:

> Huffington: There is something that we need to really pay attention to with Glenn Beck. We cannot just dismiss him. Because the truth of the matter is that there is a good reason why we have an exemption to the free speech protection by the First Amendment when we say you cannot shout fire in a crowded theater.
>
> And he's doing that every night. He's basically using images of violence to bring together with all that he's accusing the Obama administration of, which varies from racism to communism, Nazism and everything else in between. So, all that has definitely an impact. I believe words matter, language matters and he's using it in incredibly irresponsible ways night after night.
>
> Olbermann: What do you say to the argument that this country has always self-corrected, that whether Father Coughlin on the radio in the '30s or Bo[ake] Carter who was a newscaster who presented literally stuff that was made up on the hour in CBS News in the '30s or the columnist Westbook Pegler or Senator Joe McCarthy? All these people had a finale in which they exited the stage and suddenly. What is to say that that's not going to happen here?
>
> Huffington: Well, I hope it's going to happen, but it's not going to happen without people pointing out what Glenn Beck is doing.

In February 2010, Huffington had the opportunity to confront Fox News president Roger Ailes about this, when both appeared on the ABC News Sunday talk show *This Week:*

> Huffington: And aren't you concerned about the language that Glenn Beck is using, which is, after all, inciting the American

people? There is a lot of suffering out there, as you know, and when he talks about people being slaughtered, about who is going to be the next in the killing spree . . .

Ailes: Well, he was talking about Hitler and Stalin slaughtering people. So I think he was probably accurate. Also, I'm a little . . .

Huffington: No, no, he was talking about this administration.

Ailes continued to deny that Beck had used such rhetoric in reference to the Obama administration, and the next day, so did Beck: "I don't know if I've ever used the word 'slaughtered,'" he told his radio audience. But on November 4, 2009, Crooks and Liars posted a video of Beck saying this:

> I told you yesterday, buckle up your seat belt, America. Find the exit—there's one here, here, and here. Find the exit closest to you and prepare for a crash landing. Because this plane is coming down, because the pilot is intentionally steering it into the trees!
>
> Most likely, it'll happen sometime after Christmas. You're gonna see this economy come up—we're already seeing it, and now it's gonna start coming back down again. And when you see the effects of what they're doing to the economy, remember these words: We will survive. No—we'll do better than survive, we will thrive. As long as these people are not in control. They are taking you to a place to be slaughtered!

Beck tried to explain on his Fox News show, in response to Huffington, that he was only using metaphorical language—and so, because these words were simply meant to illustrate what Obama was doing to the economy, it shouldn't matter that the metaphors evoked mass death.

In reality, rhetoric that uses violent metaphors has a historical record of inspiring violent responses among its audience. People's economic well-being is nearly as vital to them and their families as their physical well-being. When you tell them that the president is going to drown them economically, or crash the economic engine of the nation, or economically slaughter them, the reaction will be every bit as visceral and violent as if they were threatened physically. As Huffington wrote in her counter to Beck's lame defense: "The crux of the matter was never whether Glenn Beck really believes Barack Obama is planning to actually slaughter Americans. It's the damage being done by the inflammatory rhetoric and imagery he constantly uses."

Confrontations such as this, however, have been rare, particularly in the mainstream media. In the absence of such self-policing, citizen journalists and progressive organizations stepped into the vacuum to produce an ongoing critique of Fox News and the right-wing punditocracy—not merely Beck, but Rush Limbaugh, Lou Dobbs, Sean Hannity, Michelle Malkin, and the seemingly endless list of right-wing talkers who had been so eagerly poisoning the public discourse with false information, vicious smears, and incendiary rhetoric and conspiracy theories. Progressive organizations like Media Matters and Think Progress, progressive media like Salon.com and the *American Prospect,* sites like Arianna's own Huffington Post, Josh Marshall's Talking Points Memo, DailyKos, and Crooks and Liars, as well as a thousand smaller-circulation blogs and the liberal blogosphere often dug out important nuggets of information and helped spread them.

This outpouring of scrutiny was not built on angry speculation and partisan disinformation, but rather was almost wholly the product of these citizen journalists' abilities to watch and record what was being said on the national airwaves and in the halls of power and to reproduce those things whole, and in context, for broad public examination. The critique infuriated the pundits on the Right, who hated above all else having their bigotry and mal-feasance played back for them—and for the public as well.

Citizen campaigns arose to force accountability on those media figures who were abusing their positions of power and author-ity with grossly irresponsible rhetoric and propagandizing. In November 2009, the chorus of voices demonstrated that their cri-tiques were not just an empty flood of discontent but a power to be reckoned with—the American Left's version, as it were, of orga-nized populism. And it was strong enough to finally overwhelm one of the icons of right-wing populism: Lou Dobbs.

◇ ◇ ◇

On Wednesday, November 11, 2009, Lou Dobbs had an unusual second segment in his nightly CNN broadcast of *Lou Dobbs Tonight* that featured an abrupt and mostly unexpected farewell:

> This will be my last broadcast here on CNN, where I have worked for most of the past 30 years and where I have many friends and colleagues whom I admire deeply and respect greatly....
>
> Over the past six months, it's become increasingly clear that strong winds of change have begun buffeting this country and affecting all of us. And some leaders in media, politics and busi-ness have been urging me to go beyond the role here at CNN and to engage in constructive problem-solving, as well as to con-tribute positively to a better understanding of the great issues of our day. And to continue to do so in the most honest and direct language possible.
>
> I've talked extensively with Jonathan Klein; Jon's the presi-dent of CNN, and as a result of those talks, Jon and I have agreed to a release from my contract that will enable me to pur-sue new opportunities.

At this point, I'm considering a number of options and directions and I assure you I will let you know when I set my course.

A few days later, it emerged that CNN had offered Dobbs an $8 million severance package to pack his bags and leave, and he had taken it. And everyone knew the reason they wanted Dobbs gone: His unrepentant wingnuttery had finally taken too much of a toll on CNN's reputation for credibility. What had hurt CNN the most was the sustained activism from progressives to force Dobbs out.

The campaign began stirring when Dobbs was still refusing to admit he had reported fake leprosy statistics to scapegoat immigrants, but it took root in July when Dobbs began reporting the "Birther" conspiracy theory as credible news. Civil-rights organizations, including the Southern Poverty Law Center, America's Voice, the National Council of La Raza, and Color of Change, as well as progressive media-watchdog groups like Media Matters and Think Progress, all played critical roles in organizing a response. They worked together to form two online-petition campaigns to have Dobbs removed and to boycott his advertisers: Basta Dobbs, a project of Presente.org (itself an offshoot of Color of Change), and Drop Dobbs, the product of a broad array of progressive organizations, including the Center for Community Change, Netroots Nation, and the National Hispanic Media Coalition. Together, these campaigns collected hundreds of thousands of signatures demanding that CNN show Dobbs the door and produced thousands of calls to CNN's advertisers asking them to drop their sponsorship of his show. The groups also organized marches and protests outside CNN studios and ran television and print ads demanding that they deal with the issue.

There was never any indication that CNN was being hurt financially by the advertiser calls, but it was becoming a public-relations nightmare. When CNN began running *Latino in America,* a sympathetic in-depth series about daily life for Hispanics, it was promptly hit with charges of hypocrisy from Latino leaders for trying to be warm and fuzzy on one hand while condoning Dobbs's incendiary brand of ethnically divisive journalism on the other. Moreover, CNN was in a downward ratings spiral, and Dobbs's ratings were some of its worst.

After the ax finally fell, the people who organized the campaign expressed satisfaction: "Our contention all along was that Lou Dobbs—who has a long record of spreading lies and conspiracy theories about immigrants and Latinos—does not belong on the 'Most Trusted Name in News,'" said Roberto Lovato, co-founder of Presente.org. "We are thrilled that Dobbs no longer has this legitimate platform from which to incite fear and hate."

Less than a week later, Dobbs was the featured guest on *The O'Reilly Factor:*

O'Reilly: Final question: Barack Obama, is he the devil?

Dobbs: He's not the devil, but he is certainly a man who is right now not making it easy to understand why he is making the public policy choices that he is. There has to be a better understanding from—and it can only result from his expression to the American people, as to what is taking so long to come to a decision on Afghanistan. Why it is so necessary to turn over a sixth of the economy to the United States government, which has not showered itself with glory on any other subject.

Among right-wing pundits and Beltway Village talkers, however, the favored talking point was that Dobbs had been the victim of a hypocritical witch hunt. On CNN's *Reliable Sources,* host Howard Kurtz invited on right-wing DC radio personality Chris Plante to hit back at Dobbs's critics:

Well, the reason Lou Dobbs was in trouble is not because he has opinions, it's because of what his opinions were and his opinions are out of lockstep with the rest of the mainstream news media. The *New York Times* in their—pretty much every report also say that he's a crusader against immigrants, or immigration and that's false. It's a misrepresentation and it speaks to their point of view. And maybe the *New York Times* should be taking a look at itself rather than Lou Dobbs.

Bill O'Reilly invited on Southern Poverty Law Center president Richard Cohen to pay off on a bet he had made with Cohen—that CNN would not fire Dobbs. O'Reilly promised to give $10,000 to Habitat for Humanity if it happened, and he made good on it. They also got into the free-speech ramifications of Dobbs's demise:

> Cohen: We had no secret pipeline to CNN, Bill. And you know, the truth of the matter is, you played an important role in the campaign. I appreciate your having me on in July, and I appreciate your acknowledging on the air to your viewers that the things that Dobbs was saying about the "Birthers" were bogus and absurd—
>
> O'Reilly: Well, some of them were bogus, but here's where we differ. And everybody should know it, Mr. Cohen. I don't want Lou Dobbs off the air. I think he's a voice that should be heard. You want him off the air. See look—I feel that you, and your organization, while you do do some good, are fascist in your approach to people with whom you disagree. Because Lou Dobbs shouldn't have been pulled off the air for his opinion— challenged, yes. I disagree, I say it! Pulled off the air? No! You shouldn't even want that. You should want, in a democracy, people to have freedom of speech and put stuff out there. If you disagree, or you think that he's inaccurate, get—that's why I give you airtime! You're welcome to come on, and say look, this is what we do, that's what we do here!

Of course, no one infringed on Lou Dobbs's free-speech rights, because having a network-TV show is not a right guaranteed by the First Amendment. No one prevented Dobbs from exercising the same right to free speech as enjoyed by everyone else in the country. What his critics insisted on was accountability to the responsibilities inherent in holding a powerful media position.

O'Reilly wanted to pretend that all speech is equal speech, but it manifestly is not: The people who are national news anchors reach millions of people—unlike, say, the ordinary citizens who are regularly demonized by the likes of Lou Dobbs.

Moreover, it's one thing to hold a contrary opinion—which, despite the claims of Dobbs and his defenders, was not the reason for the attacks against him. It's quite another to irresponsibly demagogue and demonize an entire bloc of the American population with provably false information and paranoid theories derived in large part from hate groups—which was what he was attacked for. Dobbs wasn't in trouble merely for opposing illegal immigration. A large segment of the public sought his removal because he had become an irresponsible font of disinformation and fearmongering, demonized and belittled Latino immigrants, and peddled conspiracy theories. His program had become a major conduit for right-wing extremism to filter into the mainstream.

The free press and free speech are vital to the functioning of our democracy, precisely because they are the only means by which the citizens of a democratic society can obtain the information they need to function effectively. This means that the people in the press who dispense that information have an overwhelming obligation to their audiences, and to democratic society, to report accurately, truthfully, and responsibly. And when they fail in that task, the public has not just the right but the obligation to demand accountability.

One can guess why Bill O'Reilly might be touchy about this subject and why he refused to acknowledge what the Dobbs affair was all about—because O'Reilly himself had indulged in reckless rhetoric, most infamously in the case of Dr. George Tiller, who was murdered by abortion opponent Scott Roeder (see chapter 4). And perhaps because his compadre at Fox, Glenn Beck, was making a daily spectacle of himself as the "fearmonger-in-chief," spouting wild conspiracy theories that made Dobbs look almost responsible and sedate in comparison. Clearly, Fox is not CNN. Responsible journalism is at best a secondary concern at Fox. No matter how many people protest, Glenn Beck will continue to have a home there as long as he brings in the ratings.

As the successful campaign to oust Dobbs demonstrated, calling someone to account can be an empowering thing. For the congenitally irresponsible, though, accountability is a terrifying thing.

Media accountability, as the journalistic failures of 2009 demonstrated, no longer works when left to the traditions of internal policing. An open and highly accessible medium like the Internet, though, allows readers and broadcast viewers to do their own fact checking and publish corrections online for all to see. This ability to interact means that communication is no longer a top-down affair, with journalists delivering information from their lofty perches and only rarely hearing back from those who receive it. Media pundits are now confronted with real dialogue from their audience, and when they behave irresponsibly, citizens have the power to call them out publicly for it and band together for redress.

Edward Wasserman, a professor of journalism ethics at Washington and Lee University, published a piece in the *Miami Herald* in late August examining the press's handling of the Tea Partiers' claim that the Democrats' proposals for health-care reform would have created "death panels"—bureaucratic bodies that would decide whether or not elderly people deserved their life-saving medications. (In reality, the legislation proposed a program enabling elderly and terminally ill people and their families to obtain end-of-life counseling sessions from their own doctors.) The charge had been brought in no small part by a coalition of demagoging populist figures such as Sarah Palin and lobbyists making appearances on certain cable-TV programs as guest experts, paid well by the insurance industry, who purposefully promoted misinformation about the "panels."

The existence of the panels was thoroughly debunked in the mainstream press. The problem, as Wasserman observed, was that despite the exposure of the meme as a fraud, it lived on anyway:

> Even though news organizations debunked the claim, 45 percent of respondents to an NBC poll still believe the reforms would indeed allow the federal government to halt treatment to the elderly—a staggering number.
>
> Why? Maybe because, by [Howard] Kurtz's count, Palin's "death panels" were mentioned 18 times by his own paper [the *Washington Post*], 16 times in the *New York Times* and at least 154 times on cable and network news (not including daytime news shows).
>
> Plainly, refuting a falsehood doesn't keep it from doing harm. The solution isn't some cheap fix, first giving end-of-the-world play to some incendiary fantasy and then inserting a line that says the preceding was utter rubbish. The real problem goes to the core of traditional news practices. As Greg Marx noted in a sensible *Columbia Journalism Review* posting, the solution is "making a more concerted effort not to disseminate false or dubious claims in the first place."

Achieving that goal, Wasserman contended, required resurrecting time-honored standards of the journalism business:

The problem isn't so much with reporters, it's with their bosses, the ones who insist on running the screaming footage from "town meetings," on giving dramatic lies a prominence they don't deserve—ensuring an audience, but while ensuring the lies a public life no reasoned refutation can end.

"He said, she said" has always been a dubious way to report the world. "We say" helps, but only a little. The real solution is simple: It's called news judgment.

Wasserman's point is essential for media professionals. However, part of the solution also lies in the rapidly changing nature of the media's relationship with its audience, because journalists no longer operate in a vacuum; their relationship with their readers, often to their dismay, is now much more intimate than it has ever been. As the Lou Dobbs case demonstrated, journalists need to respond to demands for accountability—pertaining both to news judgment and to equally fundamental standards like factual accuracy—in ways they never have before.

While the progressive critique of the media focused in many ways on simply correcting falsehoods and exposing smears, its cumulative effect was to attack the media for failing to uphold basic standards of journalism—particularly the media's willingness to treat palpably false information and transparently partisan hatchet jobs as genuinely newsworthy stories in the first place. For failing, in essence, to exercise the kind of responsible news judgment that the public expects.

However, confronting the media malfeasance that makes right-wing populism possible is only an important first step in meeting the challenges posed by the rise of this political pathology in American life. Ultimately, it means confronting the movement and its leaders, particularly in their embrace of conspiracy theories, falsehoods, scapegoating, and vicious eliminationist rhetoric.

Many of those leaders are indeed media figures like Glenn Beck and Rush Limbaugh, but increasingly, there are also institutional conservatives whose newfound populism empowers the Tea Partiers. Without a doubt, the most prominent of these is Sarah Palin.

◇ ◇ ◇

Near the end of 2009, the readers of PolitiFact.com—a Pulitzer-winning fact-checking site—were invited to vote on that year's "Lie of the Year." The runaway winner, with 61 percent of the vote in an eight-way competition, was Sarah Palin's "death panels" tale.

Even though the claim that health-care reform would lead to state-enforced euthanasia had, as Wasserman observed, been widely exposed as a flagrant falsehood, Palin was unrepentant: "The term I used to describe the panel making these decisions should not be taken literally," she told *National Review* editor Rich Lowry. The phrase is "a lot like when President Reagan used to refer to the Soviet Union as the 'evil empire.' He got his point across. He got people thinking and researching what he was talking about. It was quite effective. Same thing with the 'death panels.' I would characterize them like that again, in a heartbeat."

In a December 3 interview with right-wing radio host Rusty Humphries, Palin even appeared to endorse the "Birther" conspiracy theories:

> Humphries: Would you make the birth certificate an issue if you ran?
>
> Palin: Um, I think the public, rightfully, is still making it an issue. I don't have a problem with that. I don't know if I would have to bother to make it an issue, because I think enough members of the electorate still want answers.

Humphries: Do you think it's a fair question to be looking at?

Palin: I think it's a fair question, just like I think past associations, past voting records, all of that is fair game.

Palin's political career had taken a hit over the summer when she announced that she was stepping down as Alaska's governor before finishing her first term in office, but with the mid-November release of her autobiographical book, *Going Rogue: An American Life,* she managed to largely recover from the damage. The book rose to the top of the best-seller lists, and her national tour attracted long lines, with some devotees even camping out overnight at bookstores to be assured a place in line.

Palin also embarked on a tour of friendly media, most notably on Fox News, where she sat for interviews with Sean Hannity, Bill O'Reilly, and Greta Van Susteren. Much of the interviews involved papering over her mistakes in the 2008 campaign, most notably her infamous interview with Katie Couric in which she refused to say what news sources she read. In her November 18 appearance with Hannity, she finally listed some of her regular reads, some of which are well known, such as the *Wall Street Journal.* But first on Palin's list was NewsMax—the Patriot-friendly news site that in the late 1990s was peddling "Y2K apocalypse" warnings and Clinton "New World Order" conspiracy theories. NewsMax remains in much the same line of journalism: In September 2009, it published a piece by a writer named John L. Perry extolling the virtues of a military coup to remove the president: "There is a remote, although gaining, possibility America's military will intervene as a last resort to resolve the Obama problem," Perry wrote. (NewsMax eventually removed the piece from its Web site.)

It was in her interviews with O'Reilly, though, that Palin staked out her claim to leadership in the growing wave of right-wing populism—particularly in the segment that aired November 23:

> Palin: If there is a threat at all that perhaps I represent, it is that the average, everyday, hard-working American, that their voice is going to be heard, and their—what our voice is saying right now is, we're telling the federal government, and we're telling the elites who think that they are—can and should call all the shots for all the rest of us. Trust us in that we know what our federal government's role is supposed to be in our lives, it's supposed to be minimal.
>
> O'Reilly: But that sounds logical. That doesn't offend me.
>
> Palin: That's why it's perplexing as to why I would be, you know, kinda clobbered left and right—
>
> O'Reilly: You don't know—really. You're sincere about you don't know why you're the lightning rod, you don't know why?
>
> Palin: Only if it is because I'm representing a normal American who is—
>
> O'Reilly: Well, why don't they like normal Americans? Why don't the *New York Times* like normal Americans, or NBC News? Why should they have disdain for the regular folks?
>
> Palin: Because I think that, obviously they wanting so much control over our lives, I think perhaps there is a little bit of threat there, that the average American is gonna rise up and our voice is going to be louder and louder, and we're going to tell our government, "No, we expect you to work for us, we're not going to work for you, we expect things to turn around here quite quickly," even if that means the elites are not gonna be in control anymore.
>
> I'm talking about the media, I'm talking about those that are in bureaucracy that are calling the shots for us—I—that's why the Tea Party movement, I think is beautiful. And I think that

it is, it is empowering for so many of us to be watching what's going on with the Tea Party movement where we're saying— "That's—that's me!" I think it's beautiful what's going on right now. And perhaps that is threatening to some who don't want to cede any control.

Palin's media tour was met with broad approval within the Beltway Village, which agreed largely with the consensus at Fox that Palin had effectively repaired her image and positioned herself well for a presidential run in 2012. A Fox News poll showing her with a 47 percent approval rating—running at 70 percent among Republicans—was widely touted as evidence that she was becoming more popular than President Obama. Indeed, Palin's star power was unmatched within conservative political circles, and her prospects for capturing the party's vacant leadership role were brighter than those of anyone else on the scene at the end of 2009.

Whenever right-wing populist movements attempted to obtain power in the past, they inevitably fell short, in large part because they often lacked a charismatic leader capable of spearheading the movement nationally. Palin, however, clearly represents that potential for today's right-wing populists—which makes her rise all the more ominous.

It's particularly ominous for the state of our national discourse. As we have seen through the long and sordid history of right-wing populism in this country—particularly the way it has relied on scapegoating, smears, conspiracy theories, falsehoods, and unhinging rhetoric, all of which inevitably unleash violent, extremist rage—the foundations of democracy suffer at the hands of these movements.

As Democratic representative Earl Blumenauer of Oregon observed to PolitiFact in the aftermath of Palin's "death panels" lie: "It's a sobering prospect that political discourse is going to resemble hand-to-hand combat for the foreseeable future."

Blumenauer added that such a prospect bodes ill for involving average citizens in the democratic process:

> I think they're losing their appetite to wade through the vitriol, and I'm in the same boat. We are moving to a point where we drive normal people away, and everybody else gets their news and increasingly opinion prescreened, going for days never hearing an opposing viewpoint. That gives me pause.

While it has been effectively ginned up through the right-wing media and happily fueled by corporate interests, the populist anger into which Sarah Palin and Glenn Beck have tapped is very real. Americans are continuing to feel the weight of the economic downturn that began in 2008, and the only real signs of recovery were a return to good times on Wall Street. On Main Street, where unemployment was running over 10 percent, times were not so good.

The deluge of Tea Parties, hysterical disinformation, and propaganda that flowed from the conservative movement after the election, however, in many ways obscured for Americans how they got into this jam in the first place—namely, through eight years of conservative misgovernance. The chief underlying cause of the burst housing bubble and the recession that followed, after all, was widely understood by economists to have been the breakdown in regulatory oversight. Over the preceding 70 years, that oversight had largely prevented the financial sector from indulging in the reckless lending practices that ultimately caused the bubble and then its collapse. The conservative mania for deregulation—embodied most of all in the 1999 Gramm-Leach-Bliley Act, which overturned the financial safeguards created in the 1933 Glass-Steagall Act—was the ultimate source of the recession.

By late 2009, though the previous Republican administration was the culprit, more Americans believed that the recession was caused by Democrats—particularly the minority lending practices championed by liberals, such as the Community Reinvestment Act (CRA), which encouraged lending to nonwhites in redlined areas. Indeed, the CRA had almost nothing to do with the recession; the flood of mortgage defaults that burst the housing bubble came from private mortgage companies, which are not affected by CRA rules. Yet right-wing propagandists, particularly those at Fox, had flooded the airwaves with this bit of disinformation and successfully confused the public about the source of their economic misery.

For some reason, after the 2008 election progressives assumed that they had won the argument and largely ceded the field of public discourse to conservatives. Instead of reinforcing in the public's mind the reasons for their economic troubles, progressives cleared the way for conservatives to successfully muddy the waters, obscure their own culpability, and blame the progressives. Once in office, progressives needed to emphasize and push for solutions to fix the structural issues that had caused the recession. They needed to reinstate the federal regulatory powers and oversight that had prevented this kind of disaster for 70 years. Instead, thanks to the Tea Party crowd, the public was hearing that we need *less* government.

The progressives' message was lost, most likely, when after the election they focused their energies on the task of governance and figuring a way out of the mess the previous administration had created. The grass roots, the millions of ordinary people who had propelled Obama into office, were largely left behind to fend on their own as the new administration dealt with institutions and bureaucracies and the unpleasant intricacies and compromises of effectively running the country.

Yet ironically, the most powerful force in 2009 in blunting the conservative propaganda counterattack proved to be not institutional power but rather progressive grassroots action—left-wing populism, you could say. What kept the American Right in check in 2009 were the blogs, the media watchdogs, and the thousands of progressive activists who consistently exposed the miscreancy of right-wing propagandists, who turned back the tide of the Tea Parties so that health-care reform could have a chance to succeed, and who eventually forced out one of the most mendacious of the White House's critics from his network anchor's seat.

Progressive politicos and power players, however, have always undervalued the power of their own populist bloc. As a result, the Left's infrastructure has suffered—especially in comparison with the Right's. Liberal financial players pour their money into institutional power centers and leave the grass roots to scramble for funding. Unlike their counterparts on the right, progressive media outlets receive little funding. There is almost no flow of funding to the grassroots community, particularly the state and local progressive action groups that are the lifeblood of the Obama electoral base. Unlike right-wing authors, liberal writers cannot count on institutional support (especially not in terms of the mass purchasing that fuels the sales of so many right-wing best-sellers). The blogosphere, the most effective communications medium for progressives and one of the only sectors of the media landscape that progressives actually dominate, is run almost entirely on the passion and devotion of the people who dedicate themselves to citizen journalism—at least on the Left. The Right funds its bloggers.

Empowering their grassroots base lifted Democrats to political dominance in the wake of the Great Depression, and seven decades later it produced the election of the nation's first African American president. But that strategy hasn't yet translated into real dominance—and the Right's embrace of right-wing populism is the main reason why. As long as Glenn Beck and the Tea Partiers are out there working people into a hysterical anti-government frenzy, as long as mega-corporate news organizations are able to endlessly propagandize against progressive policies, and as long as the Right effectively taps into ordinary citizens' anger at the failure of the system, progressives are going to find their ability to effectively enact their agenda limited at best.

The Tea Partiers and anti-government extremists at the core of right-wing populism are effective because they deal in fear. Progressives, to counter the fearmongers and their poison, need to turn to another of the lessons from the Great Depression: "We have nothing to fear but fear itself."

There are several grave dangers arising from the Right's descent into madness that Americans need to confront. There is the obvious danger that, by descending so far into the abyss, conservatism will become permanently marginalized—which is not a healthy development for the state of our discourse. There is the danger to the rest of us posed by the innate violence that has always erupted from outbreaks of right-wing populism—manifested in 2009 by the increasing appearance of men like Richard Poplawski, Scott Roeder, and James Von Brunn.

This danger is likely to become acute in 2010, as widely expected immigration reform replaces health-care reform as the most pressing issue on the congressional plate. Unlike health care, immigration has been a significant issue around which many of the right-wing extremists have long been organizing. And these extremists have become an essential component of the Tea Party movement. Tea Party organizers began aiming protests at comprehensive immigration reform as early as November 2009. Called "Tea Parties Against Amnesty," the protests in some 50 cities were once again largely an astroturf operation, led in this case by the anti-immigration organization Americans for Legal Immigration PAC. Considering that the Tea Party protests in the summer of 2009 attracted thuggish and threatening behavior and rhetoric—and that some of the far right's most violent extremists carry a fervid animus toward immigrants—there is a powerful potential for an eruption of violence as the national debate proceeds. Things got ugly at the town-hall forums on health care, but just wait till the immigration debate gets under way.

Most of all, there is the danger that, in plunging headlong into the abyss of madness, the American Right will take the rest of us with it. That can happen only if right-wing populism is able to flourish unchallenged—if we fail to recognize it as a threat to progressive values and to democratic institutions.

To respond effectively to this challenge we must all take a stand: conservatives, liberals, centrists, and libertarians. Most of all, the only potent counter to right-wing populism during 2009 came from the work of left-wing populists, and clearly, leaving them to wither on the vine would be a fundamental mistake. The millions of ordinary people who elected Barack Obama president need to be called back to the fray, engaged anew, and empowered to take the nation down another road, one that guides us far away from the cliffs of fear.

Index

About the Authors

John Amato is the creator of the award-winning political blog Crooks and Liars, which has been featured in the *New York Times, Forbes,* the *Los Angeles Times, USA Today,* the *Washington Post,* and *Huffington Post* and which was honored as one of the top blogs of 2009 by *Time* Magazine. Known in blog circles as "the Vlogfather," Amato is recognized as a pioneer of video blogging. He is also a professional saxophonist and flutist.

David Neiwert is a journalist and author based in Seattle. His reportage on domestic terrorism for MSNBC.com won a National Press Club Award in 2000. He is the author of four books, including *The Eliminationists: How Hate Talk Radicalized the American Right* (2009). He is the managing editor of Crooks and Liars, as well as the author and editor of the award-winning weblog Orcinus.